Captured at Singapore

Captured at Singapore

A Diary of a Far East Prisoner of War

Jill Robertson & Jan Slimming

Pen & Sword
MILITARY

AN IMPRINT OF PEN & SWORD BOOKS LTD.
YORKSHIRE – PHILADELPHIA

First published in Great Britain in 2022 by
Pen & Sword Military
An imprint of
Pen & Sword Books Ltd
Yorkshire - Philadelphia

ISBN 978 1 39908 568 7

Printed and bound in England
By CPI UK Ltd.

Pen & Sword Books Ltd. incorporates the Imprints of Pen & Sword Archaeology,
Atlas, Aviation, Battleground, Discovery, Family History, History, Maritime,
Military, Naval, Politics, Railways, Select, Transport, True Crime, Fiction,
Frontline Books, Leo Cooper, Praetorian Press, Seaforth Publishing,
Wharncliffe and White Owl.

For a complete list of Pen & Sword titles please contact

PEN & SWORD BOOKS LIMITED
47 Church Street, Barnsley, South Yorkshire, S70 2AS, England
E-mail: enquiries@pen-and-sword.co.uk
Website: www.pen-and-sword.co.uk

or

PEN AND SWORD BOOKS
1950 Lawrence Rd, Havertown, PA 19083, USA
E-mail: uspen-and-sword@casematepublishers.com
Website: www.penandswordbooks.com

Dedicated to our parents and generous relatives

who gave their time during

and after the Second World War

to help in their repatriation.

With sobering thoughts, in the aftermath of war,

you realised your life's now for living,

when you've been heads down, bombs going off;

bullets flying all over.

Religiously it's remarkable to be 'chosen' to survive;

in reality it is luck, cruel luck, masses of it.

'A survivor'

Contents

Foreword

I recollect the childhood fear I experienced when German bombers flew overhead, and the excitement when a fighter plane crashed in the road just a few hundred yards from our home. I was too young then, to understand that Britain was engaged in a war of global dimensions. Certainly, too young to know that just after 5.15 p.m. on the Sunday afternoon of 15 February 1942, Lieutenant General Arthur Percival capitulated in Singapore to General Tomoyuki Yamashita of the Imperial Japanese Army.

Four years later, in 1946, following the cessation of hostilities, General Yamashita was executed for – and I quote – 'disregarding, and failing to discharge, his duty as a commander to control the acts of members of his command, by *permitting* them to commit war crimes'. This controversial decision, known today as the 'Yamashita Standard', has a precedent extending back to the sixth century BC when in Sun Tzu's *The Art of War*, he argued that a commander's duty was to ensure his subordinates conducted themselves in a civilised manner during armed conflict. However, we might well ask, 'What is civilised about warfare of any kind, engaged in or by any nation on earth?'

As a 1950s' teenager I had a job as a grocery store van-boy. One of the drivers was regarded as being a bit odd. He seemed moody, with a persistent cough. One day he failed to turn up for work, and I learned he had died. He was barely 40 years of age. I also learned that he was a former PoW under the Japanese and had suffered greatly. PTSD was never recognised as a serious disorder in those days, and I remember one former PoW telling me that following his release and repatriation, he was told to go home and not to talk about his experience of incarceration to anyone. The strain this silence imposed on that generation was significant.

At a recent commemoration, the grandson of a former PoW said he knew virtually nothing about the Second World War; the fall of Singapore in 1942 was a closed book for him. Alas, his experience is all too typical. Today relatives are encouraged to talk and share their stories, but widespread ignorance about contemporary history still exists and, therefore, it is important for all to comprehend events that have shaken the world causing untold distress to millions. If we are to work for a more peaceful world, we need to know our history. In truth, we fail lamentably to learn from the past – not attempting to learn now, is no excuse. The consequences of The Capitulation had a dramatic effect on thousands, which fundamentally changed the Far East. This book, drawn from first-hand accounts, is a valuable addition to our understanding of contemporary history. It has been written not to condemn, but to help us understand and, hopefully, learn lessons that will aid us as we attempt to build a more peaceful, civilised world. Regularly on Remembrance Day we hear 'For your tomorrow we gave our today'. We all need to ensure that their *giving* was not in vain.

Terry Waite CBE
Patron - CoFEPOW

Prologue

No more sign of anymore shells but situation getting bad. We were in a vehicle convoy; of course, the Japs came and bombed us.

They were surrounded in Singapore's urban area as they dodged bombs trying to defend the Jewel of the Empire.

There was 'ack-ack' and gunfire, and all sorts flying around, but our small arms fired and beat the little bomber off. It was amazing to see the Japanese aircraft's two cockpits and their pilots. The chap in the rear cockpit leaned out over the side of the aircraft to fire his hand pistol – at us!

As the trucks accelerated the troops held on for their lives, rocking from side to side to take them to safety. Young lads, younger than Stan, were cheering and jeering at the aggressors from beneath the khaki canopy, while Stan's co-fighters, issued with Lee & Enfield rifles, dared to return fire.

The Fading Sentence

This analogy holds a poignancy and sentiment of a bygone era, where troops were pawns in a wargame with little assistance to get them home, until two Atom bombs exploded, killing innocent Japanese people. This left FEPOW (Far East prisoners of war) children born after 1945 with a short, sharp shock as they realised they might never have existed.

Reading our father's handwritten diary, it occurred to us the definition of the faint outlines he crafted during the Second World War, were not the only emotions he sensed as a healthy young man. The tiny writing was faded and difficult to read, but its fragility endured captivity and post-war years to reveal this story.

The men were ill-treated, and malnutrition made their bodies fade in an imposed prison sentence where escape from disease and death was not an option.

For those who survived, the experience was simply expected to fade in their minds, as well as become a faded memory among future generations.

Authors' note: The diary texts of the prisoners of war in this book are written in a language during a time when, understandably, there was a deep hatred of the people who terrorised and hurt their victims in this theatre of war, some of which is now unacceptable. Terms such as 'Jap' and 'Nip' were commonplace at the time of their experience and in some instances, their later written accounts. Some have been adjusted; however, certain references remain so as not to obscure the true emotions felt at the time.

Introduction

A VIEWING CHANCE

Jill, West Sussex: May 2012

The usual Friday night ritual of cooking a meal and getting settled for a spell of *The One Show* was underway. The BBC programme, a firm household favourite, is filled with topical items and chit chat by studio presenters, with a main guest sitting on a lime green sofa. The guest must sit through all news bites, unlike other chat shows where they stay for their part and then exit; instead these guests remain for the duration. For me, this particular night would be different, with huge topical significance.

Part of the programme included the Far East during the Second World War. One of the guests, along with seventies comedian and singer Des O'Connor, was an elderly and lucid gentleman who had been a PoW for more than three years, a survival accomplishment that was difficult to achieve after the extreme conditions they experienced. He put his durability down to his skill as a magician. He was also the oldest conjurer in the Magic Circle. His name was Fergus Anckorn.

Watching and listening with interest, still trying to cook the meal, I saw a group photo showing fifty or so soldiers on the TV screen, and in a split second, I noticed a familiar face in the middle. It was someone who looked just like my father, but it wasn't him.

Memories flooded back of the time I found the tiny address book with small writing on pale blue pages in the downstairs bureau. I was 7 or 8 and wanted some paper to draw on. I got into a rotten temper when I couldn't find anything suitable in that stupid maze of a desk, except the tiny notebook with a few blank pages. In my childish anger I started to rip out the first few used pages, but luckily, guilt stopped me from ill-treating it; I knew it was wrong and felt terrible. My sister was saying stop and told on me, my mother scolded me, and I was sent to my room for days. Dad was upset. I never knew then just how important the notebook was. After all, to a young child, the 'war' seemed hundreds of years ago. We were told it held precious memories and it was returned to the bureau maze, 'never to be touched again'.

From then on, my father spoke little of his captivity in Changi. The subject was frightening, almost taboo. Later there were short conversations between him and his sons–in law who were interested in his war years, but no specific answers or real indication of exactly what happened to him, during that time in Singapore, were given. His tales were just snippets: eating rice every day, being skinny, learning to count to ten in Japanese, how to say good morning or good evening. Lighter moments, perhaps a song from a concert party or music heard on a ship, and a brief reference to Cape Town.

Within a week of the TV programme, I had written to the Magic Circle to ask for further information on the Oldest Magician of their illustrious club and started to delve into one of the saddest, forgotten episodes of the Second World War. My father had died in 2001, but this vibrant magician's story seemed similar. Could he lead me to the unspoken life and times of our father's prisoner of war years? The group photo seen on the TV programme was over seventy years old, taken in Ahmednagar, India. In 2012, I really thought there was no hope of ever speaking to any of his contemporaries, but now the magician and Ahmednagar were key. I owed it to my father to investigate, especially after spoiling his faded diary.

*   *   *

The underlying knowledge our father was a prisoner in the war was always evident throughout our childhood. 'Daddy was in Singapore.' Once a year, on Christmas Eve, we would badger him to retrieve his hardly worn thick creamy-white army socks from the bottom of his wardrobe, to hang up for Father Christmas. Waking with anticipation in the early hours of Christmas Day we were often lucky to find a penny whistle, a small doll, a teddy or a handful of nuts. Sometimes sweets and chocolate, maybe even a mini pocket-puzzle game, but always a smooth shiny tangerine at the bottom, snuggling in the toe.

We were inquisitive little girls, twins, and our annual infantile venture for the unused socks eventually led to Dad's war memorabilia. When we were older, the boredom of winter school holidays was often alleviated by the small box we found, made of thick cardboard, 8 inches by 6, with a big red cross on top.

'*The Changi treasure trove,*' he replied, when asked.

It was his gentle introduction to his 'time' in the Changi Prisoner of War Camp, Singapore. Inside the box was a strange wooden toothbrush with shiny spiky golden bristles, a blunt wooden-handled cut-throat razor, and a small gold and black Oxo tin containing two funny tarnished tags on worn-out string. Medals were also included, with brightly coloured striped ribbons, and fascinating old foreign notes:

'*Japanese "banana" money,*' he said.

Among the other items of 'treasure' was a large cartoon-like magazine with a huge palm tree on the cover. Inside were pages of musical notes, which we recognised as piano music, with words of wartime concert songs such as *Keep Smiling, Keep Singing, and My Castle in the Air.* But his jewel in the crown of precious memories, kept hidden, downstairs, at the back of the grownups' bureau, safe and out of reach for no one to see or spoil, was the cream thumb-stained booklet with the words *'Address Book'* artistically written on the front. Inside, the small treasure revealed fine and tiny faded writing in ink on delicate, pale blue paper – this, we discovered, was his wartime diary.

Propulsion to Reveal the Story:

He gave little detail in relation to his capture, too scared perhaps to remember the horrors he suffered. But in 1990, he made a precious audio recording for my sister as a wedding present. She had asked him several times and finally supplied him with tiny tapes and a Philips dictaphone. He was also prompted by the fiftieth anniversary of his conscription to the army. Stan's verbal account, where he expanded and relived the experiences noted in the faded sentences of his old diary, unsettled him for a few weeks – manoeuvres in England, his sea journeys, training in India, arrival in Singapore, temporary accommodation and facilities, the unabated noise of battle fire, capitulation to the Japanese, captivity, dreadful scenes of depravation, and the unsanitary debacle of Selarang Barracks.

In 1995 he provided more, in a letter to my son Christopher, for a show-and-tell school project, but it was not until 2012, eleven years after our father's death, that I viewed the *One Show* and began to crack open his Singapore history. We blew off the dust gathering on the 'diary' – the erstwhile address book – the tapes and the letter, and our Changi[1] artefacts were resurrected. We listened and transcribed the recordings, deciphered the faded, minute writing and read several accounts of the Far East theatre of war. We researched and purchased new publications, borrowed library books and watched plenty of video film footage. We read and re-read the works of valued authors and slowly his story unfolded in front of us with timelines and patterns of the capitulation, and the comprehension – often shocking – of what he and others endured. It was also evident from bookshop and library shelves that there was less published information on this theatre of war compared to the German invasions of Europe, desert campaigns in Africa and Normandy landings. The unplanned call-to-arms of the Far East war 1942–1945 deserved more, or as much, to reiterate the events of the last bastion of the British Empire and the Orient, and how the enemy was eventually stopped.

PART I

11.15 A.M. 3 September 1939

'This morning the British Ambassador in Berlin handed the German government a final note stating that unless we heard from them by 11 o'clock that they were prepared at once to withdraw their troops from Poland, a state of war would exist between us. I have to tell you now that no such undertaking has been received and that consequently this country is at war with Germany.'

Neville Chamberlain, Prime Minister

Chapter 1

Farewell

The smartly dressed serviceman walked in a small municipal park with two young ladies on either arm. It was dry and overcast, usual for October. The park was close to his home at 32 Edenvale Road, Mitcham, Surrey. The trio seemed cheerful and chatty, but as they pointed out mediocre flowers and trees their voices quivered in an aura of nervousness. Small talk somehow provided comfort from bitter thoughts of war, like an anaesthetic shielding them from reality. Autumn was on target. They admired the turning colour of leaves and the appearance of berries. The young soldier inanely commented, *'Bet 'cha winter'll be a hard one.'*

Feeling uncertain about the future, Stan then looked at his army footwear and tutted. *'Mud. That's all I need. I only polished them this morning.'*

The earlier rain and muddy grass underfoot had soiled his black army boots. Signing up to fight for king and country had blocked his ideas of being a suave, urbane gent and his recent purchase of a double-breasted suit and cravat from Burton's in Tooting Broadway was his pride and joy. He liked his dapper look – contrary to the itchy khaki of British regulation army issue, accompanied by the standard Northampton-made black heavy boots for the war. He longed to be back in his shiny expensive tan brogues instead. As he stroked his Clark Gable-style moustache and gave the winning smile for which he was known, tension in his shoulders reminded him of the chilling reality of what he was about to embark upon. It was 1941 and he and thousands of other young soldiers had four days' special leave before they departed – destination unknown. The women took turns to take pictures of him using the blonde lady's box Brownie camera:

'You won't forget to write regularly, will you?' she said.

'And me,' chimed the brunette, snapping the last photo.

'Of course, I'll write to you both, and all m' family,' said Stan.

It was real now, not just training. As they left the park through the black wrought iron gate that he held open for both women, Stan hoped his army combat preparation would not be necessary. But he could not discuss it with them. Instead, he said he looked forward to getting a motorbike and hoped that it wouldn't fail him when escaping from the enemy.

Stan had been called up in 1940 to undertake basic army training and manoeuvres in several places, including Kent, East Anglia and Scotland. He was now stationed at Droitwich in the Midlands, a town known for its salt spa. His eighteen months' training aimed to bring the recruits up to wartime strength, though some young men from the Home Counties were rumoured to be inadequate for combat as they only had eight weeks' instruction.

'They hadn't fired a gun or even learned how to salute!'

He was glad his training was lengthy, but wished he knew his destination. All he'd heard was that his company would go to Liverpool for an overseas posting. Nobody, except military chiefs, knew where. Now there were only a few hours left of his leave, and soon he would return to being Driver Moore, T/170638, Royal Army Service Corps (RASC). The women finished taking photographs. One was his older sister, Doris, the other his fiancée, Pat. He didn't want to say goodbye, and the 25-year-old soldier quickly dismissed the idea that he might not see them again. He had come to say farewell and reassure them he would be safe; he would return. But times were ominous, and nobody knew when loved ones would see each other again. The German invasion was real, and Stan said he wouldn't be gone for long. They all hoped the conflict would soon end.

Stan's older brother, Frank, had already wished him good luck the day before when he visited with his wife Molly and their young daughter, Valerie. Frank's job at the gas board in Croydon meant he couldn't afford extra time to see Stan on his last day at home. They didn't see much of each other now Frank was married and that upset Stan a little, but he understood. As the evening's autumnal sunshine began to set, thoughts of his brother faded as they walked home, and soon the silhouette of his mother appeared in the kitchen window. Her solid, upright frame was topped by her dark grey hair, piled high in a loose bun. Emma Moore, dressed in a white blouson and calf-length dark skirt was of late Victorian stock with strict values, dignity and pride. Now, as she turned to face him, Stan saw frowns and worry lines around her small brown, almond-shaped, eyes. Her face was white. She was sad and upset and looked older than her 50 years. *Would this be the last time he would see her? What if she died before he returned?* Stan's emotions would have been masked.

He hugged his mother as she wept. He was her youngest. His brown eyes closed for a few seconds as he shed a tear, but he soon gained composure, fearful of stumbling out of his army-trained stiff-upper-lipped character. He took Pat to her home in Tooting, and then dutifully caught the last train back to Droitwich.

Chapter 2

Called Up

October 1941 – Droitwich, Worcestershire

Stanley Albert William Moore, RASC Driver T/170638.

Stan was born 15 March 1916 in Camberwell, London, under the distant sound of Bow Bells. He was considered a cockney with a dialect he adopted while living in Trafalgar Street, Walworth. He was the third offspring of Frank Moore Snr., who owned a junk shop (nowadays called an antique emporium) and Emma Moore, a softly spoken and sought-after seamstress. Stan would often tell stories of when he was young, visiting his three 'old aunts' who lived next to and above his father's shop, where his first regular tasks were to sweep the floor and scoop up horse manure from behind his father's horse and cart. The horse was kept in the small back yard, but by the mid-1920s the family had moved to Mitcham for a healthier life, and the business was passed to his aunts.

The best education establishment for Stan, was the Graveney School in Tooting, where he managed adequately but did not enjoy the academic environment. He preferred, instead, to ride his bicycle or swim. He loved to sketch, and his penmanship was fine, if only he could spell. Mathematics was not his best subject, though he managed perfectly well with weights and measures for his job at the Royal Arsenal Co-operative Society (RACS), where he worked in the food halls as a meat counter assistant. The RACS was a large department store where he made many friends, and they all enjoyed plenty of active weekends, including swimming at Tooting Bec Lido and seeing films at the grand and ornate Tooting Granada Theatre. He also joined a cycling club, which led to short trips to the coast such as Brighton, Eastbourne or Hastings. He had met Pat in the staff cafeteria at work. She was an accounts clerk in the main office. Her given name was Daisy Lawrence, but she thought 'Daisy' 'too old fashioned' and preferred

'Pat' instead. They started 'going out' in 1933, which coincided with Stan's purchase of a second-hand sidecar for his Triumph motorbike.

As a soldier, his skills at butchering meat on the Co-op's provisions counter were no longer needed, nor was his talent for house painting, something he'd learned from his father after they moved to Mitcham. But a chance to continue riding a motorcycle was offered by the army and Stan could apply his meticulous map-reading skills. Soldiering required diligence and attention to detail, which was something he now realised was important and he happily adjusted to the new military rigour, though handling a weapon and the prospect of confronting the enemy was not something he relished. He had celebrated his twenty-fourth birthday in 1940 before enlisting at the Territorial Army on 4 April. This was in line with the 'Emergency under the provisions of the National Service (Armed Forces) Act 1939'. After a few months, he was posted for further instruction to the 141 Company at No. 5 Training Centre, Herne Bay, Kent, as a dispatch rider. Later he joined the 139 Company and the Motor Transport Depot in Norfolk.

Now in the army, his eight years in Tooting's RACS were becoming a distant memory. By August, he was posted to 538 Company, 291 then 292 Company, RASC, which meant he was then fully attached to the 18th Division. All these units accompanied Royal Artillery and Royal Engineers' operations. With previous preparation in Kent, Cambridgeshire and Norfolk, they were on the 'front line' of training manoeuvres. By January, his troop commanders had the mammoth task of moving this huge division to Scotland. The weather conditions were appalling, with deep snow, but their endurance was tested and before long they were moved to north-west England in equally freezing temperatures – unusual for Lancashire in June. They battled with the 2nd Division[1] in a faux operation, where one side would be selected for overseas transfer. The challenge was immense on the pseudo front line where all units in combat, or as backup, were tested to the full. The 2nd Division, with reduced strength after the fiasco of Dunkirk the year before, were perhaps less fit than the 18th Division who came out on top and were duly selected.

Despite exhausting conditions, they still found time for laughter and relaxation.

Stan's group of friends included 'Mac' Cothill, Gordon Hunter, Freddie Holt, Sid Cowling and Albert 'Bill' Weeks, also known as 'Trigger'. They used Sid's box Brownie camera to take several photos to cheer themselves up at Brook House, their quarters in Knutsford. Smiles did not last long for Stan, however:

> *While we were there a fellow accidentally kicked me in the mouth during manoeuvres and badly cracked my front teeth. They were awful anyway – too many sweets as a child – they needed attention.*

Stan was admitted to Tabley House on the outskirts of Manchester, a war hospital supply depot on a large country estate.

'The dentist's motto seemed to be "remove one, remove the lot",' said Stan, *'and out they all came, substituted with false teeth'.*

Lucky for Stan, no more manoeuvres!

He had two weeks in hospital and another week of sick leave and felt he owed a debt of gratitude to the chap who kicked him in the scramble.

At that point he thought he was in for an easy time, but little did he know the die was already cast when they 'defeated' the 2nd Division.

They continued regular training, enjoying 'rest times' and getting paid. A soldier's wage was 14s 1d per week. Even in hospital, Stan was paid 8s 6d per week. Captain Horner and Captain Cowell signed off their pay books, but there was never any news of where they would go next. They only knew they were scheduled for overseas duty and awaited further orders, all the while questioning what was in store for them.

With special embarkation leave granted to all, Stan had returned home to his family and his fiancée to say farewell. Ten months earlier, on Christmas Eve, he had purchased a solitaire diamond ring in a little red leather box and proposed to Pat. She said yes, and in that special moment they started to plan their lives together. But the future was uncertain – where would army life take him and for how long? In their last few hours Stan asked her to wait for him.

Departing had its mixed feelings, and tensions were high, but Stan's sister Doris had helped to lighten the mood with her exuberant and extrovert ways, making fun of any tableau. Some might call her irreverent, but two years older than Stan, she was always entertaining, confident and happy. He would miss his family and Pat, but his army duties were about to follow another path to places unknown and new adventures. It was harsh but exciting and they would soon be on their way.

Stan returned to Droitwich and his army pals. It was then he had the idea to use a small handmade notebook for their addresses. The folded thick card, with stapled pale blue paper, fitted perfectly in his uniform breast pocket. Gordon wrote his address first. Stan also thought it a good idea to keep diary notes in the back, to relay to Pat when he returned, though whether he would tell all was uncertain. Some of his army mates, he noted, frequented the Winter Gardens, a local dance hall. Their dance partners were girls from the ATS (Auxiliary Territorial Service), the female version of the British Army, who had to be in by 9 p.m.

If you were attached to one you walked them home to their barracks in a large [commissioned] *hotel, where their Sergeant Major used to come out and say – 'come on girls, time to be in bed.' The soldiers, who had a pass to stay out late, would then go straight back to the Winter Gardens to dance with the local lasses.*

After spending eighteen months of training, at Droitwich, we were stationed in requisitioned council houses taken over by the army. This particular morning, we were called out on parade by the corporal for the sergeant major's inspection. When all of a sudden one of the fellows called out that he didn't have his tin hat or respirator. Then he remembered, 'Blimey. I think I've left it behind the bike shed at the local dance hall – I better dash and get it right away.'

He rushed to the hall and back in time before the SM showed up. He didn't get into any bother; he was a risk taker and one of the lucky ones!

The parade was for our final instructions for embarkation and the following day we set off by coach to Droitwich station and from there by train to Liverpool. A coach then took us to Seaforth Barracks. Around midday we were allocated our billets and allowed to have the rest of the day to ourselves.

The following morning, we were ordered to do a bit of 'square bashing', just for the amusement of our sergeant major, a regular soldier who joined up during boys' service. He was a right so-and-so, 'a spit and polish merchant', and bragged about his time there. He and a friend regularly used to make each other a cup of tea on alternate mornings, then one day he was promoted and the following day his friend still brought him a cup of tea, upon which he promptly put him on a charge for breaking the rules!

Stan was shocked that they were instantly on different levels.

By 26 October 1941, his group was given final instructions for embarkation as part of 54th Brigade, 18th Division, under command of Lieutenant General M. B. Beckwith-Smith DSO, MC, GOC.[2] Stan's role as a serious soldier had begun.

The scratchy fabric of their heavy khaki uniform heightened their nervous state as they mustered in the early hours of 27 October, at 0200hrs. The chill of the October night under blackout conditions was bleak and foreboding, compensated only by the closeness of the soldiers marching in columns and the echo of their black army boots hitting the ground in unison. Moist trails of warm breath coiled from their mouths, as dark amber and crimson leaves fluttered across the usually quiet roads in front of them.

At Droitwich station ATS women smiled as they served breakfast for the troops. This was sombrely eaten in the station's stark canteen, a facility painted years earlier with cream and drab green paint. The men boarded their scheduled train and departed for Liverpool at 0400hrs.

For two days we followed the usual regime of marches, food and sleep until the third day when we were coached to Liverpool docks and boarded HMT Andes.

Some men were coached to Liverpool docks,[3] while others marched to the station.

Our small unit of the CRA/CRE [the Company of Royal Artillery and the Company of Royal Engineers] *and 4th Royal Norfolks, were shown into a converted smoke room with bunks. They were really comfortable. We were worried we might have hammocks but there were none.*

At 0800hrs on 30 October 1941, we set sail northbound towards the Clyde, where we met the rest of our convoy, in all five ships – liner types or troop carriers. We sailed around the north coast of Ireland and the sea was 'a bit rolly'.

We were making our way into the Atlantic and met up with three British destroyers who would escort us across the ocean.

Stan and his division still did not know where they were going, but they were part of a secret convoy – code named 'William Sail' WS-12X. Unaware of how secret and critical this sailing was, the men were kept engaged by their army commanders who ordered PT and fire drills every day. Officers also put on shows for everyone's entertainment and the soldiers indulged in on-board activities, games and treats.

One of the luxuries we enjoyed was the fact we could buy bars of milk chocolate from the NAAFI canteen, and therefore, we made pigs of ourselves. It was funny and told on a lot of us. Some were very seasick. Chocolate had been rationed for months and we were not used to its richness.

*   *   *

Fergus Anckorn embarked on the same journey. At 21, he had been called to Royal Artillery training in Bulford, Wiltshire, under the official Military Training Bill. This scheme required all fit young men to complete six months' preparation and afterwards join the Territorial Reserve. Anckorn, a tall, healthy blond man, outwardly fitted the requirements of strength and ability, but inwardly he preferred to be a driver because he held a driving licence. In October 1939, this was still quite a rare skill and, as a driver, he wouldn't need to kill anyone. He had applied to the RASC but found himself reporting to the Royal Artillery instead.

After war had been declared, stringent blackout regulations were imposed that autumn, and life in Britain started to change. However, Fergus thought the war would never progress, until the day air raids came closer to his home in Sevenoaks, Kent. His local office job, at Marley Roof Tiles, had also disappeared when he and other enlisted staff were declared *sacked*. They were called into the managing director's office in groups of five where their boss, Mr Aisher, delivered a profound and shocking oratory predicting their fate:

> Whatever you think now, or whatever you're doing now, whatever your life is now, it will change inexorably from what it is now. Your life from this moment is going to be a different life from anything you've ever had or thought of. Some of you will come back colonels. Some will come back as majors. Some of you won't come back at all. Whatever happens if you get back, you'll always have a job here.

Strangely, his earlier orders to Bulford were rescinded and instead he was assigned to Woolwich Barracks. On 18 October, he queued with others to sign up and receive his army number: 947555, attesting to the 118th Field Regiment Royal Artillery.

A year passed. Russia had bombed Helsinki and invaded Finland. Germany penetrated countries in Europe without a fight, then stormed into France. The Prime Minister, Neville Chamberlain, resigned and Winston Churchill took over. Within weeks came disaster at Dunkirk and a massive rescue of British Expeditionary Forces was needed, involving military and private vessels of all sizes, to save Allied troops from the occupied shores of northern France.

In Britain, on the undulating coastline at Bexhill, Sussex, Gunner Anckorn was on high alert and ready to 'single-handedly' avert a Nazi invasion during his midnight sentry duties. He had to report any unusual sightings, but instead, in peaceful darkness, there was only the sound of wildlife.

Not long afterwards, his 12th Division regiment moved to Norfolk to join the 18th Infantry Division. Though disturbing for him at the time, this was a good move as while in Norwich a call went out to audition for the army concert party. Fergus was an entertainer and, as a teenager, he had perfected his hobby of magic. In 1936, he was the youngest member of the Magic Circle. He passed the army's audition and was proud to be accepted to perform in front of commanders, colonels, brigadiers and generals – a full 'table' of authority – where his confidence abounded. He was no longer a mere gunner but 'Wizardus', and his audience appreciated his remarkable skill, which concluded with the seamless flourish of an experienced magician. It was a stellar performance, especially for the man in the centre, Major General Beckwith-Smith.

A troupe was formed from many regiments, including pianists, George Appleton and Cyril Wycherley. George improvised with incidental music at the start of Fergus's act, then played something more dramatic throughout, ending in an obligatory drum roll. Completing the act were violinist, Denis East, and Fred Cole on accordion – both top rated in their fields – plus two singers and an impersonator. They called themselves 'The Optimists'. The concert parties were part of ENSA, which meant they were excused from everyday soldiering and did not wear a uniform! Their friends were envious, but others in their division probably thought they were civilians. ENSA stood for Entertainments National Service Association; also known as 'Every Night Something Awful'!

Fergus's troupe played to the public as well as the armed forces, during which time the 18th Division moved to Scotland in January 1941; a thousand mechanised army vehicles of the CRE/CRA regiments travelled unprecedented distances to the Borders region of Melrose and Newtown St Boswell. It was cold with heavy snow at one point, which delayed them considerably; nevertheless, the concert party managed to entertain the billeted troops. Life in the north of the country was peaceful for a while, away from bombs; you could even buy a cream tea! But it wasn't long before enemy attacks began. When the unit started to move south in the spring, the concert party was disbanded, though it felt as if it could have continued forever.

By the summer of 1941, it was back to soldiering for Gunner Anckorn. Fergus's section of the 18th Division was sent to North Wales for more manoeuvres near Ffestiniog, a cold and desolate place and always wet. His division was away from the bombs in London, but there were many reasons to fight on. Winston Churchill would not appease Hitler by having talks, as the nation resisted invasion. Defeat was not an option. Word in their camp said they would be mobilised for action in a 'tropical climate' – but North Wales was not what they had in mind. By order, all embarkation leave was to be completed by 20 October. Their division was now part of another brigade. For a while they decamped to the Midlands, near Uttoxeter, and after a few weeks 118th Field Regiment, as part of the 55th Infantry Brigade, was placed for shipment overseas on 22 October 1941. The 18th Division was about to set out on an unknown mission. It was terrifying.

Fergus and his fellow troops were heavy-hearted as they mustered, with their belongings, for their march to Uttoxeter station at 0200hrs. It was wet and slow in the dark; some realised they had unnecessary items, such as musical instruments, and left them abandoned by the roadside. The march usually took forty-five minutes, but today it was longer. A commissioned train awaited to deliver them to Liverpool.

Two hours later, at the Liverpool dockside, hired military transport HMT *Orcades*, a 23,000-tonne troop ship from the Oriental Line, loomed in the harbour shadows. This ship was also part of WS-12X. Gunner Fergus Anckorn boarded the *Orcades*, and Mr. Aisher's words flooded back:

'... some of you won't come back at all.' He decided then that no matter what, he would again set foot on English soil, but when? He had no idea.

Chapter 3

Leaving: Convoys

From HMT *Andes* to USS *Wakefield*, 3 November

Long grey days at sea were accepted with resignation. Stan and his army pal, Gordon Hunter, helped each other deal with bouts of dizziness and vomiting as the swell of the Atlantic tossed them around the decks. Their captain, Ronald Horner, braved the discomfort and suffered alongside his men. They didn't know how long they would be at sea; all they could do was get used to the heaving colossal waves. When they recovered, Horner would fend off his men's flippant jokes, then one day the scene changed, as Stan recorded in his tiny notebook:

> *After* [four] *days at sea, we sighted another flotilla. There were battleships in the distance, and this turned out to be the Americans who had come to escort us across the remainder of the Atlantic and into Halifax, Nova Scotia. It was a large complement including an aircraft carrier. The aircraft guided us into the new convoy, HS-124.[1] The destroyers swung away, and the nine remaining troopships formed into 'line ahead' ready for sailing into Halifax Harbour.*

The naval orchestration was magnificent, with the Stars and Stripes fluttering as they led the convoy. America was not involved in the European conflict and this help was a surprise. Invigorated and with boosted morale, new formation orders were detailed:

Destroyers x 3
Duchess of Atholl/MV *Sobieski*/MV *Dunbar Castle*/Battleship/Destroyer
Destroyer/Carrier/HMT *Andes*/*Duchess of Bedford*/Cruiser/Destroyer>Ahead
MV *Reina del Pacifico*/SS *Oronsay*/HMT *Orcades*/Cruiser
Destroyers x 3

Three days later, the convoy crossed the remainder of the Atlantic to their destination.

> *Halifax was a beautiful sight, swinging into the harbour. We seemed to spend the rest of the day on the Andes sailing up and down but as to why, was unknown. The port, lit up at night, was a grand sight as we'd not been used to seeing streetlights, due to the blackout at home.*

The wonderful panorama of the harbour was intriguing and enhanced their spirits. Their time on board was spent playing 'housey-housey' and staring up at the great ships that towered above them. Instructions from Captain Horner were to report to the cargo hold at 2300hrs for night unloading. The irony of working in a blackout situation was not lost on this band of army baggage handlers. Stan continued:

> *Our ship docked the following morning and we were told to standby for disembarkation. I'd had very little sleep. I was assigned as part of the detail for the baggage party which meant being allowed ashore before the rest of the company.*

Under Horner's orders, they unloaded the baggage from the Andes then reloaded on to the USS *Wakefield*.[2] There were around 6,000 troops preparing to board.

Stan noticed the incredible streetlights. The troops from 'Blighty' had not seen such a sparkling display for a long time, but when the lights went off at 11 p.m. their task became dangerously difficult. Only a ray of torchlight provided respite from the shadows; meantime, fingers and toes were crushed when others' feet or heavy crates landed on extremities. Hard army boots sustained a lot of toe stubbing that night, but despite the hazards the dedicated team completed the task.

> *We went into one of the warehouses and in the corner, we saw several broken hoop and sacks of ground nuts – peanuts! We thought this a luxury as we'd not seen peanuts for a long while, so we took quite a*

few bags back to the ship and later distributed them among the rest of the lads. We thought they were great, but soon we found out they were for the pigs! Eventually we unloaded everything and headed out to our new ship, the USS Wakefield. There we settled into our bunks, which for our section were hammocks strung across the promenade deck, but they were comfortable – very comfortable to be precise, at least we weren't below deck. That day we had a long delay for our dinner, but it was well worth the wait. The Yanks certainly knew how to dish out food to the troops.

Stan was delighted to be part of the baggage team; they were always first off. Under Horner's charge for administration and wages, they were a fit and able group. Eventually, 20,000 troops boarded six convoy ships under cover of darkness: London Cockneys,[3] Irish, Scots and Welsh. Quite a mix.

*   *   *

Fergus Anckorn observed the scene from the bow of the troopship, SS *Orcades*, and wondered why American vessels were leading the convoy. The troops had been trained for desert warfare, with the objective, they thought, of a mission in Egypt. It was top secret due to the tremendous risk of submarine attacks in the Mediterranean and the Atlantic by German Wolf Packs.[4] Was the 18th Division sailing halfway round the world only to reach Cairo via the Suez Canal?

But as they followed the additional escort westward, they realised they were not going to the Mediterranean or the Suez Canal. This was a puzzling move, and the troops had many questions. Either way, they disembarked and Fergus's troop reloaded and boarded a different ship, the USS *West Point*. The mission, William Sail WS-12X, was now HS-124, pulling out of Halifax Harbour. The mystery deepened, but soon the second convoy was underway, sailing south down the east coast of America.

Portside
3 x Destroyers
Fleet Oil Tanker/Cruiser
Destroyer/*Orizaba*/*J T Dickman*/*Leonard Wood*/Destroyer>Ahead
Aircraft Carrier/Cruiser
West Point/*Wakefield*/*Mount Vernon*
3 x Destroyers
Starboard
Smaller vessels to portside, larger to starboard.

The USS *Manhattan* passenger liner, now USS *Wakefield*, was named after George Washington's birthplace, Wakefield Manor. It had many seafaring knots in its history: 'The primary mission of the USS *Wakefield* is to provide safe and expeditious overseas transportation for personnel materiel between established ports and bases.'

Having two previous Admirals in command: Admiral Russell Randolph Waeshe and Rear Admiral Wilfred Neville Derby, the role of command for this posting now fell to Rear Admiral William Kirk Scammell, of the US Coast Guard.

The convoy was later joined by aircraft carrier USS *Ranger*[5] and heavy cruisers USS *Vincennes*[6] and USS *Quincy*[7] with a division of eight destroyers. As the many vessels moved into the Caribbean Sea, the destroyers reloaded their depth charges – another reminder of war.

Trinidad Harbour

Stan pulled his diary from the pocket of his shorts and continued to write:

On 9 November we set sail, but we didn't know where. This journey seemed very pleasant: a good variety of chicken and pork [well-fed on peanuts no doubt] *which we'd not seen in the British Isles for ages. On the 10th we woke up to find the crew had changed into their white drill uniforms suitable for tropical weather. The sun was very hot. On 18 November we arrived at Trinidad Harbour. A fuel tanker came along side to refuel. A Commodore also came on board but that was to only tell us that we still had no shore leave. Not that any of us were terribly worried. Most of the journey my friends and I spent sunbathing – sounds like a summer cruise!*

He also noticed things he hadn't seen before: no one sat down for meals! The British troops and other enlisted personnel stood up to eat at 4ft-high counters, row upon row at chest height. Queues seemed normal, meal to meal, but many catering crews came from the Caribbean and their joviality eased the long wait. Even the US crews would stand to eat with everyone else. Now, as well as fresh fruit for breakfast, they had sugar and butter. Some put sugar in their pockets! Due to rationing, the British troops hadn't seen these commodities for months. The quality of food was impressive and despite unnecessary portion control lectures from British brigadiers, the lads had a feast of plenty.

The American penchant for fun and music could not be faulted. With a gramophone and a PA system, Glenn Miller's orchestra played cruise overtures, including *Moonlight Serenade*, *Little Brown Jug*, *My Prayer*, *Tuxedo Junction* and *Chattanooga Choo Choo*. Enthusiastic high spirits were the order of most days. The only irritating problem was the boats were 'dry'. While Stan's buddy, Gordon, missed his wee dram of whisky, it was senior officers who were the least pleased.

But all was not quite as peaceful on board, as the US Coast Guard continued to complain about the enormity of mealtimes. Only one dining room and no lounges, apart from the officers' mess room, meant long queues and soldiers lying everywhere. Some senior officers used their shaded cabins, but lower ranks sat most of the day on the sun deck. The ship was under command of the US Coast Guard, but US Navy personnel were also aboard.

As they approached Trinidad, the sound of Catalina flying boats was heard, and the planes came along side to greet them. These incredible amphibious aircraft, the men learned, would be a regular feature in the coming months.

The Gulf of Paria was a vivid blue with calm waters and the convoy dropped anchors 7 miles offshore. Daily news sheets from officers said little about future destinations, but here, with the Port of Spain so close, men were dismayed to find they were prohibited from going ashore. It was noticed though, that two people with special privileges did. Few men saw them leave in the officials' tender; Stan and Gordon wondered why they could go ashore when others couldn't. American crew said they weren't missing much as the town was hot and dusty with only one hotel, The Queen's Park. Nonetheless, it was an opportunity to send letters home via the 18th Division's postal unit, who liaised with Port of Spain officials.

On 22 November, at 1400hrs, the anchors under Convoy HS-124 were raised in Trinidad and the fleet headed south. It was a magnificent sight of imposing vessels. The secret mission had docked four days to replenish fuel and supplies before slipping away again, leaving its army passengers on board in awe of the mastery of incredible seamanship as well as the luscious Caribbean scenery. The verdant islands were stunning; some said reminiscent of England's green and pleasant land emerging from a turquoise sea of warmth and peacefulness. Other scenes were quite unworldly for the parochial homeland troops confronted with geographic spectacles; one amazed army private described vast deposits of red mud from the Orinoco River as 'an incredible natural terracotta panorama'.

The course was set via Tobago, but the weather had changed and visibility was poor. Troops knew the island was close but could see nothing. Slowly they headed out into the Atlantic. They wondered where they would be going next as the roar of a plane took off from its flight-deck and circled overhead. The majestic aircraft carrier USS *Ranger* was leaving HS-124 as the vessels once more manoeuvred from column formation to line abreast. US Coast Guard Officials deemed protection from the mighty *Ranger* no longer necessary.

As we headed towards the equator on Monday, 24 November, we had several 'crossing the line' ceremonies.[8] This is a navy tradition where each time the equatorial line is crossed there is an expected prank of some kind performed on equatorial novices. A lot of ducking and diving went on. The month was creeping past and we were getting browned off being sailors, more than soldiers!

Clearly, Stan wanted nothing to do with this.

Almost everyone on board was a novice 'Pollywog'. Initiation was seen to be fun, except if you were the novice or the target. In this case a large black American cook was the obliging 'Royal Baby', with his big pot belly on view for all first-timers to kiss his bellybutton. Presiding over the ceremony was Neptune, traditionally the ship's captain. Many troops refused but the crew insisted; even the captain hadn't crossed the equator before and had to kiss the Royal Baby's bellybutton! The ceremony took hours with much coercion. Frightened by the mariners' myth – that their ship would sink to the depths of Neptune's watery world – many new 'sailors' complied. Each of the zigzagging detours across the equator hoped to avoid U-boats. The monotonous ceremonies were frequent, but many lives of sailors and soldiers were saved by these actions.

* * *

The heaving swells of the southern Atlantic were mastered by the experienced coast guard crew of Fergus's ship, the USS *West Point*. The vessel was originally USS *America*, built in Newport, Virginia, in 1937. Its interior was one of few maritime projects by Smyth, Urquhart and Marckwald, a New York design team consisting mostly of women. The huge first-class cruise ship, launched by the First Lady, Eleanor Roosevelt, was now converted for wartime operations – drab on the outside but luxurious within. State cabins remained, with gold taps, plus a gymnasium, steam cubicles and new electrical appliances. A large swimming pool rested deep in the bowels, designed to withstand the pitching and rolling of the high seas. Troops could even have suits made by an on-board tailor. There was a dry cleaner, shops for cigars, confectionery, even ice-cream, a distant memory of pre-war Britain. Eight levels were served by lifts operated by smart Caribbean attendants, sharp in white uniforms. It had everything including storage spaces the size of warehouses, operating with forklift trucks. It took a week to acclimatise.

On this fabulous ship, Fergus heard a tannoy call for a magician.

'Anyone here 'do' conjury?'

Mesmerised by his surroundings, Fergus remembered that he was a magician and could 'do' conjury.

He made himself known to the announcements office and was introduced to a gentleman called Ray Hafler, an American entertainer and magician. They swapped ideas on different techniques. Hafler had a bias towards the mental style of sorcery, Fergus was more practical. Once again, he would be part of a concert party to entertain troops, as they sailed across the ocean.

The troops were considered passengers, totally disconnected from nautical operations. But throughout they were reminded on several occasions there was a war on. At times this was easy to forget with perfect cruising weather and glorious food. One officer worried about the size and richness of American portions and demanded rationing, but was told, 'soldiers are guests of the US Navy', and that he should stop trying to restrict their diets.

A certain amount of free time was given and sometimes this got them into scrapes. One night, Fergus smelled a pleasing aroma of roast chicken and followed its source to a large kitchen near his cabin. Inside he could see a pile of roast chicken pieces and asked the cook what would happen to all the food?

'Leftovers,' came the reply, 'We're about to chuck it overboard.' To avoid food poisoning, the crew immediately disposed of surplus cooked food.

Horrified by the waste, he vehemently complained and was subsequently invited to take some, which he did, enough for the whole of his mess. Soon several others, including Red Cap army police, followed the aroma trail and participated. Nothing would be wasted. After the meat was devoured, Fergus went up two decks, found a port hole and pushed the bones into the sea, but the next day he learned that was a massive error.

Dropping chicken bones into the sea could have provided the perfect trail for a U-boat attack, not just his ship but the full convoy. Even tossing out orange peel had its dangers. Luckily, he was not reported and avoided the punishment of a court martial. Waste from kitchens, he learned, was always significantly reduced in a specific procedure to minimise the risk of food trails. The convoy continued and after several more days they approached Cape Town for refuelling.

Chapter 4

Cape Town

Stan noted the beginning of his short stay in South Africa in his diary:

We arrived at Cape Town's harbour on 9 December 1941. What a welcome we had! There were so many people to greet us. I went ashore in the evening with my friend Gordon. We had a few beers, which was a change as the American ships were dry. I bought some chocolate, and we went to the cinema; the Carlton I believe.

The expectation of setting foot on land was heaven after six weeks on the Atlantic, but as the convoy approached the tip of Africa the weather turned. Large walls of relentless waves pounded the vessels. Troops were advised to shelter in their bunks, from which they would not emerge for another thirty-six hours. The cruel sea battered the cruiser USS *Vincennes*, a heavy convoy ship, which lost a motor whaleboat. Biplanes were ripped from other carriers, but no lives were lost.

The storm abated and under blue skies HS-124 'Winston's Special', William Sail 12X, sailed into the harbour at Cape Town. The troops were told the HMS *Prince of Wales* had docked there previously on 25 October, an event that was jubilantly celebrated by the Cape Town residents. The troops had a good welcome then, and this new battalion looked forward to similar treatment.

The convoy radioed ahead 1,500 miles from land and Gordon was excited to send a postal unit cable to his brother and sister informing them of his forty-eight hours shore leave. As dawn broke and the fleet approached, the excited troops were incredulous at the expanding scene before them. They had woken early and assembled on the decks, as the silhouette of Cape Town's Table Mountain grew to reveal the huge flat-topped rocky mass against the blue South African sky. Many had never seen such an arresting sight, or such an imposing backdrop for a capital city. Drawing closer, flurries of people and colourful cars on the harbour rushed around in immense excitement, and claxon noise from both the harbour and fleet was completely deafening.

Stan was lucky to have Gordon with him as he had family in Cape Town able to play host while they were on shore.

When they disembarked at 1 p.m. the following day, Hughy, Gordon's brother, met them at the port and they had a glorious afternoon exploring the sights, buying and eating chocolate, going to the cinema and nipping into Delmonico's,[1] the place to 'be' in Cape Town. Stan imbibed one lager and a whisky and felt quite tipsy after; a result of the dry American ship which left most of the troops, deprived of alcohol for several weeks, now unable to hold their drink.

The next day, they arranged to meet Hughy at the gates again, but he didn't show. They waited some time, and eventually decided to stick to the plan to visit Gordon's sister, Cissy. Gordon had the address and led the way. But Hughy wasn't there either. Nonetheless, Cissy was delighted to see them and had bowls of strawberries and cream ready, which the pair hungrily demolished; they had not eaten strawberries in months. Still uncertain about Hughy, they all went to St James Beach at Muizenberg, next to the Indian Ocean. They walked on the soft sand, meeting other troops, and watched as surfers demonstrated intriguing water skills. Stan and Gordon swam in the ocean and tried surfing on their stomachs. Stan loved to swim and was the fitter of the two; having dark hair he was also extremely tanned. Gordon, on the other hand, was fair skinned and burned easily. They returned to Cissy's for tea – still no Hughy – then went back to the disembarkation gate, where they found him. Nobody was more pleased. Hughy had worried he might never see them again. The meeting place had been misconstrued, but there was still time to revisit Delmonico's. Cape Towners were incredible, providing troops with free use of their transport system and free confectionery from shop owners. It was astounding.

*   *   *

Stan and Gordon then heard terrible news from their American crew, about a Japanese bomb attack on Pearl Harbor on 7 December. The US Naval Fleet in Hawaii had been decimated. These times were worrying for a soldier at sea, but on 11 December, they brushed aside their concerns to concentrate on the journey ahead and arranged to meet Hughy again at the gates; no misunderstandings this time. They all agreed a 'refresher' was necessary with more beers, swimming and sunbathing, and photographs as reminders of the wonderful time they were having, far from Britain's blackouts and bombings. They were also pleased to be away from regimental orders. For the final hurrah, they revisited their favourite shops and Delmonico's for a grand supper. Hughy treated them to schnapps!

But their joy ended abruptly when they heard of another bombing by the Japanese in the South China Sea. This time it was the HMS *Prince of Wales*[2]. In November, the hero ship had been in Cape Town and the residents felt they personally knew every soldier and sailor. All were in disbelief. On 10 December the vessel had sunk within an hour. The ship had been in open waters near Kuantan, as part of naval mission fleet, Force Z, when Japan launched its catastrophic air attack. With HMS *Repulse*, it was one of the first British capital ships sunk by enemy aircraft. Unfortunately, the British government had been unable to provide sufficient aircraft reinforcement to protect them. Two thousand survivors were picked up; 850 men died.

*   *   *

Gordon was sad to leave his older siblings on the dock and, as they bid farewell to Hughy and Cissy, Stan felt the same emotion. There was little conversation on the *Wakefield* as their ship pulled away. The two men waved at the place where they thought Gordon's brother and sister were standing, until their arms ached.

Stan leaned on the ship's railings and smiled, thinking about the great time they'd had. Hughy lived in Accra on the west Gold Coast, though he never spoke about his job, and Cissy, his older sister, had been in Cape Town for some time. Stan couldn't thank Gordon enough for his family's hospitality and the pair planned a return visit to Cape Town with their respective wives after the war.

Stan had met Gordon during manoeuvres in Norfolk. He was younger, from Scotland, and in January 1941 had married Lizzie, his sweetheart from Paisley. When they met up again on the *Andes*, they were delighted to be in the same unit and maintained an unspoken sense of family as pangs of homesickness were pushed aside to face the reality of their situation.

As the bright and beautiful magnificence of Table Mountain gradually faded to a pink and purple hue against clear blue sky, Stan pinched the top of his nose and screwed up his eyes for a split second to control his emotions. Soon the proud mass disappeared completely as the ship sped away from the Cape of Good Hope. The name made him wonder if their next stop could fulfil that promise.

The colourful South African stopover was an unexpected experience, filled with generosity and friendliness, a stark contrast to the war-torn sadness of the Britain they'd left two months earlier. But with the kindness came whispers of sympathy, especially as the convoy's American sailors were now involved. President Roosevelt had declared war on Japan on 8 December and South Africans feared for the young troops, especially after the shock of losing the HMS *Prince of Wales*. Would they also perish in the same way?

* * *

Most of the troops in the convoy had never heard of Pearl Harbor, including some Americans. The surprise attack on the island of Oahu, Hawaii, had taken place on Sunday, 7 December at 0745. Nineteen ships were sunk with more than 2,400 lives lost. The incident brought America firmly into the war. Reports said it was an unprovoked raid, but tensions had been brewing for several years between Japan and America over land disputes with China.

A state of war now existed between the United States and the Japanese Empire. President Roosevelt's speech broadcast to America on 8 December was crystal clear: 'December 7th, 1941 – a date that will live in infamy ... No matter how long it may take us to overcome this pre-meditated invasion ... The American people in their righteous might, will win through to absolute victory.'[3]

Churchill promised that Britain would also declare war on Japan within the hour. Japan countered with its own declaration: 'The entire nation will immobilise its entire strength, so that nothing will miscarry in our attainment of our war aims.'

With the depressing news, the Allied troops and sailors had no doubt they were truly in a world war. Moods changed and as the convoy departed Cape Town for Mombasa on Saturday, 13 December, Stan recorded:

> *We headed north towards Durban and Suez, or so we thought, but after Madagascar, we discovered this was wrong. Our direction was now easterly, and again we would have to pass over the equator!*

With new declarations of war, their purpose moved to a different and more serious level. None of the troops knew their destination, but the fear of impending battle was now extremely troubling. A different escort destroyer, HMS *Dorsetshire* – identified by its camouflage, a pink painted bow and black funnels, known as *'the Dorset'*[4] – made a surprise move in the Mozambique Channel and peeled away towards the African coast, leading *Orizaba* and *Mount Vernon* west for refuelling in Mombasa.

The remainder of the convoy stayed on an easterly course, but on Christmas Day the *Dorset* returned to the middle of the Indian Ocean. Alongside the *West Point* and *Wakefield*, its marine brass band, in full white uniform and helmets, played patriotic music and festive tunes to raise the troops' spirits. For many it was their first Christmas away from home, but Stan indicated sea life was once more bearable.

> *The meal was great – turkey with all the trimmings. The old man, Winston Churchill, gave us a gift of 100 cigarettes and matches, with sweets.[5] Senior officers rallied round to give the commanders presents of army socks filled with the government gifts and their own contributions, to show appreciation.*

Major General Beckwith-Smith, known as 'Becky', was delighted and wasted no time in showing his appreciation for such kindness from his men. There was a panto on deck and Stan wrote:

It was quite a good show.' The Dorset's brass band provided a rousing festive celebration with renditions of 'A Nightingale Sang in Berkeley Square', 'Bless 'em All', *and* 'Whispering Grass', *among others. It was memorable for all but sadly the familiar tunes from home would be the last some would hear.*

After the joyful Christmas and camaraderie, the *Dorset* returned to the *Orizaba* and *Mount Vernon*. The men then realised they had no escort, except for a Royal Navy cruiser. A tannoy announcement confirmed their small convoy was heading towards India. It was further unwanted news which indicated they would train in jungle warfare to fight the Japanese. The attack on Pearl Harbor was the main reason. The troops of the 18th Division were in a state of numbness as their life compass suddenly changed and they learned they would be the defending army for the Far East. Left to fend for themselves, the under-protected seafaring troops of the *Wakefield* and *West Point* felt forgotten and alone. As they sped towards an unknown port,[6] Stan wrote: *'After more boring and silly days at sea, crossing the equator, we felt helpless but eventually became resigned to our fate, there was nothing we could do but follow orders.'*

They approached the coast of Bombay a few days later, ready to obey High Command and 'serve' in India. With courage and steadfastness, the troops drilled themselves mentally for serious warfare. But the reality of fear in battle was yet to surface. Their natural zest for fun was rekindled after the thrill of the ocean and the thought of a new country and new adventure. They even felt they knew what to expect in India because they'd seen pictures on Pathé News.

* * *

But while they enjoyed Christmas music in the Indian Ocean, they were unaware of carnage taking place at St Stephens College Hospital, Hong Kong, as soldiers of the Imperial Japanese Army rampaged through, brutally killing patients and medical staff. Heavy casualties revealed the Nippon savagery as horrific details were reported by survivors. They witnessed unspeakable scenes of murder and were herded into tiny hospital rooms where they were left to die. Many of those slaughtered were commissioned nurses, self-sufficient respected women with an inspiring commitment to professional duty. There was no indication of danger and they believed this was an adventure offering tantalising 'freedom', away from battle-weary Britain and rationing. Those who survived were sent to North Point prison camp, eastern Hong Kong.[7]

Chapter 5

Ahmednagar, India

Under Major General Beckwith-Smith, overall general commanding officer of the 18th Division, Captain Ronald Horner had orders issued by Brigadier E. H. W. Backhouse to take charge of entraining cargo from the *Wakefield* and the *West Point* via rail to the barracks at Ahmednagar. Stan and Gordon were once again part of his team, assisting a smooth and speedy transition of supplies on Bombay's dockside.

Horner was the 'supreme' organiser of supplies and now, under the major general, was responsible for moving the division's baggage and supplies to barracks at Ahmednagar. This also incorporated the 54th and the 55th brigades.[1] Brigadier Backhouse[2] had insisted Horner resume the position he'd held since October in Liverpool, as ship's baggage officer. At the time, Horner admitted he'd taken a dim view, as it was not an easy job but, as Backhouse later pointed out – when he apologised for asking him to undertake the task yet again – Horner was the one who knew all the ropes; speedy unloading at the next destination was essential.

Captain Horner was a seasoned soldier, having attested to the Royal Artillery in 1939 while a recruit of the Officer Cadet Reserves. But in an urgent appeal for drivers, he later transferred to the RASC. He lived in St Albans, Hertfordshire, with his wife Florence, and their young daughter Elizabeth – whose small black and white photos were nestled between the banknotes in his wallet. He was called up in February 1940 and as part of B Troop on the *Amazone*, helped evacuate troops at Dunkirk in May and June of that year. He was commissioned again in July and elevated to the rank of captain, responsible for 292 Supply Company. This was an accountable position he'd sought for a while and, in Norfolk, was charged with a sizeable number of military novices. He just hoped they were all trained adequately to assist him with the dispatches and deliveries of all kinds. He feared the young men might be rather callow. The enormity of the task in accurately disseminating messages, food, catering, fuel, armaments and equipment for multiple troop units was a satisfying challenge.[3] Changing ships in Halifax had been a surprise, but as captain he was informed a couple of days in advance, and his group managed well in the darkness. Now, approaching India, he prepared for another experience altogether and had another screed of instructions with advance information.

At the scene, Stan explained:

> *We arrived at Bombay on 27 December 1941. Gordon, myself, and a few others were detailed to see the baggage off the ship; quite an easy job in comparison, as most of the work was done by local labour. Our duties consisted of guarding the baggage and general cargo, so the natives wouldn't pinch it! While there we had the opportunity of eating bacon and beans with hamburgers, fresh butter and hot sweet tea. Actually, eating and drinking* [he said, laughing] *was the main topic in the army, we found.*

> *Around 28 December, we finished unloading our ship's cargo on to the train. The unloading consisted of bicycles, electrical equipment, mainly light stuff. We finished about 1700hrs that day. Afterwards we had a rather uncomfortable journey on the Indian train, all slab wooden seats; made our bums sore! We disembarked from the train near Ahmednagar and had breakfast at the side of the track, hard-boiled eggs, more bread and butter and hot sweet tea. Just the job.*

> *After this our unit marched off to the so-called fort. Gordon and I stayed behind to keep control of the various bits of baggage. We arrived at the fort sometime in the afternoon. It was a bit of a lousy billet. The Indian boys used to come in and clean the billets and the equipment, but they caught* [robbed] *us right left and centre; we were real rookies!*

Another so-called rookie was Freddie Holt. Stan and he were friends during army training in Knutsford and Droitwich, and one could say he was part of the baggage team too since he was Captain Horner's batman. Stan and the others would have received hints from Freddie on what might happen next, though not in detail. Stan liked this arrangement.

* * *

It was a four-hour train journey to the city of Ahmednagar, north-east of Pune in the state of Maharashtra. Ahmed Nizam Shah founded the town in the late 1490s on the site of a medieval city. Englishman, Arthur Wellesley Wellington (later Duke of Wellington, Battle of Waterloo), defeated the Maratha forces in 1803 to gain control of the fort by the East India Company, where the army then provided protection.

> *Ahmednagar, 29 December. On parade in the morning, we were allocated our duties; with another couple I had to do night guard – blooming cold! Later we moved out to proper billets. Gordon and I fiddled a guard job that night in the headquarters office which was cushy. All we had to do was show the natives – called beasties – the job they should do and how to do it.*

The days drifted by slowly for the British lads, from the warm sunrise call of the bugle to the evocative strains of the Last Post at sunset, echoes of military life rang in their ears, and Stan and Gordon would always try to pick the easy stint – the night-time lookout. To forget the night's cold, they reminisced about meals from home: a roast, a tasty stew, a hotpot or a haggis. The memory was, no doubt, culinary torture and probably harangued their taste buds, transporting them back to New Year celebrations at home. *'Come New Year's Eve we made the best of it as we could, only drinking lemonade or tea.'*

For Gordon it would soon be a year since he married Lizzie. Life in the hot January Indian climate was a million miles from the almost sub-zero temperatures of Scotland, and there were days he yearned for Scotland's chill on his face. The cool of the Indian evenings helped. The young soldiers had little to worry about, then, but knew their roles as RASC on the front line of battle might soon be tested. They were worlds away from the stark atmosphere of Great Britain and their training now was extremely strict; the fort had been their temporary base for more than two weeks and Stan's diary was filling up:

We had various duties to do. Myself, I used to go on the rations wagon. [This entailed] a trip down to Ahmednagar City to pick up the rations [he chuckled] on a bullock cart; it took us all day to collect and deliver. It was all experience.

India was full of evocative experiences. For this they would have to lift and shift jute sacks and wooden crates using a two or four-wheeled jinker[4] cart – pulled by a bullock or two – an ancient means of transport still used in some parts of the world, especially for carrying goods.

The only real bore was the RSM's parade at 0700hrs. After breakfast we often went down to the bazaar for various daily duties, and in the evening, as the canteen had opened, we could eat chicken.

Some evenings they got up to all sorts of high jinks.

We had a rather unusual incident in Ahmednaga city one evening. Three of us lads had hired bikes and rode into the city, but we had no lights and a Sikh policeman stopped us, to complain. We said: 'We're very sorry.'

He said: 'Just a moment, I'll bring my sergeant.'

This was right outside the police station! He went in to get his sergeant and we just rode off out of the way quickly. We never saw him again.

It was dark and they barely knew where they were but did get back to their billet.

During this time the Royal Artillery regularly arranged formal group photographs in front of the fort. The photographer would direct and correct the troops' posture for the professional regiment record, but some disobeyed. The 118th Field Regiment, RA, had an unruly soldier who refused to cross his arms. He was Fergus Anckorn.

Meanwhile, Stan and Gordon's three-week stay in Ahmednagar turned out to be quite reasonable, but they were soon on the move again. The baggage team diligently ensured all their supplies and equipment were correct as they loaded everything back on to rickety carriages.

On 14th January, we left Ahmednagar by train about midnight, with the advance party, heading again for Bombay. After unloading onto the dockside, a lighter came alongside the docks loaded with all our gear [jungle warfare kit], *several lighters that is, and blow me, we went straight back to USS Wakefield which we'd left 3 weeks ago!*

Dhows or 'lighters' are boats that deliver to ships in deeper waters. Dealing with sea vessels' cargo was additional to their training, but the entraining of thousands of kits and equipment was efficient and well established. The next train to arrive was also loaded with gear for the Royal Artillery regiment from the *West Point*. Most were for Bombay, but some 18th Division units went to a Deolali base, still in Maharashtra, about an hour's drive further north. The Divisional Reconnaissance Battalion and the 125th Anti-Tank Regiment, would follow later.

The soldiers observed again the shocking down-trodden existence of people living in squalor by the railway during their return journey to Bombay. How could people be forced to live in such terrible poverty? But then the men remembered these subjects lived under British rule. It was a shameful situation, but they too were inclined to turn their backs and run from the dirt and sickly stench of rotting vegetation, sewage, pungent spices and sweat that constantly lingered.

At Bombay's vast and ornate Victorian terracotta railway station, scenes of deprivation persisted. Empire buildings crumbled in filth and disrepair, and street urchins begged for rupees in the hustle and bustle, while the long warbling calls of Tamil market traders rang out selling food, to those who could afford to buy, next to the dusty roadside. The cacophony mingled with caged squawking chickens, about to be sold for slaughter, while car horns shrilled and drivers yelled, and tuk-tuk vehicles kicked up dust as they deftly weaved through traffic.

In the mayhem, flashes of brightly coloured saris, with cream tones of tunics and turbans lifted the scene through the heat and dust, against a promising backdrop of blue sky. Bombay was busy! The station conditions were cramped, and one could hear the scratchy noise of a gramophone record playing, while a peeling film poster caught Stan and Gordon's attention. The music was from the film *Khandan*.[5] As they waited in line for roll call in front of the station, where the big Victorian clock struck every fifteen minutes, the sound of the chimes and Indian music might have prompted them to dance, but they had serious soldiering to do, and flippancy was not permitted.

They stayed in Bombay for about four days and nights and, although the light-hearted film *Pictures of Tonga* entertained them briefly, the Western troops continued to be staggered by the poverty around them. Watching from their ship's deck one night, they were alarmed to see that some of the lighters were literally alight, and rather too close for comfort.

> *The sight was incredible. The navy did no more than put a line to the boat and towed it away from the ship to let it burn in the bay, where it finally sank.*
>
> *I don't know what happened to the natives aboard!*

The fires were caused by the constant high temperatures and charcoal, which locals burnt to cook their meals on board. Witnessing the portside challenges was unbelievable and, at times, amusing for the young soldiers.

*   *   *

Horner had also left Ahmednagar fort with the advance baggage party on 14 January, heading for Bombay. They had changed at Dhown,[6] where he lunched with the Railway Transport Officer (RTO) and observed the curious habits of passengers arriving and departing on a long-distance train. The filth and dust of basic third-class crowded travelling conditions was equally shocking – 'interesting yet primitive', wrote Horner. After a short stop at Poona, they reached Bombay at 2030hrs and Horner met with his army friends, 'Trader' Horn and Denis Pearl. But among the excessive dust and pungent smells, duties had to be completed in preparation for the next part of their voyage.

As baggage officer, Horner knew the *Wakefield's* holds like the back of his hand, as did his team of able lads. At the Bombay dockside, they separated the Royal Artillery's baggage from RASC and loaded it on to cranes; there were two for separating 'wanted' or 'not wanted' items. Ammunition was also loaded, which had its own dhow and guard. There seemed to be a hundred coolies helping, but they wanted to put *Wakefield* baggage on to the West Point. In the confusion, the reloading took over thirty-six hours. They managed a few hours' sleep, and by 1115hrs they were alongside the *Wakefield*, lying out in the stream. The dhows were then tethered alongside the correct holds: an awkward job with strong tides and waves as they loaded continuously until the last item was on board at 0230 hrs.

Right from the beginning, labels indicated artillery vehicles were destined for 'Singapore'. Some loaders thought it a 'military ruse' but now this seemed to be true.[7]

During the final hour in Bombay, Stan remembered:

> *The rest of our company arrived the next day and they all boarded the Wakefield, but we stayed ashore and were lucky enough to spend an evening in the town with two ORs and two officers. We went to the pictures but couldn't do much else because we didn't have enough money.*[8]

> *We had a good meal at the NAAFI that evening, but it was terrible to see the natives sleeping on the pavements, just covered with loin cloths. All the regiments had embarked on 'lighters' at the dock and were taken aboard the Wakefield or the West Point. We boarded on the 18th at midday, back to the same bunks we had prior to arriving in Bombay, which made it very convenient. We were glad to get back to the ship's food!*

The *West Point* and *Wakefield* were fully loaded with troops and cargo by 0100 hrs on 9 January. Other ships in the convoy were the *Empire Star*, the *Duchess of Bedford* and the *Empress of Japan*. They set sail from Bombay, now part of convoy BM11. Lying in his familiar bunk on board, Stan scribbled:

> '*Sailing due South. We're going to have a go at the Japs*', and later lamented, '*Little did we know what was in store for us*'.

The news was confirmed by the ship's ubiquitous tannoy announcements as their convoy turned east. The 18th Division would not be Desert Rats, but instead re-routed and partially re-trained, to fight the Japanese Army pouring through the jungles of Malaysia. The fun part was nearly over.

Chapter 6

Somewhere Beyond the Indian Ocean

BM11 Convoy sailed from Bombay 19.1.1942:
5 Light ack-acks (AA) Batteries, 1 Light Tank Squadron,
Railway Company.
(18th Div. less 53rd Brigade group of 17000 troops & stores).
USS *West Point*, USS *Wakefield*, RMS *Empress of Japan*,
MV *Empire Star*,
SS *Duchess of Bedford*.
Escort ships: *Exeter, Dragon, Durban, Glasgow, Thanet, Tenedos, Express,
Electra, Caledon.*
Reached Singapore 29.1.1942.[1]

Mid-January 1942 – Tranquillity Before Tension

Horner was certain they were either going to Burma, Java, Sumatra,
Singapore or Australia, with the first three places being more likely. HMS
Hampshire had left the convoy and turned towards Ceylon.[2]

On the USS *Wakefield*, Horner, Stan and Gordon had plenty of time to write
in their diaries, and life on board was eventful with many concerts to keep
up the troops' morale. These were always held on 'B' Deck aft and organised
by the British with the Americans joining in. The national anthems of both
countries were played and the hymn *Abide with Me*,[3] was sung at the end of
the evening as ships rolled across the ocean. It was peaceful; *'the sound of it
all was lovely and tranquil.'*

> *Abide with me, fast falls the eventide. The darkness deepens, Lord
> with me abide.*

Between 22 and 26 January, Stan recalled:

> *Crossed the equator line again. (That was getting rather monotonous.)*
> *Paravanes* [detectors] *were put out on either side of the ships to detect*
> *any mines laid by the Japanese.*

This was worrisome, but interesting, nonetheless. Buoyed by strong escorts their route was set: they appeared to be heading towards Singapore.

* * *

On 23 January 1942, a sister convoy, BM12 departed Bombay for Singapore with 3,800 men from the 9th and 11th Northumberland Fusiliers and their associated supplies. It consisted of the *Empress of Asia*, *Felix Roussel*, the Dutch vessel *Plancius*, the *Devonshire* and later the *City of Canterbury* (which was involved in the mutiny at Durban, and later joined the convoy early in 1942, off Batavia). The *Felix Roussel* primarily carried stores and supplies. The convoy was protected by a strong naval presence, including HMS *Exeter*, the makeup of the escort changed as the voyage progressed.

BM12 Convoy Sailed from Bombay 23.1.1942:

Drafts for 9th & 11th DIVISIONS 3800 TROOPS & STORES.

DIV TROOPS for 18th DIVISION.[4]

Empress of Asia – Felix Roussel – Devonshire – Plancius

ESCORTS: *Encounter – Exeter – Danae – Sutlej – Yarra*

(*City of Canterbury*)

Reached Singapore 5.2.1942

Effective techniques to skirt around U-boat threats in the Atlantic had been successfully engaged with the help of British Intelligence. Now, similarly, the troopship decelerated their route to Java, in Japanese-controlled waters around the Malay Peninsula. From Ceylon, across the Bay of Bengal, Andaman Sea and down the Straits of Malacca, skilled, but time-consuming, dogleg routes via western Sumatra and the Sunda Strait, were employed instead.

This third leg of the voyage[5] was a laborious 200-mile detour, but the landscape provided incredible distractions, including Krakatoa, the imposing volcano between Sumatra and Java, and the Berahla Straits. Picturesque scenes of Sumatran life were observed in verdant jungle and on mangrove shores, where fishermen and their families lived in hastily erected huts on spindly stilts. As they zigzagged back and forth, the convoy crossed the equator line again. Each time the sailors' debunking tradition continued. Most soldiers hated the intrusion and tired of the ritual, but some enjoyed the spectacle.

On 27 January, the troops were given respite from their daily drills and the seaworthy men had time to reflect on their journey. It certainly was full of fond life-changing memories which, they felt, would last forever, and as they sped cleanly across the water under clear equatorial skies, the sun glinted on crested waves, making them feel exhilarated and that life was good.

In the distance, one could still pick out the sharp, but skewed, monumental silhouette of Krakatoa. Stan felt amazing sights such as these would probably never be seen again once he was back in chilly England. The evening weather closed in and ahead looked stormy. It was nearly nine days after leaving Bombay, when the convoy[6] turned north into the Bangka Straits. As they passed the south-eastern tip of Sumatra and turned north towards Singapore, the convoy vessels fell in line. Land was nearby. Destroyers positioned themselves on each end of the convoy as the vessels followed each other through the narrow stretch of water. The guns on the warships were fully manned. The troops returned to their bunks knowing their destination was on the horizon.

A few hours later, Stan wrote: '*28 January – an enemy plane sighted. AA opened up. One paravane found the bottom of the strait* [snaps a derrick].'

Without warning, a single Japanese aircraft had flown over and 'dropped a stick of bombs'. They missed the ships, but the sea erupted from the explosions and the rapid movement of the convoy's destroyer as it returned fire. One AA burst lifted a wing off the plane but there was no retaliation until later; it probably failed to reach its base. As their convoy line remained stationary in the straits that day, they were 'an ideal target with no room for manoeuvre'.[7] It was a small glimpse of what they were later to experience with erratic shows of Japanese intentions.

Nothing more attacked, and peace returned to the idyllic scene of bright sunshine and blue, but choppy, sea. The troops later heard the area was shark infested!

They continued without further harassment in the darkness, but visibility was good enough to see land, as they passed through narrow waterways between the islands. The *West Point* and the *Wakefield* moved ahead in the strait, travelling at full speed with *Empress of Japan* close behind. The starlit night framed a hazy moon and shone on the frothing wake of the silent ships. Only the sound of water reverberating on the rocks could be heard. With great stealth, the convoy steered through deep waters and land-mass obstacles. It was breathtaking, as the crews expertly navigated the strait at full speed towards Singapore.

Briefings were held on board, which all troops were ordered to attend. Colonels revealed strategic information by way of a Far East map dotted in red to represent British Army units on the Malay Peninsula. The position of the 53rd Brigade, who had gone ahead, was also marked with red dots but surrounding these were yellow dots indicating the Japanese Army. Morale of the troops at that point was considerably reduced and jocular attempts were made to bolster spirits with derogatory comments about the Japanese – but they were not amused, just alarmed and demoralised.

Winston's Specials – BM11 and BM12 – addressed as Task Force 14.2, approached Singapore's Empire Docks, Keppel Harbour, at the end of January and into February.

THE 17 DAY BATTLE

JANUARY 1942

Order of Battle – 18th Division Singaporc 1942[1]

Officer commanding: Major General M. B. Beckwith-Smith.

Royal Artillery: 88th, 118th, 135th & 148th Field Regiments,
85th & 125th Anti-Tank Regiments

Royal Engineers: 287, 288 & 560 Field Companies, 251 Field Park Coy.

Royal Army Service Corps: Headquarters, 53rd, 54th, & 55th Brigade
Group Companies; 18th Division Troops Company, 16th Mobile Bath Unit.

Royal Army Ordnance Corps: 18th Div. Ordnance Workshops,
18th Div. Field Park.

Royal Army Medical Corps: 186th, 197th & 198th Field Ambulances.

53rd Infantry Brigade: Brigadier C L Duke

Headquarters

5th Royal Norfolk Regiment, 6th Royal Norfolk Regiment,
2nd Cambridgeshire Regiment.

54th Infantry Brigade: Brigadier E H W Backhouse

Headquarters

4th Royal Norfolk Regiment, 4th Suffolk Regiment, 5th Suffolk Regiment.

55th Infantry Brigade: Brigadier T. H. Massey-Beresford

Headquarters

5th Beds and Herts Regiment, 1/5th Sherwood Foresters,
1st Cambridgeshire Regiment.

18th Divisional Troops

9th & 11th Royal Northumberland Fusiliers.

Recce Corps (5th Loyals).

Chapter 7

Keppel Harbour

I n Keppel Harbour, destruction and attrition were distinctly visible. Bomb craters and blemishes from spattered gunfire along the harbour walls, greeted the troops as they disembarked.

We arrived in Singapore [Keppel] Harbour on 29 January. Soon after we docked the sirens went off. The AA opened again as bombs dropped. The main party disembarked and set off for Tanglin Barracks. Gordon and I, and the rest of the baggage party, and two other men, stayed behind to supervise unloading the gear. The officers' kits were moved first, the majority for Tanglin. I was left on my own to finish the job. Not a very pleasant task knowing the Japs were making for the docks, with their bombs dropping nearby every now and again.

Stan wrote about joyful events, but most others were distressing:

We got to the barracks with the baggage about 1700hrs that day. While I was there Gordon gave me two cables, one from Pat and one from my mother. They made me very happy.

When they docked at Keppel Harbour earlier that morning, around 0900hrs, 29 January, Horner and his team were first ashore and contacted the Embarkation Staff Officer (ESO) to arrange baggage and cargo off-loading. The quayside and go-downs (warehouses) were crammed with supplies of all sorts and the job was difficult due to lack of space. Interruptions were frequent, as at every alert both Chinese coolies and US Coast Guards downed tools. Into the night the men and their helpers had been quite blasé, but they soon dived for cover as more sticks of bombs were delivered. Searchlights picked up other Japanese bomber aircraft following them across the sky, but no fighter planes appeared and no AA. Unloading cargo was a massive task, now with added safety considerations.

> *30 January: The Japs made a* [bombing] *raid on the dockside and one of our party was there. They dropped a bomb clean down the funnel of the Wakefield. One of our corporals, Percy, got his face blackened but that was all.*

Stan was referring to Percy Warnes, a private from the Norfolks.

When the docks were targeted by Japanese pattern bombing and the *Wakefield* was hit at 1100hrs on 'B' deck, Horner saw the burst and thought the bomb had gone straight down No.2 hold, where his party was working. Along with an assisting officer from the Suffolk regiment, he rushed on board and was pleased to see most of his baggage party lads emerging from the stairs, blackened with smoke but uninjured.

But one scorched man shouted, 'Someone is still in the hold, hurry!'

The damage was now visible, and they could see where the bomb had penetrated the deck 12ft to the portside of the hold. Underneath was the ship's hospital where a fire raged and other damaged routes were inaccessible, excepting an interior staircase that provided access for the officers where they found two US medical orderlies trying to lift a stretcher patient out of the burning area. The man was not part of Stan and Horner's party, but all around endured intense smoke and heat, cloying black ash and the smell of burning flesh that restricted their breathing. Horner did not know if the young patient survived. Six died in the attack. After accounting for his party on the quayside, all returned to the ship to complete the task of unloading.[1]

They managed somehow and worked all night, eventually finishing at 1630hrs on 30 January. It was an horrendous hit and a dramatic near miss – too close for comfort – Stan and Gordon could have been killed.

*   *   *

The GOC (General Officer Commanding) Malaya Command was Lieutenant General Arthur E. Percival, a First World War veteran. He had served in Ireland, against the Irish Republican Army during the Anglo-Irish War, as a commander, and latterly as an intelligence officer in the Battalion of the Essex Regiment in Kinsale, County Cork. He proved to be an energetic counter-guerrilla officer with a noted talent for gathering intelligence. Between the wars, he delivered lectures on his experiences in Ireland and subsequent studies at the Staff College in Camberley, where he was one of eight students accelerated for promotion. He was appointed major with the Cheshire Regiment and spent four years in the Nigerian Regiment of the Royal West African Frontier Force. Soon after, he received brevet promotion to lieutenant colonel in 1929, followed by another year of study in 1930 at the Royal Naval College, Greenwich. His progression over the next ten years led his mentor to say: 'Percival has an outstanding ability, wide military knowledge, good judgement and is a very quick and accurate worker.' He added, however, 'He has not altogether an impressive presence and one may therefore fail, at first meeting him, to appreciate his sterling worth.'[2]

His connection to Malaya began when additional mainland forces were needed to prevent Japan from creating bases to attack Singapore. Percival was appointed full colonel in March 1936, General Staff Officer Grade 1, Chief of Staff to General Dobbie, GOC. At this time, he realised Singapore no longer held the position of an isolated fortress, and the threat of Japanese forces attacking from Siam (Thailand)[3] was real. Consequently, he provided an appraisal to the War Office. By the time war was declared in 1939, Percival had been appointed Brigadier General Staff of I Corps, British Expeditionary Force, commanded by General Sir John Dill, his mentor from the Royal Naval College. Among other positions of rank, Percival also held the post of acting major general, GOC 43 (Wessex) Division and Assistant Chief of the Imperial General Staff at the War Office. In April 1941, Percival was promoted to acting lieutenant general and GOC Malaya.

Much of the information reaching commands and headquarters was muddled. The resident Malay Command – The Manchesters – expected nothing to happen, in a careless air of idealistic oblivion. It was unthinkable to some that the jewel in the empire's crown, Singapore, could be invaded.

Others thought the causeway should be blown to stop the advancing Japanese. But troops were unable to halt them at Gemas and were outflanked by Japanese guard divisions down the west coast at Port Swettenham and Port Dixon. Defences crumbled and a shambled retreat towards the south began. With the fall of Endow and more casualties to the east on 16 January, Lieutenant General Percival and his troops were in an impossible position, with enemy aircraft bomb attacks originating from recently captured British airfields.

In less than two months, the Japanese had advanced and controlled over 500 miles of British Empire territory. Spirited and desperate defence attempts were made by Australians at the River Muar, but they were forced to break and retreat. Percival ordered a retreat across the Johor Strait to the island on 25 January, and the last of the British and Empire troops crossed on 1 February. The mainland link, the causeway, was destroyed. Now 80,000 troops (including the new 18th Division) joined a million civilians on the small land mass, the size of the Isle of Wight, wondering where the next attack would come from.

To cover and defend, Percival split the island into three sectors: north and north-east coasts, where the fresh reinforcements of the 18th Division were deployed with the 11th Indian Division, the 8th Indian Brigade and the 29th Australian Brigade; in the west were the Australian 8th and the 44th Indian; the 1st and 2nd Malaya brigades defended the south and Singapore City.

* * *

Stan and Gordon worked as a team. When all were 'hands-on-deck', or 'off-deck' as Stan liked to joke, they knew the risks were high. They now knew the threat of Japanese bombers was genuine. Their group went on to complete thirty-six hours of unloading in dire conditions. Enemy plane attacks and the whine of bombs and subsequent explosions around them were frightening. Death or injury now seemed very real. When the attacks stopped, the weary pair yearned for sustenance and sleep.

On the last day of January, the overriding feeling of the men was that they were being sacrificed. Their military 'force' had arrived in boats from a faraway garrison, directly into battle. It was a mess. There were no orders, and no one knew what would happen next.

One direct call to duty, however, was for Tanglin Barracks' drivers to collect their motorbikes for dispatch duties. '[While] *I was busy with reserve composite rationing, I also received my brand-new motorbike.*'

The Composite Ration or 'compo ration' Stan spoke of were comparable to American 10-in-1 basic standard food portions, popular with the troops. One of their favourites was a biscuit with marmalade resembling the bread portion of the American C ration. But forgetting their stomachs, Stan and his other driver friends were more than happy with their new machines and couldn't wait to be out on the road. The British Army had commissioned BSA M20 motorcycles early in the war and their success was proven time and again. The sought-after fast and reliable transport was always recognisable, painted in fuel-proof green Khaki Drab, known as KD. Each army dispatch rider was issued one with a census number of six or seven digits painted on the petrol tank. Their top speed was 60 miles per hour. A simple knob controlled the lights: T for tail, L for side, and H for headlights; handlebars were covered with canvas and there was a dust filter. Two panniers carried dispatch papers.

In between attacks, the troops marvelled at the beauty of the new land, filled with vibrant colours, exotic flowers, shrubs and tall palm trees against an azure sky. Their motorbike journeys were exhilarating, and Stan and Gordon must have relished their first day of dispatch duties, especially with new aromas, and even the pungent smell of *blachang* (native fish paste) that hung in the air.

*   *   *

The young soldiers, however, were shocked to hear stories from part of the 53rd Brigade who had arrived mid-January in Singapore on the USS *Mount Vernon*, one of the ships that had separated from their convoy in December. The brigade had found themselves assigned to Malaya to face the aggressor. They had disembarked and spent two days on the racecourse before crossing the causeway to the mainland and Batu-Phat, where they confronted the

Japanese for the first time. They were instructed to withdraw at Pontis Ketchik, on desperate orders, 'every man for himself!' Four hundred or so reached Singapore, swimming back across the strait.[4] Several of the survivors now undertook dockside duties at Keppel Harbour and retold their harrowing stories. They had set up camp around the town in the south of Singapore, but were bereft of equipment as this was destroyed when the *Empress of Asia* was hit by Japanese incendiaries and caught fire off Pulo Bukum, 11 miles west of Singapore. The brigade on board had been sent for additional training in Deolali and had left Bombay three days after the *Wakefield* departed.

On 5 February, as the *Empress* approached Singapore, it received six bombs down the deck; there were men screaming and on fire. The ship keeled over. Around fifteen men perished. Singapore was also under heavy attack with enemy bombardment, and that February morning the blazing vessel was alone. Its cargo held many troop belongings, particularly those from the *West Point*. They had no ammunition to retaliate, therefore the only choice was to abandon ship. The captain was forced to anchor close to Sultan Shoal Lighthouse. The ship's company amounted to 416, with 120 civilians and 2,235 troops. One trooper, Bert Warne RE, M.E. CEN, escaped from the sickbay. A medic had yelled for anyone who could swim, to do so. They opened the 2ft wide portholes and swam out and up as the ship began to sink. 'My father told me, if I found myself in this situation, to always swim away from the vessel to avoid the propellers and any vortex. If the portholes hadn't been as big as they were in those days, and if I hadn't found a rope to cling to, I wouldn't have got out. The lifebelts were made of cork back then – I saw one and grabbed it. Then a boat came by, the *Yarra*, and it took me to the lighthouse.'

As crew and troops abandoned the vessel in the western Johor Straits, other convoy escorts and lifeboats – burnt and punctured from shrapnel – helped them to safety. HMS *Yarra* assisted 1,000 troops, while others were rescued by HMS *Sutlej*, HMS *Danae* and a motor launch. The *Empress of Asia* had carried excess CRA military equipment and many gunners' possessions from units on the *West Point* – the 125 Anti-tank regiment and the Reconnaissance Battalion. Its destruction was a major loss, both personally and strategically. With no salvageable weapons, the men were now infantry.[5]

The newly arrived 54th Brigade troops heard heroic accounts of their fellow fighters, including the Australians on the coast and the Argylls in the

Bukit Timah region, revealing they were tied with barbed wire and bayoneted. One soldier played dead and was helped to safety by a sympathetic Chinese. The listening young soldiers, Stan, Gordon and Fergus, were shocked by the news they heard.

With more incoming supplies and troops, both brigades' permanence in the Far East theatre of war was now a certainty. Further troops later approached Singapore unaware they were soon to be delivered straight to the hands of the Japanese who had the dubious reputation of killing with no remorse.

There was more distressing news of Japanese armies advancing towards the Straits of Johor and across to the north of the island. The British Army concluded their defences in the north were not up to full strength; indeed, some military personnel were seen boarding ships to escape via Keppel Harbour in the south. Some were RAF personnel. Their departure reduced the confidence of the 18th Division: there would be no air support! Their situation was dire, and their only defence was to blow up the causeway, the single link that joined Singapore to Johor on the mainland.

As RAF personnel fled, civilian evacuation commenced as soon as the order came from General Percival. Their vehicles were haphazardly left on the dockside, as they raced to board waiting ships. Distressing scenes of women, children and nurses littered the port as they said farewell to their menfolk in the certain knowledge that they would never see each other again. Panic ensued under the terrifying conditions as the island's long-standing ex-pat community, whose livelihoods relied on colonial industries in Malaya, escaped. Their lives were in jeopardy as fear and the reality of a Japanese invasion spread. Families – RAF engineers, medics, dentists and clergy – from northern cities such as Kuala Lumpur, Ipoh and Tai Ping had left hurriedly weeks earlier and squeezed into Singapore. Now they crowded the port. Malay people, employed by old colonial growers and used to idyllic and peaceful countryside scenes, were deeply shocked by what was happening in their country and swiftly planned to escape by whatever means possible to save themselves and their families.

One man changed his family name to begin with 'A' instead of 'S', to get his wife and four children ahead in the boarding queue of the *Felix Roussel*. Another had driven at top speed in the early hours of the morning to ensure his wife and young son had a place on the *Duchess of Bedford*. Once they were issued with boarding cards they were accepted for the journey. The wife, with babe-in-arms, was allowed a multi-bunk cabin, sharing with two other mothers and their young children. Others made do with corridor benches or comfortable corners on deck. Some slept on lifebelts. Bedding was scarce. Possessions were restricted due to unprecedented numbers of passengers and, of course, there was little time to prepare for departure.

The last Singapore days were terrifying and upsetting as people left behind the families, friends, heirlooms, photographs and pets. Some handed over belongings to staff – a cook boy, an amah or driver.[6] Then, as they boarded rescue vessels, they were forced to deal with filthy and degrading conditions – the legacy of the thousands of troops who had just arrived. The lavatories were disgusting but were soon tackled by the female community. Only small amounts of picnic food were permitted – hardly enough for a week's voyage to India – but worst of all was fear of the unknown. Enemy aircraft bombed the port and gunners counterattacked as women and children escaped. Stress and anxiety reigned as naval crews hurried to turn their ships from danger, but some did not survive.

*   *   *

Stan and his group settled into Tanglin Barracks after the bombing. It had hampered the transfer of baggage and supplies from ship to shore and took twice as long to complete. Looking back over the last eleven days, however, he felt his introduction to war had been less dangerous than others.

> *One of the first things we had to do was get used to the climate. The sea breeze on our seafaring journey was definitely different to what we now experienced.*

Stifling Singapore. Hot was an understatement. There were few shaded places to cool off and body sweat lingered all day. Stan had never experienced such extreme heat before. Evening rain helped, but the humidity only meant more perspiration. They had avoided serious attacks, despite constant air-raid threats and distant bombs over the city, but the close proximity of assault was stressful. After their hard graft, they were always glad of a cold lager at the SD (Supply Depot).

The worrying rumour there, however, was: 'The Japs have landed...!'

News of the *Empress of Asia* was also uppermost. The ship carrying the troops and divisional equipment had allegedly lost fifteen men.

* * *

SD rumours continued, and troops were dumbfounded when they heard the causeway blast left only a 12-foot gash in the side. 'That won't stop anything from crossing. What were they thinking? They should've blown up the bloody lot, they had 13 tons of explosives!'

Stan's intermittent jottings between 1 and 5 February indicated that after the first days of action:

> *... dispatch riding in the strange country was very strange. In fact, there were no signposts, although they may have been in Chinese and not English, but a fairly pleasant country, really wonderful. We spent days in parades and in the evenings at the swimming baths at Tanglin Barracks.*

In the calm before the storm, he recorded:

> *Most of my dispatch riding took place in the evening. But when I was out on my bike on duty, on the 5 February, the Japs bombed our barracks, and I knew nothing about it until I got back. That night, we moved out of the barracks and went under canvas in a rubber plantation, Paya Lebar.*

In a wartime newsreel it is thought Stan can be seen with his co-ranks, walking in triple column along a country road, behind his company officer, as troops moved encampments.[7]

Despite writing '*Under canvas, not so good,*' the following day Stan wrote a letter to Pat. He described his arrival in Singapore and his new motorcycle; he was very proud but at no time did he hint to her about the bombing, carnage and devastation around him.

H.Q. R.A.S.C., 18th Div.,

Malaya

6/Feb/1942

Dearest Pat,

I had already started a letter to you when our office brought these folders to us, so I think it just as well I send you this instead, as it will most likely reach you a lot quicker.

I've sent you a cable telling you I received your cable and P.C.

We've been here in Singapore about 6 days. It's not too bad. The Japs are a bit of a pest during the day with their bombers, but apart from that we are all O.K. I hope soon we shall be able to finish this war and get back home to you.

I was issued with a motorcycle the second day we got here. It did seem strange travelling in a country which you know nothing about. The first day three of us went out to find our way around inland and it took us till 2.30 in the morning to find our way back to the camp. If it hadn't been a moonlit night, we may not have got back till breakfast time.

I've been hoping to see something of Jack Sanford during my travels but have not been lucky enough yet. Tell Doris Sanford I'm here, if you see her, it may interest her.

Had better close now as it looks like rain and I've got some washing out on the line.

So, cheerio Darling, keep well.

All my love

Stan x x x x x x x x x x

Dr Moore S. T/170638

Pat wouldn't receive his letter until 23 April 1942.

Stan's earlier freedom, pleasantly motorcycling around the countryside of Singapore, had abruptly ceased when a high degree of vigilance was enforced during daylight hours. Bomb threats and the Japanese invasion meant evenings were best for briefings. It was also the quietest and safest time to be travelling alone collecting and delivering orders to and from the outposts and HQ.

Troop movement instructions for different units were given over several days – no two routes were the same. The CRA and CRE were split into various defence positions, mainly in the north-east. After the attacks, the 18th Division RASC HQ moved from Tanglin Barracks and its comfortable country club feel with a swimming pool, as the barracks in the south were considered too close to the docks. The whole unit marched steadily on foot further east to Paya Lebar. This time 'home' was under canvas beneath peaceful rows of cathedral-like palm canopies that towered above. Its reverential quietness, with soft limestone and green moss underfoot, pierced by sharp rays of sunlight, however, did not last long. Stan's diary of events grew:

February 7th

The guns were going, and huge fires could be seen around the island. I imagine it was to do with the oil stores.

February 8ᵗʰ Sunday morning.

Been sinking tents in the ground for safety's sake. Japs surprised us with a few shots. We were busy digging ourselves in at the rubber plantation and pitching our tents over the holes. The holes were a square arrangement, but you only had to go down about 18 inches and you got full of water. As you can imagine, Singapore is built on a swamp, so we didn't have to go far down to find water! During the day, we heard gunfire and thought 'Ah! Our artillery had opened up on the [air raiding] Japs,' but it was getting nearer and nearer, and in the end, we found out it was Japanese shells bursting in the rubber. One fellow in our camp got a splinter in the leg; that put him out of action for a little while. Guess who was first in the trenches directly the shells started bursting? Yep, you guessed it – the RSM! [The former boys' service soldier from the unit's Droitwich days.]

Japanese infantry forces pressed southward. They were now in control of Johor Palace, where a tower overlooked the entire island of Singapore and across the southerly straits. As darkness fell, the Japanese plan fell into place with a convoy of cars heading east, towards the island of Palau Ubin, headlights glaring. The British expected the enemy and were prepared, under orders from Lieutenant General Percival. The 18th Division, positioned on the north-eastern side of Singapore, waited.

As the week went by, Stan delivered to other units and learned more news of horrific battles, which he relayed to his fellow compatriots. The Japanese attacks were getting closer; all of Malaya was under siege and Singapore and the Allies were a clear target. Australian forces saw Japanese activity across the straits in the west, but British forces and their intelligence only saw night activity in the east, where lines of enemy trucks shone their headlights, as if transporting troops and equipment. The British assumed an invasion would take place in north-east Singapore, via the island of Palau Ubin. General Percival positioned the 18th Division accordingly on the opposite bank of the waterway, ready to counter-attack.[8]

Several days of threats, skirmishes and defence positions consistently changed, causing orders to be dispatched on a speedy rota. One dispatcher came back to report he'd delivered to C and D companies, based at Serangoon Creek in the north-east. The 4th Royal Norfolk Regiment, who patrolled the north-east straits, heard rumours of the Japanese being there and this seemed to be true as they successfully made their fake presence known with headlight activity at night; it was the perfect decoy. However, this dangerous speculation ultimately damaged British strategy. The defending 4th Royal Norfolks, battalion C and D under the command of Major John Packard, soon discovered the enemy's alarming, but shrewd, strategy: On 8 February the Japanese armies had landed successfully on the north-west side of the island instead. The surprise attack drove the Australians back from the north-west shores. The Japanese invasion of Singapore had commenced.

Safe but defeated, remaining troops from the mainland fell back behind the Allies' front line. The 18th Division units formed a special-forces resistance. One was 'Tom Force' under command of Colonel Thomas, Northumberland Fusiliers, another was 'Massy Force' under Major Massy-Beresford of the 55th Brigade. By now, a brigade in this context was often no more than a few hundred men who had survived and were aided by untrained reinforcements or logistic troops pressed into service.[9]

The troops hoped American reinforcements were on their way after the attack on Pearl Harbor. But where were they? Nothing had been heard.

Beach defences to the south and east were lacking; forces' administration thought it bad for morale to see preparation for a Japanese landing. Neither HQ Western Area nor British Malay Command thought it would be more than a few days' bombardment and naively made assumptions, swayed by Singapore's commerce and businessmen's opinions and avarice. They grossly underestimated the enemy – their ability, their strength and their tactics. The British were no match for Japanese technique, strategic planning, and sheer cunning. Orders to retaliate were not issued in time by the government, and they were simply caught out, with little fighting.

*   *   *

At the time, the young British soldiers would not have known of the fierce fighting and other atrocities in the village of Parit Sulong in the north-west, as defeated Australian units fell back and left their wounded behind. More than 160 Australian and Indian troops were slaughtered, drowned or burnt alive on orders of Japanese General Takuma Nishimura.

The same day, the Australians and the Gordons withdrew from the mainland, along with the remaining ninety survivors of the Argyll and Sutherland Highlanders. They were ordered to retreat across the causeway, prior to its destruction. As the last men stepped on to the island, their chief pipers played traditional bagpipes and *Hielan' Laddie*, in an act of defiance.

The low-level causeway built on a barrier of rocks, rose no more than 4ft above the water and took just six minutes to traverse by car. The short distance from Kranji Creek to Johor also served as a single-track railway as well as vital access, but it was a small deterrent to invasion. The strait after all, was narrow – only 300 yards wide in places.

*   *   *

Despite the atrocities, the retreating troops felt confident extra fighters would benefit the 18th Division. But were they right? Now the army was a mix of different brigades and regiments with disparity over how to defend a small island. Surely it was impenetrable. But no. The British naval base was destroyed to prevent the Japanese from using the facility and the force that was bearing down on them seemed unstoppable. Morale of the Allies was at its lowest. Orders from the Prime Minister, Winston Churchill, revealed there was no longer an effective force to defend the Empire Island of Singapore. It was the end.

As multitudes of escaping civilians and deserting soldiers ran for their lives, drunken, unruly Australians roamed the city with no respect for anything. There was no protection. Civilians needed air-raid shelters; there were none. Lawlessness and chaos ensued, with looting and general panic. Many used open sewer channels and drains as safe routes to reach the port. Australian troops had protected Singapore for the last few months, but they were the first to board the waiting ships, ahead of civilians, some climbing ropes to board. Senior officers were also culprits when they abandoned their platoons. The island's oil stores were destroyed to prevent the enemy from procuring army fuel. How would the army operate their vehicles now, provide power? Even replenishing troops seemed senseless, and Allied soldiers wasted their time in the north-east instead of providing accurate surveillance and protection in the north-west of the island.

*   *   *

Before the causeway was destroyed, many deliveries of resources to units came through providing a good ten days of supplies. The reserves were held at Bukit Timah, Joo Seng, the racecourse and Robertson Quay. But fair distribution became complicated when gunners, sappers, and periphery volunteers, attached to the 18th Division, were then re-attached elsewhere. Keeping on top of who should have what, and how much, became a difficult task.

There was a constant threat of attack, and troops kept a low profile to complete their assignments. When raids of multiple aircraft in V formation came over – 54, 27 or 9 – they would instinctively dive for cover. The planes dropped 50kg anti-personnel devices which burst on impact, scorching deep along road surfaces, causing vehicles to swerve and crash into ditches. Abandoned trucks, cars and debris became a familiar post-raid sight. Malay Command had nothing. Any RAF engineers left were specifically detailed to service Hurricanes, but they never came.

The Order of Battle on land under General Percival was Malay Command 1 and Command 2 Infantry brigades, and the 12th Indian brigade. The 8th Australian Division was under Major General Bennett and General Heath was in charge of the 3rd India Corps.

But defence of Malaya and Singapore had just 130,000 troops with only 450 guns and 110 aircraft – Brewster Buffaloes[10] and other out-dated equipment. As battle progressed, the Japanese bombarded from the north over to the city of Singapore, until it was almost flattened. Wave after wave of attack couldn't be matched. It was hopeless. Preparations were useless and equipment extremely out of date.

> Artillery were issued 3' guns, made mobile on an under carriage with wheels, from World War One. The Gunnery Instructor was nicknamed 'Bow and Arrow Archibald.'[11]

*   *   *

The British government only saw Singapore as a lost cause and threatened to turn her ships around to start evacuating the island. But Churchill declared: 'Obviously, it depends if Singapore Island can be maintained, if it is only for a few weeks. It is not worth losing all our reinforcements and aircraft.'

However, the Australian Prime Minister, John Curtin, saw Singapore as Australia's front line: 'After all the assurances we have been given, the evacuation of Singapore would be regarded here and elsewhere as an inexcusable betrayal.'[12]

An order came from General Sir Archibald Wavell, CCB CMG MC, who now directed all ranks through their commanding officers. Wavell famously said he would welcome an attack on Singapore. The order declared that some troop units had not shown the 'fighting spirit' expected of the British Empire soldiers and that it would be considered a lasting disgrace should they be defeated by 'an army of clever gangsters, less in numbers than the Allied forces', and that 'The spirit of aggression and determination to stick it out must be inculcated in all ranks.'[13]

Chapter 8

Move of Many

'They train you but do not TELL you about the noise in action; the shells, the mortars, the guns going off. It was stupefying!'

By 5 February, Fergus Anckorn was responsible for a gun-driving detail. On 10 February he was transporting a large weapon and a projectile shell on his camouflaged quad lorry with, unusually, a consignment of beetroot. But this wasn't going to be an ordinary day, as was evident when twenty-seven bombers came over from behind. He was on Compton Road, and he was their target. Under direct fire, he was bombed and shot at … 'blown about all over the place … like in a biscuit tin, tossed around on the road by the erupting earth, and skewered in a thousand places by shrapnel.'

Badly injured he managed to kick open the door and fell to the ground. He had been hit but propelled himself onward; standing, limping yet running, colliding with others, English voices called out in the confusion:

'Where are you going?'

Fergus didn't know. He tripped and fell into a monsoon ditch and passed out. He regained consciousness, unaware of how long he had been there – having been out cold. He crawled, between periods of pain and blackout, eventually dragging his body from the concrete channel, thinking his unit would fear 'poor old Gus' was dead!

* * *

Under similar life-threatening conditions, Stan endeavoured to add more to his diary.

9 February 1942

We moved out of the plantation; it was getting a bit too hot. We went to a site called Hill 110, just outside Teck Hock.[1] Our artillery behind the hill started firing; lobbing shells at the Japs' position on the opposite

*side. I was on guard duty that night, a bit scary because a lot of fireflies
and also wild boar. You'd hear a shuffle and a scuffle and see a few
lights and you didn't know if it was a Jap or what!*

*After we left the comfortable Tanglin Barracks, we always seemed to
be digging holes, pitching tents, taking them down, then moving off
somewhere else, digging more holes, pitching more tents again ... and
that's how it went.*

Moving through swamp conditions, phosphorescent fungus shimmering in
the dark tricked the eye, and during the day the Japanese shelled heavily.
They had the range of the road at Somapah and along Tampines Road. There
was little sleep for the next two nights. Gunners were all around with a
25-pounder battery, 400 yards abreast, with a further 75mm battery just to
the south, which seemed to sweep shells across the treetops.

Horner's team in their 40lb tents felt the reverberation of the bombard-
ments, and smaller tents were in danger of collapsing. During the day,
ammunition was drawn from one of the dumps at Joo Chiat under Horner's
supervision. Carrying ammunition – as they had to – he never felt secure
with Japanese aircraft overhead.

Stan: 11 February

*No sign of anymore shells, but situation is getting bad. Moved off Hill
110 at about 1400hrs to Newton Road. During the move we were in
convoy – of course, the Japs came and bombed us. There was 'ack-ack'
and gunfire, and all sorts flying around, but our small arms fired and
beat the little bomber off. But it was amazing you could see the small
aircraft's two cockpits and the jap chap in the rear cockpit leaning over
the side of the aircraft, firing his small arms at us! The next day, we
moved to a private house.[2] We had guard duties to do.*

The two-day episode was terrifying for Stan and his unit. They were only
facilitators and yet they were fully targeted.

* * *

The closeness of the danger was frightening as Stan's 18th Rear Division HQ awaited more ferocious attacks. Their change of address and retreat to the suburbs took them from unsecure plantation camping to an empty Chinese businessman's home. The requisitioned white house of sizeable proportions was central to the city at 39 Newton Road. With other 18th Division HQ staff and their postal unit as neighbours, they were a quarter mile from the battle and Advanced Divisional headquarters, under Major General Beckwith-Smith. An escape party was formed, including RASC HQ men, Divisional Ammunitions Officer Bill Cowell, Intelligence Officer Harold Atcherley and Colonel George Rossall. It was intense. Four days had passed since the Japanese landed in the north.

Number 39 was no fortress. The home had two large reception rooms, with arched 'Georgian-style' windows that once looked on to peaceful gardens and a curved driveway. The imposing doorway led to a wide hall featuring an over-sized staircase that supported a low banister of solid wrought iron railings and wooden newel posts carved in art-deco symmetry. The stairs led to six good-sized bedrooms where thirty officers and soldiers squeezed in trying to make themselves comfortable.

The room Stan shared with six others was at the front with tall arched windows. There was no time for niceties or room planning. Each claimed a spot as they entered and dumped worn kits on the floor to mark their zones. Putrid feet and body odour were no doubt the 'elephants in the room' after days of active troop life, where hygiene played second fiddle. The most poignant sight was an array of hurriedly discarded toys that once belonged to infants. Someone collected them together and put them in a box.

Orders were given to keep the windows closed and to stay low in case of attack. The officers elected three rear rooms, where each had a window and a door connected to a long narrow balcony. The balcony's low concrete wall was interspersed with square openings, and some took cover behind the solid screen to peer through the gaps, their weapons ready.

From this vantage position the men surveyed the area as the battle continued. Whining bullets, smoke, fire and loud shell explosions were in the distance. Gunners from the Indian Mountain Regiment's Charlie Battery were 200 yards in front of them. It was a comfort to know they were there, though some wished they weren't so close when excruciatingly loud counter-battery fire engaged at each barrage from the attackers.

* * *

Japanese night-time diversionary tactics were successful. Multiple seacraft with 13,000 Japanese soldiers raced across the 300 yards of water, from the Johor coast north-western strait to land between Tanjong Buloh and Tanjong Murai.[3] Allied chiefs had been tricked into thinking a stronger defence was unnecessary. Instead, aggressive scenes of intense fighting followed with bayoneting, decapitation, grim death and destruction. The Japanese advanced.

After the Hong Kong massacre, Singaporean local civilians, mostly Chinese, joined 'Dalforce',[4] a volunteer militia defence, led by Lieutenant Colonel John D. Dalley of the Federated Malaya States Police. The well-meaning group of more than 4,000, plus Australian troops, desperately battled on the beaches of Kranji, but under excessive shelling their lines of communication were cut and contact with command lost. Outnumbered and with poorly trained local men they suffered many casualties and ultimately lost the battle.

Last-minute plans made by the Allies were gradually falling apart as the IJA (Imperial Japanese Army) conquered western Singapore. Then Japanese aerial bombardment hit the main bunker at Fort Canning in the centre of the city. This was a secret underground shelter and headquarters for counter-battle plans and the Royal Corps of Signals, as well as some RASC strategic staff. The signals intelligence officers of FECB (Far East Combined Bureau) had escaped to other secret and safe intelligence bases before the invasion.

* * *

As military chiefs inspected the battlefields and strategised, General Archibald Wavell issued a last order to all divisions on 10 February.[5] He advised the Japanese had crossed the straits and their mission now was to destroy the enemy: British Empire honour was at stake. He spoke of America holding Bastan, the Russians turning back the Germans and the Chinese fighting Japanese aggression for four and a half years. The missive's tone warned that failure in holding Fort Singapore would be an embarrassment. There was to be 'no sparing of troops or civilians, no mercy to be shown', and that 'commanders must die with their units: fight to the end.'

Lieutenant General Percival responded[6] to Wavell's order by alerting the commanders of 5th Indian Corps, A.E.F. and the Southern Area. In his missive, he also stressed the need to inculcate a fighting spirit within all ranks, with no thought of withdrawal. Every available fighting man, from the back ranks forward, had to do what was necessary and fight to the death. The truth was bitter.

It is said that Wavell left the island soon after issuing his order on 11 February 1942, when he accidentally fell over a sea wall into barbed wire and was hospitalised for three days. During this time there was much confusion, and it appears he left Singapore without further duty, or delay, and eventually returned to India.[7]

Two thousand civilians died daily as the Japanese continued to attack relentlessly. Now Governor Shenton Thomas[8] cabled London reporting that a million people were crammed into a radius of 3 miles; many were dead and had been left in the streets with no prospect of burial. Contamination was rife, and the city's damaged water system would only add to disease.

*   *   *

Along with other ranks, on 11 February officers had taken breakfast at the Polo Ground where the perfect terrain of the immaculate racecourse was destroyed by troops digging in and aerial bomb attacks. The 18th Division's Supply Depot, operated by the 4th Norfolk Regiment, was the best place to buy an ice-cold beer on tap. The Norfolks were given orders to retire but they were still in action for a while longer.

The attacks had been a 'hot' session, with nine Japanese bombers unloading their bombs on the petrol dump, while on the ground they were sniped at by Japanese infantry or Malay 5th Columnists. No casualties, but on their return, iced lager had never tasted so good. The men were living on tenterhooks.

On 12 February, Japanese tanks broke through from the north to the middle of the island. 'Eighty thousand troops were now packed in a perimeter with a radius of some five miles from Singapore [City],' wrote Horner.

The manoeuvre hardly increased the reputation of Malaya Command's traffic control. Soon the 18th Division was on the move again, and they had to share a crossroad with the 11th Indian Division, resulting in chaos when the two groups met.

On 13 February, Percival cabled Wavell for permission to surrender, hoping to avoid further carnage and destruction from urban warfare if they continued to defend Singapore.[9]

13 February 1942

The Nips got the range of our house and lobbed a few mortars into it. Wall is strong. Jonny's room and two on fire around the outer building. Feeling a bit shaky. Things were getting too 'hot' for comfort. Captain Horner, one of our officers, copped a shell straight into the room with his camp bed; luckily, he wasn't in it. In fact, the shell, a dead one, landed on the bed, but no one was injured at that time.

The identity of 'Jonny' is still unknown. Horner, who shared a room with Denis Pearl, described the incident differently, 'Just as I was leaving the room the shell burst on impact. The furthest wall was hit, and it wrecked the room behind. Fortunately, no one was there, and no casualties occurred.

Stan continued:

Just across the road from us a dugout received a direct hit by a shell and six fellows were badly injured. I was sent out with my motorbike to find an ambulance. I found one abandoned, no driver, so I managed to get a voluntary reserve fella to drive it back to where we were at the house, and all six fellas were taken off to the hospital in Singapore city. That little episode helped straighten me up a bit.

An urgent conference of all officers was called regarding the selected personnel who would attempt to escape. The officers and soldiers would rendezvous at Keppel Harbour at midnight.

> *During the night of 13ᵗʰ February our colonel and a party of other people – chosen people – made an attempt to get off the island via the navy.*

Colonel Rossall, Bill Cowell and Majors Knowles and Hodgkinson left Newton Road about 2330hrs and attempted to make a getaway.

> *But the Japs made the area so hot the navy couldn't get in to take our fellas off and they came back to us during the night.*

* * *

A selection from 600 men tried to get away. They were chosen for their intelligence, leadership and ammunition skills. Undercover, they were told to make their way to a point near the docks – the former YMCA – where they awaited orders. But fierce bombing and shelling meant persistent danger; it was too risky to dispatch many men at once. When there was an opportunity to go, lots were drawn in reduced numbers, and those with the winning tickets were dispatched immediately to the docks. Those remaining endured more bomb attacks, some within inches of their lives. Rossall, Cowell and Atcherley were ultimately ordered back to their units.[10]

That day, Fergus saw his officer, Sergeant Ludgate, dressed in his full uniform, hoping to scarper with the escape party. He had also been the man who wrenched off Fergus's dog tags, believing him a victim of the lorry bomb attack. This resulted in a distressing false report for his family where he was declared dead. In fact, another bombardier found 'Gus' and took him to a field hospital, and successive transfers to the Fullerton Post Office Hospital and the Alexandra Military Hospital.

The Admonition of Peace

On the other side of the battlefield, the Nippon army typed a warning on behalf of the commanding officers.[11] With war-like authority and 'honour' they presented a document to the British Army, which they supposed was within the sphere of Nippon Samurai Spirit.

Nippon Navy, Army and Air Force had conquered the Philippine Islands, Hong Kong and the British Extreme Oriental Fleet in the Southern Seas. The document dated 13 February 1942, advised the war 'has almost been settled already and Malay is under Nippon Power'. They aimed to establish a New Order and zone of mutual prosperity in the East Orient saying, 'the British could not deny – in their hearts – that it will be divine and humanity to give happiness to thousands of East Orientals who are mourning under exploitation and persecution'!

The long missive (see p.6 of photo plate section) written in poor English declared in part:

> The state of mind of you who have as well done your duty, isolated and without rescuer, and now surrender by our armies how much more could they not sincerely sympathise with the British Army.

They dared the Allied forces to make peace with the Japanese Commander, who directed Percival and his commanders to consider and agree to The Admonition:

> Upon my word we won't kill you, trust you as officers and soldiers if you come to it. But if you resist against us, we will give swords.

* * *

Stan wrote:

> *14 February 1942 Air full of whinging shots and mortar bombs. Colonel comes back with stuff intact.*
>
> *I had the duty of taking the dispatch to the general hospital with Lieutenant Hines. After I delivered the message, I made my way back to the unit.*

The Newton Road HQ had converted to an ADS (Advanced Dressing Station), where Medical Officer Lieutenant Emery tended casualties.

Horner recalled:

> The HQ cook, Driver Palmer, was also quite amazing. He churned
> out hot sweet tea for the wounded and a meal for us at 1300hrs,
> despite shells being dropped around the house. Two fell either side
> of the cookhouse, plastering the outside walls with deep pitted holes.

Malay Chinese civilians ran with possessions in all directions, unsure of
the safest route. Fires and columns of smoke enveloped the vicinity as more
death and destruction occurred. Horrific slaughter of civilians, women and
children was taking place below their Newton Road balcony. Bodies, some
whole, some in pieces, lay strewn across pavements and roads. The alarming
attack was the second life-threatening incident Horner witnessed that day.
Earlier, he had the gruelling experience of standing on the 8th floor of the
Cathay Building[12] in the city, where the 3rd Corps had their HQ, and saw
and heard shells about to strike, but the missiles hit the roads and houses in
front of him; he couldn't stomach the death and destruction. It was carnage.[13]
Horner and his men couldn't look anymore.

*   *   *

From the northern Kranji beaches, down through Sime Road and Bukit
Timah and to Thomson Road and the city, the once perfect terrain was now
devastated. The racecourse and polo club had been built for 'the sport of
kings' and the British way of life, in a time when Singapore's countryside
was a playground for the rich and glamorous. There were many clubs and
associations, and the area featured a new-style dual carriageway, one of the
first of its kind, with a central reservation growing succulent plants and
flowers to divide two opposing lanes of traffic.

Part of the area was named after Scotsman John Sime, who founded Sime,
Darby & Co. in 1910, when he went to Malaya with his brother. In 1915,
he transferred to Singapore where the company became successful agents
for five rubber plantations covering 12,437 acres; they later diversified into
timber, preservatives and motor insurance. John Sime was an active member
of the Singapore Golf Club but left the area before the war. Now the club

house was requisitioned, originally by the Royal Air Force until the end of December 1941, when the property transferred to British Army HQ, and where Percival ran military operations.

* * *

Japanese forces had swept into Singapore on 8 February 1942, but it had taken them several days to advance a mile to Sime Road. The once blissful countryside, with its green valleys and undulating hills, held strategic positions for the Allies, but now it was a major battleground and Percival and his men were forced to abandon the area to retreat to their Fort Canning HQ on one of the higher points of Singapore overlooking the south. The governor's nineteenth-century residence, an imposing building, was renovated when the city of Singapore was transformed to a fortress to counter growing Japanese threats. Surrounding woodland gave natural cover to its raised position and its visiting high-ranking officials. But now the house and grounds showed signs of dilapidation, and where immaculate plants once grew, army vehicles churned the lawns and decimated the flowerbeds. Strong walls dominated the fortress perimeter, supported by impregnable gates and guards' sentry boxes, to protect the steep and winding roads of its two entrances.

Lessons were learned after the horrors of Hong Kong and all women and children were immediately ordered by the Fort Canning Command to leave Singapore. It was unprecedented that nurses should abandon their patients, but in February they obeyed authority and left with little time to spare. Their ships departed on 12 and 13 February.

As the terrified nurses made their way to the docks from the British Military Hospital – an 8-mile dash – they crawled to safety through the open sewer culverts of the Singapore Cricket Club, another bastion of the rich. Smoke from fires aided their cover but at times hindered their escape as they ran through the concrete drains to waiting vessels. Women with crying children queued hoping to board, while defending troops held the advancing enemy. In mass confusion, all nurses were relieved to board, but the *Empire Star,* with 2,500 passengers, was under constant attack in the harbour until it sailed.

* * *

Orders were issued for troops to advance to the front lines. On the outskirts of Bukit Timah where the Royal Norfolks dug in for the night, there was an overriding feeling of exhaustion. Permission was given to sleep anywhere, and a good defensive position on a gentle slope with trees and bushes overlooking a green valley seemed peaceful for a while. But at dawn the troops, holed-up in their pit, heard unusual voices. Was it the enemy? In the relative peace, two officers, an NCO and a captain, carefully moved forward to investigate. They returned laughing. The cause for alarm was a local Indian field bakery, busy making bread. When they heard the news of a battle about to start, they broke all records running to a safer place, and left their wares behind. It was no surprise therefore, that several freshly baked loaves found their way into numerous troops' rucksacks.

Further instructions were given to advance over the racecourse, following the pipeline until Japanese frontline units were met. Sporadic gunshot greeted them as they carried out the mission. Orders were to attack; drive them back.

Following Company 'A', with 'B' and 'C' Companies in reserve to the left, the 4th Suffolks held their position on the right. Captain Reginald Burton of the Norfolks advanced up hill, as the Japanese increased their fire. Soon 'A' Company retreated with injuries and blood-spattered uniforms. The Allied advance wavered as some injured soldiers were relatives or friends, but the men had to find their inner strength to move forward into battle and ignore their instincts to help the wounded.

As enemy aircraft roared above, dropping bombs, Allies on the ground took immediate cover. Japanese pilots flew so low the troops could see their faces. The exploding missiles made the earth shudder and the quaking landscape undulate in such a way that it resembled green jelly. Trying to stand, walk or run under fire was almost impossible; dugouts at the front line provided refuge, but these were often full of Chinese coolies taking cover. More 'A' Company men retreated. Two service men returned on one delivery bicycle, one lay seriously wounded across the front pannier box, while the other pedalled frantically to find him medical attention.[14]

On Friday, 13 February 1942, the 4th Battalion of Suffolk Regiment, supported by the Cambridgeshires and the Norfolks, had fought the Japanese on the Bukit Timah Golf Course. Many men were lost with one colonel suggesting they were bayonet-charged. Soldiers were cut to ribbons.[15]

* * *

On 14 February, Churchill relented and gave Percival permission to make the final decision. Meanwhile, High Command received a handwritten note from Lieutenant General Tomoyuki Yamashita, High Commander of the Nippon Army.[16]

> To the High Commander of the British Army in Malaya.
>
> The High Commander of the Nippon Army is ready to accept the surrender of the British Forces in Malaya. So that, the British High Commander has requested, fulfilling all the required conditions specified in the separation sheet. To present himself by 5.30 p.m. 15th February (Japanese Time). To have an interview with the Nippon High Commander at the appointed place (Time). Where his parliamentaire has been dispatched.
>
> He should be accompanied by his staff necessary for negotiations.
>
> (Sgd.) Lieut. General Tomoyuki Yamashita
>
> His High Commander of Nippon Army.

Considering no battle commander would give away his strategy to the enemy, it seems the Japanese knew the right moment to send the handwritten note and the prior Admonition of Peace. The aggressors, however, also knew their own resources were almost depleted and played their 'poker-hand' to demand the Allies concede. The situation was futile for both sides and it was a chance the Japanese took.

Although British commanding officers and Churchill said fight to the last man, the anticipated victory had not included scenes of deprivation and pestilence. Communication between Churchill and Wavell was by a series of telegrams or cables, designed to churn commanders into instructing their men to fight, no matter what. But the decision ended with Percival, who chose humanity over death, to save the lives of his troops facing dire conditions and exhaustion. The IJA, however, had fewer troops, not much better materiel and found their role as jailers of many more prisoners than expected, wanting.

*   *   *

Troops were horrified by the massacre at the British Military Hospital – also known as Alexandra Barracks or Alexandra Military Hospital. On 14 February 1942, the Imperial Japanese Army 18th Division, code named Chrysanthemum Division, had advanced through Kent Ridge down Pasir Panjang Road to the facility where they began attacking patients and medical staff. The protecting British 1st Malaya infantry brigade retaliated, but then retreated through the hospital to the west while they covered with more machine-gun fire. When a lieutenant prepared to surrender on behalf of the non-combatants, with a Red Cross brassard and white flag, he was killed immediately. The Japanese continued bayonetting and decapitating patients, many of whom were recovering survivors from other battles and warships. Two hundred and fifty died and another 400 were captured and imprisoned in a small room, where many suffocated. On upper wards, patients escaped when a Japanese officer ordered his men to assemble in the hospital grounds. This action prevented further brutalities and left some patients and staff alive to retell their horrific stories.

Fergus Anckorn, who was there, believed he was the only one to survive the attack. With serious injuries he had been moved from a makeshift hospital at the Fullerton post office to Alexandra Hospital. Concussed but coming out of a haze, the place seemed empty, but something had woken him. Drifting in and out of consciousness he saw the wounded men, their hands bound with barbed wire, being pushed by Japanese soldiers wielding charged bayonets. Delirious, he wasn't sure what was happening, but could hear the thud, thud, thud of impaling bayonets and thought he would be next.

'I remembered waking up again, alone in the quiet ward. There was blood on my chest from a tourniquet, they must have thought they had already bayoneted me. It was a lucky escape; extraordinary,' he said.

THE SURRENDER

15 February 1942

'We had to decide between Russia and Libya on the one hand and Singapore on the other.

It is difficult to form any opinion of the correctness of the decision, because we simply do not know the fact which is needed in order to determine the accuracy of our strategy.'

Commander King Hall, House of Commons speech,
24 February 1942

Chapter 9

Capitulation

The troops' lifeline of a clean drinking water supply was rapidly diminishing. All they had were battle-damaged water pipes. What would happen to them now?

Weary from battle, the days had taken their toll. They fought, ran and hid to save their lives. They weren't gunners, they were just young men. Bursting latex in plantations seemed to drip from rubber trees. Adrenaline prolonged the fear. The stark reality of combat mingled with the sound and smell of battle – a pungent odour of acrid smoke, reminiscent of a November bonfire night back home, was not exciting, nor was it a celebration. Between illuminated explosions and enemy fire, alternating rallies of weaponry and moments of silence were heightened by the sound of clicking insects. Men of all ranks protected each other and ran with aid wherever possible. Their earlier summer training was code named 'The War of the Roses',[1] but that did not match this experience. Hot terror had nothing to do with roses, or fireworks. The day of 'throwing in the towel' or being 'in the bag', whatever one called it, was not the best St Valentine's Day memory.

* * *

In the officers' quarters of British High Command, a memorandum was being typed.[2] A few hours later, a prominent Rolls Royce cavalcade, displaying British Colours and the white flag of surrender, sped along Bukit Timah Road to the Ford Motor Company Factory.

The state-of-the-art premises had been captured and was now headquarters to the Imperial Japanese Army. Lieutenant General Percival and Major Cyril Wild, who spoke Japanese, carried the Union Jack and flag of truce into the building. They were accompanied by Allied commanding officers and interpreters and Lieutenant General Yamashita laid down the Japanese terms for unconditional surrender.

* * *

After the surrender, a dispatcher was summoned to collect and deliver orders. This was Stan. The assignment was not one of his happier deliveries on his beloved BSA Triumph, but he adhered to the task and conveyed the status of battle to senior officers. Only Stan could write this contribution to history in his diary for the morning of 15 February:

> *I was out on my motorbike and saw a car speeding along with a white flag and Union Jack on either side, turning up the Bukit Timah Road.* [I] *guessed what for! The Orders of Capitulation. The water supply had been cut off, so we were without water, and the causeway had been blown* [again] *to prevent the Japs from getting over, but to no avail. I had the job of taking the Orders of Capitulation to our Colonel. At that time, he was at the DSD* [Divisional Supply Depot], *supervising the distribution of rum* [or destroying it – one way or other]! *The Order was to cease fire at 1600hrs on 15 February, that day.*

In preceding days, the DSD was the place where troops grabbed a cool lager at the end of stressful duties, but that day, shocking sounds and scenes of anger pierced the torrid atmosphere, as soldiers frantically destroyed their alcohol supplies to prevent them falling into enemy hands. The shattering glass of beer bottles was deafening as armfuls were smashed into bombshell holes. Beer and brown glass flew everywhere. Rumour had spread like wildfire prior to the order being read to the men, and the colonel had marched in to stop the destruction. Only a short time before, his command had received the worst possible news: the Orders of Capitulation from the British High Command had been delivered by Driver T/170638, Stan Moore, to the 18th Division HQ, along with an explanation from Percival. Fighting was to cease at 1600hrs. Once silence was restored, the colonel read the following dispatch:

Cmd. 5 Indian Corps. B.R.A.
    Cmd. Southern Area. C.E.
    Cmd. A.I.F. C.S.C.
    D.D.S.T.
    D.D.S.S.
    C.A.A.D. D.D.O.S
    D.P.E.
    G (1)

Staff Message Control.

It has been necessary to give up the struggle, but I want the reason explained to all ranks. The forward troops continue to hold their ground, but the essentials of war have run short. In a few days we shall have neither petrol nor food. Many types of ammunition are short and the water supply, on which the vast civilian population and many of the fighting troops are dependent, threatens to fail. This situation had been brought about partly by being driven off our dumps and partly by hostile air and artillery action. Without these sinews of war, we cannot carry on.

I thank all Ranks for their efforts throughout this campaign.

(Sgd.) A. E. Percival.
Lieut. General
General Officer Commanding, Malaya Command.
'G' (Ops).
15.Feb.42.

Stan described their raw emotion from where he stood to this pivotal news in history:

We were handed a tot of rum by the order of our colonel. Some of the chaps didn't drink alcohol, so those who didn't drink gave it to others,

and after a while some of the fellas had more than they could manage
and were thoroughly upset, in fact some began to cry [from the strain
they'd been through].

Wrecking the drink supplies ensured nothing would be left for the Japanese
to impound for themselves and prevented havoc. It was a safety measure –
particularly in helping to protect civilian women. The colonel also ordered
the men to drink some of the rum. They were to congratulate themselves for
their days of hard battle and commiserate for those who had fallen. A tot for
each man. Portions declined by those who did not drink were solemnly, but
gladly, drunk by others. After, remaining bottles continued to be destroyed.
With a sting in their throats permeating to their chests, the sweet spicy
spirit swept over their bodies. The fighting had stopped but their ferocious
anger held a torrent of wilful destruction in the battle of the bottles. In that
moment they were ambivalent to the perils of what was next, but anxiety
began to surface; now a different type of courage was needed. As reality hit,
they became deflated and, yes, even the toughest wept.

Meanwhile, bomb blasts and shell firing could still be heard in the
distance; ceasefire was still a couple of hours away. Stan continued:

I was sent out with another order. I can't remember where to; it wasn't a
long journey. By the time I came back the Japs were already in among
our unit, rounding them up, collecting all the arms. I drove in on my
bike. A Jap came up to me and gestured for me to get off: I gave him
my revolver – less the rounds – because any rounds I had I threw away
on my last trip out. I had to fall in line with the rest of the lads and on
16 February, we were herded on to a lorry and taken down to a large
football field, just outside the town, with what looked like thousands of
fellas, all on this one field, just sitting, standing, talking and wondering
what was going to happen next.

Stan was sorry to hand over his cherished motorcycle, but that was the least of
his worries. Gordon and other dispatch riders had also surrendered their pistols
and ammunition to Japanese soldiers who now controlled 39 Newton Road.

They had little idea of how long the terror would continue, or how close to death they would come through disease and starvation.

*   *   *

Horner recalled:

> At the Polo Ground on 15 February, we learned the Staff Car bearing a white flag had gone through the 5th Suffolk lines to negotiate a cessation of hostilities at about 1100hrs. Later a message from Divisional HQ arrived stating that a ceasefire was to be called at 1630hrs. Actually, that was a mistake; 1800hrs was the correct time, because of the Japanese time zone change. There was no positive purpose in fighting on. Further battle would have resulted in a massacre. Disposition of troops and lack of strength, the Japanese had broken through at Alexandra and down the Changi Road within 24 hours. Insufficient troops only remained to hold them back as capitulation came. At the time there was a serious shortage of water and ammunition, the supply system was chaotic. It was apparent the Malay Command had no idea what was happening. The drone of planes, crackle of rifle and machine-gun fire, warfare sounds became increasingly audible, as battles continued. It was feared the Japanese would come through in the night, despite the agreement they were not supposed to until 0800hrs the next day.

On 16 February, the victors arrived after breakfast. Lorries whisked officers to a field adjoining the main Bukit Timah Road to join their troops and some, who had nothing, made a risky return to obtain their kits and those of others from their previous accommodation. Stan's diary confirms:

> *The football field was just off the Bukit Timah Road. We were all being fairly well fed, okay for those who could eat. I, myself, was off food.*

On the field they sat wherever a space allowed, and quietly spoke to others nearby. Senior officers tried to keep order. There was a form of roll call and the supply division dished out food which they'd managed to transfer. The former baggage team witnessed exhausted emotions as they now ladled out meat stew to others. There was an overriding feeling of worthlessness: Sailing for miles, climate assimilation, all for a few days of fighting; many dead, no chance of victory. What was it all for? They slept on the field overnight.

After many nights of duty, with fractious nerves on full alert, the soft football field seemed a godsend. Gradually, the bomb blasts and gunfire stopped. Ceasefire. The RASC discussed the deaths and injuries of their friends and the frightening clashes they had experienced. They had been makeshift stretcher bearers and ambulance drivers while the battle was full on, taking casualties to advance dressing units and carrying out the depressing duties of burial. Captain Horner, in a moment of reflection, felt it better to die than be severely disfigured. He'd seen officers and men during his hospital visits who were so badly wounded they would always be helpless and unrecognisable even if they survived.

Stan wrote in his little diary and perhaps wondered where the diaries of the dead were. The small address book he'd started in Droitwich had survived, safe in his top pocket. Gordon and he spoke quietly about the unlucky gunners on the front lines, the earth-shattering explosions, the blood and death. They both knew prodding sticks would be used to find survivors or bodies but overcome by sadness and fatigue they succumbed to desperately needed sleep. It was the best they'd had since arriving in Singapore. Stan wrote on 17 February:

> *Woke in the early hours of the morning. It was quite a pleasant sleep in the field on the grass, a bit damp underneath, but the best sleep I'd had for about ten days. Prior to that nobody had had much sleep.*

> *Eventually the whole field was lined up at 1600hrs by the Japs and was told we had to march to Changi, which was a 17-mile march, in tropical heat and to carry whatever you could carry.*

They began the long march to Singapore's north-eastern corner to Changi, and the gaol, on 17 February. The sun scorched as they marched past the distressing sights of corpses and carcasses of animals that had been shot or blown up with all sorts crawling out, burnt-out buildings and vehicles. Foot-sore and weary they reached Changi at 2000hrs.

> *I can tell you it was a hell of a march; it was a long trail of men and as we walked along there were various dead bodies of those who'd been shot and killed by shell fire. Along the other side of the road there were bits of equipment just abandoned. Everyone was fairly dejected. It took us nearly four hours continuous marching to get to Changi. There were some fellows who got there first; apparently, they got a lift by lorry. They gave us some dry rations, so we had something to eat, then had another night's kip on another football field.*

Japanese soldiers took their valuables: fountain pens, watches, rings and pencils; one man hid his wedding ring on a pencil in his underwear. They were told they were on Tokyo time, an hour and a half ahead.[3] This seemed irrelevant to their plight. 'Why bother?' they grumbled. The winners in this theatre of war had taken two weeks of their lives and now they were stealing their time as well as their watches!

*   *   *

Prior to the march, there was a laborious long wait in the searing sun as Japanese guards repeatedly examined the rows of terrified captives, confiscating anything of value including cigarettes, though many continued to deftly stow precious belongings in private places. After much disorganisation on the part of the Japanese, British Command ordered two columns to march, as instructed by their captors, through the centre of the city. Japanese guards, so-called liberators of Malaya and Singapore, strutted beside the prisoners as they herded them along. Defeated, their heads hung low in dejection, failure and shame. The slow march formation to Changi for the 52,500 men was confused, and so were their minds. They attempted to keep in units, but some had to stop while others marched stoically on. At Farrer Park, another 35,000 Indian Army PoWs joined their group, making the total more than 87,000 men. During the arduous trek, many found themselves alongside other ranks as stragglers trailed behind. Conversation was prohibited, but from surreptitious comments and whispers, under hats and behind hands, the captives learned of Fort Canning personnel and their Command's escape, and the atrocities at the Alexandra Military Hospital after the retreat of the 44th Indian Brigade. The stronghold of the 11th Indian Division upheld the raised enclave at Bukit Chandra, within the radius of the military hospital and the Bukit Timah Road, but aggrieved Japanese soldiers decided that shots had come from the hospital grounds and embarked on a rampage. Dr Bill Frankland, an RAMC (Royal Army Medical Corps) attached to an Indian hospital, tossed a coin to decide where he should be detailed for duty: either at Tanglin or Alexandra Hospital. Heads meant he went to Tanglin while the other MO went to the hospital.[4]

The PoWs heard that a small group of Japanese had defeated Singaporean troops when they chased them over the railway into the hospital. They had bayoneted medical and nursing staff, as well as bedridden patients and defenceless people on operating tables. The massacre continued as the walking wounded were corralled into small hospital rooms to die or were openly attacked in the hospital gardens. The news was sickening.

The marchers' boots rubbed against their threadbare socks and the men wondered where they might be led. Were these horror tales their fate too? Death seemed real. At Malaya Command Headquarters,[5] commanders were taken prisoner at Fort Canning bunker and General Percival's operations staff were rounded up at bayonet point. Faces were slapped for no reason; epaulettes and shoulder rank badges were ripped off. Caps were torn from heads and thrown to the ground in disdain. There was no respect.

Terror was chilling as fear enveloped them in a pulsating membrane of cold sweat. They knew, in the eyes of the world, they were part of a massive military disaster, trapped in a hot foul-smelling land where the atmosphere was stifling. Civilians jeered en route. To them, capture of the 'colonials' was a good idea. Locals now considered Japan the rightful keeper of the Island; colonialism was over. Defeated in one stroke; the Australians couldn't understand how Singapore, ruled for years by the British Empire, was no longer. Fight to the end they were told. No one believed this could happen and blame was apportioned in all directions. British commanders cited the slow laid-back attitude of the Australians and their lack of awareness in the north-west. Now Singaporeans waved Japan's white flag with the solid red circle, while Chinese civilians quietly sang, 'There'll always be an England.'

In 1937, well before the declaration of war in 1939, First World War veteran, Air Chief Marshal Henry Robert Moore Brooke-Popham, was asked by the British government to leave retirement and his governor's post in Kenya to become commander-in-chief of British Far East Command and the fortress of Singapore.[6] His remit was to investigate, assess and recommend a way forward since the area was deficient in military protection, particularly in respect of aerial defence. But unfortunately, his report citing serious security needs went unheeded when he was unable to convince the government during political infighting and personality clashes. His recommendations to annex Siam[7] and deploy troops to help deflect a Japanese invasion were also ignored. Brooke-Popham was incredulous at the War Ministry's denial, but he also made poor decisions saying: 'We can get on all right with (Brewster) Buffaloes out here...,' and 'Let England have the Super Spitfires and Hyper Hurricanes.'

Political division led to his replacement by Lieutenant General Henry Pownall on 27 December 1941. But his post was also short-lived when, on arrival in Singapore, he found himself demoted to Chief of Staff, reporting to General Sir Archibald Wavell in the newly formed Allied initiative ABDACOM (American, British, Dutch, Australian Command). Responsibility for the Far East then fell to Lieutenant General Lewis Heath who reported to Wavell and Percival.[8] Meanwhile, an air of frivolity, inefficiency and denial prevailed while governing parties believed that 'nothing would happen there'.

Instead, 'Operation Matador' was an offensive plan to defend beaches in Siam and northern Malaya. Troops were to be ordered across Siam in all directions to stop a Japanese invasion; a move that could take twenty-four hours. Invasion in the north, through thick mangrove swamps, was considered impossible. New defences at Changi's naval fortress were installed in 1938 at a cost of £60 million, but these were set towards the sea in the south of Singapore, a costly mistake. The island was deemed impregnable; the cannons would withstand a seaborne attack, backed by reinforcements at four airfields. General Percival was told to prepare but received no orders to move. Matador was abandoned. Why?

As bombs dropped on Pearl Harbor, a simultaneous Japanese invasion on the beaches of Siam and northern Malaya was taking place. There was no resistance and Singapore was bombed four hours later. Churchill cabled a message to Wavell at Fort Canning:

'There must be no thought of saving the troops or sparing the population. The Battle must be fought to the bitter end at all costs. The honour of the British Empire and the British Army is at stake.'[9]

Wavell told his troops they would be a disgrace if they did not fight to the end and Fortress Singapore was lost. However, defence was severely lacking, with fewer than 200, mostly obsolete planes, and Singapore's airspace and reservoirs under Japanese threat, fresh water supplies would be depleted for troops and civilians.

*   *   *

Gunner Fergus Anckorn had survived the Japanese air attack, as he transported the large weapon, and the Alexandra Hospital massacre. Still dazed from his injuries and rough treatment, he discovered the war was over, and that he was a prisoner, when he woke in a makeshift recuperation ward at a Chinese high school. Somehow, he had cheated death. He remembered being thrown on to a stretcher and into a lorry with other prisoners. All the patients were being poorly man-handled by Japanese soldiers, as corralling great numbers of sick and injured had been an unforeseen task for them. He recalled the assembly at the racecourse, the night before he transported the large camouflaged gun, and the relayed words of Wavell, via senior officers. He had asserted that they should consider themselves 'death or glory boys', finishing with '... those of you not willing to die are not fit to live!'

Willing to die? Willing! No. He decided then he was not going to die. But he nearly did.

The ethos of the British Empire lay decaying under deadly battlegrounds, bad management, debris and destruction as the eastern jewel was besieged by a greed-driven enemy. Japan aimed to plunder the rich resources of the Malay Peninsula and control the Silk Road trade route to India. When Japanese troops ransacked Fort Canning, they helped themselves to the small pickings left behind. Earlier, Percival had issued orders to destroy all secret and technical equipment, ciphers, codes, top-secret documents and heavy guns.

The captives witnessed ghastly sights as they marched through the city and had to quash the impulse to retch. The repulsive horrors were examples of the barbaric regime. Decapitated heads on spikes in the Chinese quarter, a deterrent for those thinking of retaliation; the smell of rotting flesh and discarded bodies was sickening. This could happen to them. But slowly they continued. No tunes, no talking. Just terror and worry, and constant intimidation by the Japanese guards. Now they bore the degrading label of 'Prisoners of War'. Their bodies threatened to collapse from dehydration, hunger and pain. Some locals spat at them – Sikhs, Tamils and Malays mostly, as they waved Japanese flags.

Mile on mile they marched the dusty route into darkness. Recognisable sights were a blur as the men shuffled along. One building was the Fullerton,[10] the island's main post office, now a medical station for the wounded. Their feet needed medical treatment, but only the brutal blow of a rifle butt was administered; prisoner's feet were not important to the scruffy armed guards.

Soon cool evening air relieved the searing heat of the afternoon; at least they were still alive but, still petrified, they gradually began to accept the vile situation.

*   *   *

In the redness of the evening sun, the emblematic Japanese flag was hoisted on the thirteenth floor of the Cathay Building – then the tallest in Singapore. The high-principled power of the British Empire had plummeted, and virtues of sixteenth-century samurai customs came into effect. *Bushido* – the Way of the Warrior.[11] The system only honoured the morals of ancient Japanese; the alternative was death.

*   *   *

During the fall-out days of capitulation, other sights one could never have imagined, took place. Mark Felton in *The Coolie Generals* refers to a scene of disillusionment and displacement as civilians were also forced to parade through the streets.

> Passing Kantong, we saw a cantonment of separated women and children civilians. They made a forlorn group, abandoned with no purpose, their belongings loaded into prams; infants and property teetering on top. A dignitary, Colonial Officer Governor Sir Shenton Thomas, led them. Shenton was a special case for the Japanese to humiliate, providing a pleasing sight for those Indian, Malay, Chinese and Asians aggravated by the power of the rich middle-class, now a tragic group. But some civilians intercepted the group with offerings of biscuits and water, as they passed the Sea View Hotel.[12]

*   *   *

Background reasons for their plight would not be revealed for decades. They knew of the attacks on America at Pearl Harbor, and that HMS *Repulse* and HMS *Prince of Wales* had both been sunk, but had few details. The British Naval Squadron, under command of Admiral Sir Tom Spencer Vaughan Phillips, had gathered on 2 December 1941, as Force Z, consisting of the two battleships and destroyers *Electra, Express, Tenedos* and *Vampire*. But the fleet was deficient in air support after the new, illustrious-class, aircraft carrier HMS *Indomitable*[13] had run aground far away at Port Royal, a coral reef on a spit of land in Jamaica. Clear skies in the South China Sea exposed the two capital ships and Japanese bombardment sank the vessels with the loss of 850 men, including Admiral Phillips. The destroyer escorts picked up more than 2,000 survivors.

The Japanese land attack was launched from Indo-China on the island of Hainan. It was directed by General Tomoyuki Yamashita, Commander of the 25th Division, with only three other divisions under Lieutenant Generals Matsui, 5th Division; Mutaguchi, 28th Division, and Nishimura from the Imperial Guard Division (IGD). The 56th Division was held in reserve but not needed. Along with a cruiser squadron and the Southern Force, 60,000 Japanese troops, 200 tanks and more than 600 aircraft assembled in the

Gulf of Thailand. There, the attack began on thirty-eight Allied battalions and led to the eventual capture of Singapore.[14] From 8 December, the IJA took less than two months to cover 500 miles over the Malay Peninsula and British-held territory. They overpowered the 9th India Division in the east to take Kota Baru, Singora and Pattani and, in a surprising tactic, their armies progressed rapidly towards the south – using bicycles! Entire regiments moved quickly and smoothly through dense jungle, causing a chaotic Allied retreat. Japanese forces gained a foothold in Kuala Lumpur after advancing over hazardous mountain terrain using pack mules, but they did not enter the city, instead they pressed on to Kampar forcing British defenders – the 3rd Indian Division – to withdraw westward to the Slim River area. The Allies were outflanked.

A diluted resistance on the eastern coastline provided a valiant final attempt at victory, but their stretched forces were severely hindered by poor communication and contradictory orders. On 16 January, desperate efforts to hang on at the river Muar by the 11th Division commanded by General Lewis Heath and the Australian 8th Division, under General Gordon Bennett, were unsuccessful. On 21 January, General Wavell sent the prime minister a devastating message:

> I am anxious that you should not have a false impression of the defence of Singapore Island. I did not realise myself until lately how entirely defences were planned against a seaward attack only.

Forced to break and retreat to Singapore, orders were given to abandon Malaya on 25 January.[15] The remaining island defence was then divided into three areas: Under Percival, Malaya Command consisted of Malaya 1st and Malaya 2nd infantry brigades in the south and the city. Under General Gordon Bennett in the north-west, was 8th Australian Brigade and 12th and 44th Indian brigades. Under General Heath in the north-east was 3rd Indian Corps, 8th Indian Brigade, 11th Indian Division and 29th Australian Brigade. With Heath was Major General Beckwith-Smith and the 18th Division. Defence of Malaya and Singapore consisted only of 130,000 men armed with 450 guns and 110 aircraft. Armoured cars were used but no tanks were available. In Churchill's memoirs, there was a twinge of guilt and bitterness:

> I ought to have known. My advisers ought to have known and I ought to have been told or I ought to have asked. The reason I had not asked about this matter amid the thousands of questions I put, was that the possibility of Singapore having no landward defences no more entered my mind than that a battleship would be launched without a bottom.[16]

The Fall of Singapore, the British Empire's 'Gibraltar of the East' was, in Winston Churchill's sombre words, 'The greatest disaster and capitulation in British history'. Over 120,000 captives held the same thought. Singapore Island was naked.

> We had no aircraft whatsoever and the Japanese always bombed with twenty-seven planes; we always said they must have only one bomb aimer, so they blanket bombed us. We had three planes – American Brewster Buffaloes – as soon as the Japanese came over, they took off and disappeared – out of the way.[17]

Chapter 10

Beginning PoW Life

18 February 1942. We moved to attap huts in Changi called India Lines. We had to more or less, and accept the fact that we were settling in for a spot of PoW life. During the month of March there were people in these lines who settled down to make the place more habitable. We were under our own administration, being our own officers. That kept us busy – you know – having parades of a morning, instructions and orders, which gave us something to occupy ourselves, I suppose.

With a sense of foreboding and abject desolation, the degrading and devastating situation hung over them like a black cloud. They were sad, angry and felt totally helpless. The worst thing was the dire sanitary conditions. Barracks nearby were already full of sewage, but now there were no toilets at India Lines. With dysentery, some just defecated where they stood. No one tried to escape, though many considered such action. The Japanese surrounded the perimeter with large machine guns, aimed at the men. If anyone tried to escape, alone or en masse, the result would have been a ghastly massacre. The prisoners stood long hours in the camp the first day and when night fell, they lay on the ground. Escape was not an option.

In the warm Changi morning, on the 18 February, RASC prisoners came around with buckets of food for breakfast. They ladled out portions into mess tins which the supply corps had brought along. It was a stew of just green vegetables. Ravenous, they enjoyed the offering but didn't realise it would be the last 'good meal' they'd have for a long time. The next night, as prisoners in confined quarters, some were lucky to sleep on bamboo camp beds. They were unfamiliar and uncomfortable, but still a blessing. Stan and his group were fortunate to be in a hut close to their HQ officers who were housed nearby.

First off, we found our way to what we thought was a nice big swimming pool, but it wasn't a swimming pool. It was a tidal sewerage drain. When the tide came in it filled the drain up and appeared to become a big wide pool. We were stopped, obviously, from going in there! Later, the Japs gave instructions to our engineer units to collect wire from various depots around the island, being huge coils of Dannert[1] wire, barbed wire; we wired ourselves in under Japanese instructions, guards were placed on one or two exits around the wire, and later those guards were replaced by Sikh soldiers who had gone over to the Japanese side.

Confined for the next few months, March to July, the Japanese made the men's lives as horrible as possible, since they now found themselves responsible for 'entertaining' multiple numbers of foreign prisoners; an enormous problem they had not envisaged. How the Japanese authorities would deal with so many captives was a deep concern for discussion.

As well as taking prisoners' valuables, officers' badges and ribbons were ripped off making rank and file indistinguishable from captains and commanders. Some could wear a regimental star pinned to the right breast pocket, denoting a higher rank, but all were considered equal in imprisonment, all were followers. The captors were begrudging leaders and, so far, not one Japanese commander had been seen.

Coconut palms and papaya trees peppered the area where British officers settled into their accommodation at India Lines. The two-storey building dominated a field and boasted elegant white verandas, shuttered windows and doors that lead to empty rooms. Banana plants and trees, with long runner bean-type pods called 'Flames of the Forest', grew beside the palms along with edible coconuts. A mangrove swamp ran down to the sea. On the other side of the small padang, where the prisoners played football, were attap huts. Officers were not totally separated from their men due to such large numbers in confined spaces, but these were their quarters for now.

There was plenty of work for the men of the RASC. They were responsible for collecting rations from the city and the produce grown outside or within the camp. Everything was sorted in the Gun Park and distributed by them using hand trucks tied to a two- or four-wheel car chassis. Their roaming space within the Dannert wire was adequate. They knew their boundaries and felt lucky to have a good deal of legroom. The four formations of the captive troops were: 18th Division, 11th Indian Division, AIF (Australian Imperial Force) and Command, and Garrison troops (Southern area). Each had its own location and internal administration with a Malaya Command link. The most surprising aspect for all PoWs was that they were expected to organise their own captivity. Administratively, officers looked after other ranks 'as usual', while their captors gave access to food rations.

*   *   *

While the men of the RASC and the 18th Division were held captive in relative 'luxury', the Japanese Army committed barbaric murder of so-called Chinese opponents. From 21 February to 5 March 1942, a system of 'Purging through purification' was carried out close to India Lines. Alistair Urquhart, in *The Forgotten Highlander*, wrote: 'Another group of Chinese dressed in white shirts and shorts were forced to the beach by the Japanese.'

They, it was later heard, were gunned down along with hundreds of others on the beach at Changi. Consequently, the British PoWs – a specific work party – had to dig mass graves for the bodies one week later.[2] More than 50,000 people were murdered by the Japanese Army.

*   *   *

Fergus found himself going through the gates of Changi Gaol on the back of a transporter. His group of fellow patients were now starving, dehydrated and exhausted. He was lifted off the truck to the ground, and tried to walk, but with his left leg so damaged he could only crawl. He felt he resembled an injured spider. Sleeping on the ground, he thought he must have looked like a beggar in India. For two days, he looked for somebody he knew but eventually a gunner sergeant found him and took him to the sergeants' mess, where an air of normality appeared to reign. But as he was helped through a pair of swing doors, one swung back and hit his injured arm and wrist. The pain he felt was excruciating and his old wound split open spurting blood everywhere. The sergeant immediately took him to Roberts Hospital in another part of the camp. It had been ten days since the bomb hit his gun lorry, now proper treatment for his injuries was at last being administered.

As doctors unwrapped his filthy bandage from Alexandra Hospital and broke the news that he had gangrene, he feared the worst and thought he would lose his entire arm and hand – his magician's hand. But strangely there was a remedy – maggots! The medics applied the squirming grubs deep inside his wound where they feasted on the bad flesh. This type of treatment throughout incarceration saved many lives and limbs.[3]

* * *

The commander-in-chief of the IJA, General Yamashita, was astounded by the number of troops captured. Over 54,000 men of all ranks had survived. A major general was put in charge of each formation, and brigadiers took charge of sub-divisions. At the start of Stan's confinement, Major General Merton Beckwith-Smith, DSO, MC, GOC[4] was in overall charge of the 18th Division PoWs in Changi. Their commanding officer was Brigadier Goodman.[5]

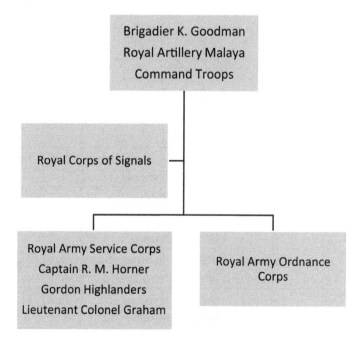

BRITISH AND COMMONWEALTH GENERAL OFFICERS –
Imprisoned 1941–1945.[6]

NAME	RANK	AREA	CAMPS
Percival, A.	Lieutenant. General	GOC Malaya	CH,KA,TA,T5,MA
Heath, Sir L.	Lieutenant. General	GOC II Indian Corps	CH,KA,TA,T5,MA
Beckwith-Smith, M.	Major General	GOC 18th Division	CH,KA
Callaghan, C.	Major General	GOC 8th AIF Division	CH,KA,TA,SH,MA
Keith Simmons, F.	Major General	GOC Southern Area	CH,KA,TA,MA
Key, R. S. W.	Major General	GOC 11th Indian Division	CH,KA,TA,SH,MA
Maltby, C. M.	Major General	GOC Hong Kong	SO,AR,SH,MA
Sitwell, H. D. W.	Major General	GOC Java	BI,KA,MA
Backhouse, E. H. W.	Brigadier	Brigade Command. 54th Inf. Brigade	CH,KA,TA,SH,MA
Ballentine, C. G.	Brigadier	Brigade Command. 44th Inf. Brigade	CH,KA,TA,SH,MA
Blackburn, A.	Brigadier	Command. 'Black Force', AIF, Java	BI,KA,TA,SH,MA
Challen, B. S.	Brigadier	Brigade Command 15th Indian Inf. Brigade	CH,KA,TA,SH,MA
Crawford, K. B. S.	Brigadier	III Indian Corps	CH,KA,TA,SH,MA
Curtis, A. D.	Brigadier	Command Fixed Defences, Malaya	CH,KA,TA,SH,MA
Dalby, A.	Brigadier	Brigade Command. West Brigade. Hong Kong	SO,AR,SH,MA
Duke, C. L. B.	Brigadier	Brigade Command 53rd Infantry Brigade	CH,KA,TA,SH,MA

NAME	RANK	AREA	CAMPS
Evelegh, G. C.	Brigadier	Deputy Director Ordnance Service Malaya	CH,KA,TA,SH,MA
Fraser, F. H.	Brigadier	Brigade Command. 6th Indian Inf. Brigade	CH,KA,TA,SH,MA
Goodman, E. W.	Brigadier	Brigade Royal Artillery, Malaya	CH,KA,TA,SH,MA
Lay, W. O.	Brigadier	Brigade Command 6th Indian Infantry Brigade	CH,KA,TA,SH,MA
Lucas, H. F.	Brigadier	Administrative HQ Malaya	CH,KA,TA,SH,MA
MacLeod, T.	Brigadier	Command. Royal Artillery, Hong Kong	SO,AR,SH,MA
Massy-Beresford, T.	Brigadier	Brigade Command 55th Infantry Brigade	CH,KA,TA,MA
Maxwell, D. S.	Brigadier	Brigade Command 27th AIF Infantry Brigade	CH,KA,TA,SH,MA
McLeod, L.	Brigadier	Royal Artillery, Hong Kong	SO,AR,SH,MA
Moir, R. G.	Brigadier	Brigade Command Federated Malay States Volunteer Forces	CH,KA,TA,SH,MA
Newbigging, T. K.	Brigadier	Director Of Administration Malaya	CH,KA,TA,SH,MA
Painter, G. W. A.	Brigadier	Brigade Command 22nd Indian Infantry Brigade	CH,KA,TA,SH,MA
Pearson, S. R.	Brigadier	Brigade Command 16th Anti-Aircraft Brigade. Java	BI,KA,TA,SH,MA
Peffers, A.	Brigadier	ADO, Hong Kong	SO,AR,SH,MA
Richards, C. W.	Brigadier	DDST, Malaya	CH,KA,TA,SH,MA
Rusher, A. E.	Brigadier	Command Royal Artillery, 11th Indian Division	CH,KA,TA,SH,MA

NAME	RANK	AREA	CAMPS
Selby, W. R.	Brigadier	Brigade Command 28th Indian Inf. Brigade	CH,KA,TA,SH,MA
Servaes, H. C.	Brigadier	Command. Royal Artillery, 18th Division	CH,KA,TA,SH,MA
Simson, I. J.	Brigadier	Chief Engineer, Malaya	CH,KA,TA,SH,MA
Stringer, C. H.	Brigadier	Deputy Director Medical Services, Malaya	CH,KA,TA,SH,MA
Taylor, H. B.	Brigadier	Brigade Command 22th AIF Inf. Brigade	CH,KA,TA,SH,MA
Torrance, K. S.	Brigadier	BGS, Malaya	CH,KA,TA,SH,MA
Trott, W. A.	Brigadier	Brigade Command 8th Indian Inf. Brigade	CH,KA,TA,SH,MA
Wallis, C.	Brigadier	Brigade Command.East Brigade Hong Kong	NP,AR,SH,MA
Wildey, A.W.G.	Brigadier	Command Anti-aircraft Def. Malaya	CH,KA,TA,SH,MA
Williams G.G.R.	Brigadier	Brigade Command. 1st Malayan Infantry Brigade	CH,KA,TA,SH,MA

Key:

- SO – Shamshuipo Camp, Hong Kong
- AR – Argyle Street, Officers Camp, Hong Kong
- NP – North Point Camp, Hong Kong
- CH – Changi Camp, Singapore
- BI – Bicycle Camp, Java
- KA – Karenko Camp, Taiwan
- TA – Tamazato Camp, Taiwan
- T5 – Taihoku No.5 Camp, Taiwan
- SH – Shirakawa Camp, Taiwan
- MA – Manchuria, China

(Taiwan formerly known as Formosa during the Second World War)

Before the Capitulation, Brigadier Goodman had reported on defences held by the 18th Division at Fairy Point Hill, Changi, Sungei and Seletar. He noted the west side of the causeway was guarded by the 11th Indian Division, and that Australian troops covered the area north of Paya Lebar, but felt there was no command with gravitas, or knowledge of the plan to carry out orders.

'It was impossible to get information out of the regiments while the battle went on. The formation of the 18th Division almost ceased to be, but they did as well as could be expected.'

Throughout the night of 14 February, when the Japanese had continued to press against the Allied perimeter, the military supply had rapidly deteriorated and the water system was damaged, with doubtful continuous supply. Rations were low, petrol for military vehicles was depleted and ammunition rounds for field artillery were few. Anti-aircraft guns were also drained and unable to disrupt Japanese air attacks which caused heavy casualties in the city. Few air-raid shelters had been built and looting and desertion of Allied troops added to their chaos.[7]

Goodman attended the conference in the Battle Box, 'a large air-conditioned dug out', and at the meeting of generals, a decision was made not to carry on; food, water and ammunition supplies were all but exhausted. That night he slept at Fort Canning after helping to arrange the details of surrender. Lieutenant General Percival's senior artillery officer, Malaya Command. Brigadier T. K. Newbigging carried the Union Jack and Major C. Wild,[8] a Japanese speaker, carried the white flag of truce to the new Japanese Army headquarters at the Ford Motor Company.[9] He later said he'd found it difficult to register the calamity of their defeat, but that changed when he returned to the Fort Canning stores and the NAAFI canteen for supplies and a Japanese guard prevented entry by pointing a gun at his stomach.

At capitulation, Goodman was given his own small HQ and command of 2,000 men from RASC, RAOC and Royal Corps of Signals, assisted by Lieutenant Colonel Graham of the Gordon Highlanders. The realisation of the enormity of their situation suddenly hit him, especially when he saw thousands of captives and heard horrific stories. One came from a fellow brigadier, Ivan Simson, a senior Royal Engineer. He was coerced to ride in a car with two young Japanese officers who took him through the city to witness the devastation. At the docks he was forced to look at a group of coolies rounded up for looting; their hands tied behind their backs with barbed wire. The guard in charge, on seeing the officers' car with British officers inside, did no more than raise his samurai sword and behead all the coolies, one after the other. In sickening horror, Simson turned his head from the barbaric act, found only in ancient cultures, but he fully understood their message. Sights in the city and the Chinese Quarter were repulsive. There would be no leniency from the Japanese.

Chapter 11

Prisoners on the Padang

'I speak to you all under the shadow of a heavy and far-reaching military defeat; Singapore has fallen.'

Churchill spoke of the worst disaster and largest capitulation in British history, but his grave words were not heard by the captives as they reluctantly wired themselves into an area encompassing India Lines, Selarang, Roberts and Kitchener Barracks. Their captors had little or no organisational planning, except to disrespectfully strip officers of their disciplinary powers, of which some prisoners took advantage.

On the first Sunday, 22 February, an impressive open-air church service was held on the Padang. Everyone, from senior officers to the most junior of soldiers worshipped, giving solemn thanks for having at least survived the ordeal of the last twenty-two days. Around 55,000 attended. Many had also lost friends days after the battle, from lethal wounds. By early March, many argued over space; in fact, officers were the worst offenders. The Emergency Commissioned Officers (ECOs) seemed to be the main culprits, as the selfish side of human nature reared its ugly head. Meagre food supplies were also meted out from a central supply depot, but cheating was discovered, and a general feeling of mistrust ensued.

The defeated troops were treated as labourers to clean up the city. The RE (Royal Engineer) PoWs repaired the reservoirs and water supplies and reconnected electricity to the hospital and other civilian places. They were not liked by some Singaporeans, but others were brave enough to help them when they could. Ultimately, however, this was a concern for British officers as, if discovered, all involved would be punished. It was illegal for civilians to approach captives as the Japanese were worried that PoWs would reveal their ill-treatment. Everything was guarded.

In truth, reminds Ernest Warwick (a vocal ex-PoW), the Japanese military did not know what to do with the massive number of prisoners. Those captured in the first days of the battle were of value for intelligence reasons and sent to Saigon where they were severely tortured, but the rest were a greater problem.[1]

Stan's Early Days in Changi

We used to have working parties go to the city of Singapore to do various jobs. It was soon after capitulation. In Raffles Square there was a row of native severed heads on [wooden] pikes and a notice saying this is what happens to people who loot buildings and do not co-operate with the Japanese. They were not a very humane race – not then anyway.

I witnessed a Malay or Chinese outside the gates of our camp at Changi. We were on our way out to the rubber plantation for tree felling. We used to have to halt at the gate while the Korean guard checked our numbers to make sure the right number was going out, escorted by other guards. This particular time we were waiting outside the sentry shed/ guard room, and there was this poor Chinese knelt down, his head held back hard [with them] pouring hot water up his nose as a form of torture. They said he'd been caught talking to one of the prisoners.

During the very early stages of confinement, the Japs ordered some of our fellows (engineers) to go to the beaches for bits of barbed Dannert wire. In one incident, the working party went on a big old Ford, all-steel, lorry, picking up wire but they ran over a land mine which blew up the lorry! Our fellows standing on the back, just behind the cab, had their ankles shattered. This wasn't a good thing to happen, [considering] the conditions we were living in. I suppose the fact the lorry had an all-steel body, protected them a certain amount – they could have been killed.

Another favourite of the Japanese, if you were caught doing something you shouldn't be doing – or THEY thought you shouldn't be doing –

*was to make you stand in the sun holding a heavy weight above your
head, such as a big heavy log. On one occasion I saw a fellow holding
an earthenware sink above. You had to keep your arms stretched most
of the time, if you didn't the Japanese would come along and give you
a kick or do something like that. Mainly just for punishment.*

*   *   *

Stories from other soldiers also recounted barbaric acts. One of a British
soldier held naked for five days and nights, upside down, locked inside a metal
coffin, tied to a tree. His only crime was trying to save an elderly Chinese
woman. She was in her seventies and being beaten by a Japanese guard for
selling chapatis to a PoW.

A Jap guard had walked by and kicked the lady's legs apart. There was an
old iron bar which he made her hold above her head, but she wasn't strong
enough. She was crying and frightened. The Jap belt-slashed her face and
blood gushed from her wound, but the soldier punched him to the ground and
the woman ran away saying, "God bless you son." Eight other Jap guards ran
to the scene and the soldier admitted the incident. He was stripped and beaten
with sticks for five days and tied to the tree. A badly written notice was left at
the foot implying that if anyone attempts to help; death would be the penalty.

The prisoner thought about his family – his mother – and hoped something
might save him. He wasn't religious, but anything would have helped; he was
numb from his injuries and sore from the ropes. Several days passed before a
commander from the Japanese Army came by with a British medical officer.
Colonel Harvey pointed at the tortured prisoner saying, 'You are murdering
this man; he should be cut free.'

The commander was General Yamashita, who immediately ordered his
release. The PoWs cut their fellow prisoner down and put him in the back of
a pick-up truck and took him to River Valley camp. There, Australian PoWs
revived and nourished him and gave him clothes. He had survived the awful
ordeal.[2]

*   *   *

The RE division, like the RASC, who distributed food, had immediately provided essential sanitary facilities for the overcrowded Changi campus. The parties were housed in two other camps bound by River Valley and Havelock roads, known as the River Valley Road Camp.[3] Before the war (in the event of a presumed attack from the south), temporary military camps had been built by colonial authorities on the banks of the Singapore River. PoW parties were sent from there daily, to other parts of the island and across the causeway to Johor. The camp also housed civilian refugees, European, Australian, Indian and local PoW internees. Once a swamp, its abandoned huts were occupied by the IJA. Its accommodation consisted of attap huts, mostly large with two-tiered sleeping platforms on each side, a cook house, sufficient for the numbers in both camps, and even sanitary facilities, including showers. The camps were divided by the narrow river and PoWs were at liberty to wander across the bridge between the two, exchanging visits and more. The camp had no hospital facilities, therefore cases of dysentery, avitaminosis (long-term vitamin deficiencies), recurring fever and other ailments were sent to Roberts Barracks Hospital, elevated on a small hill inside the Changi compound. Before long, on 13 March 1942, Major W. A. J. Spear and Second Lieutenant B. McD. Buchanan (288th Field Company) bravely marched a healthier contingent of sappers back to River Valley Road.

Some PoWs here painted encampment scenes or drew caricatures for a small fee. It was part of the Changi black-market profiteering. You could even buy a penknife or a gun. These internees were controlled less by the Japanese guards. As time passed, there were rumours and concerns that some PoWs operated as spies for the Japanese. If someone was summoned to their office and came out unscathed, they were immediately under suspicion. Even if a medic provided a minor manicure or foot massage, it led to that person being labelled 'Jap Happy'. Tongues wagged and speculation was rife. But those who worked in the Japanese kitchens seemed to be exempt from the tag of 'Jap Happy'; it was more a case of 'good luck to them'. They were, of course, better fed, being closer to the food.

* * *

Forced working parties were taken to areas such as the docks, in commandeered trucks that once belonged to the British. Guarded by Japanese soldiers, about forty men were packed inside each vehicle. Some were driven through the city of Singapore to other places such as Pasir Panjang[4] in the west of the island. Later, some 6,000 captives went 'up-country' for hard labour, leaving around 45,000 in the southern prison camps. This was the first wave of troops to be transported north to Malaya in working parties.

The main Changi prison compound had been built by the British six years earlier, to hold a maximum of 5,000 prisoners. Some buildings were three storeys with verandas, and in normal times inmates had extraordinary roomy conditions. Now 50-55,000 were expected to survive in overcrowded, sordid and degrading conditions.

> *There was no room,* recorded Stan, *several men shared cells, taking it in turns to sleep on the floor. But under the circumstances, we were fortunate when we went with our HQ, to the internment area of India Lines, near Roberts Barracks.*

The rustic attap huts were a welcome sight after forced work from daybreak to sundown – if one was lucky enough to survive. Prisoners were ordered into working parties for the city. Sometimes they unloaded stores from ships, such as rice, meat, sugar and rotting vegetables. The Japanese controlled the supplies, but the captives didn't know where they went. Some dockside parties took what they could, but it was risky and some paid with their lives for stealing a handful of rice. Hunger was the main hurdle to survival. Japanese guards beat the pilferers with iron bars, staves and pickaxe handles, often leaving them blind, paralysed or dead. It was a crime to steal, even if you were starving.

* * *

Some officers tried to intervene in the torture of Chinese locals as they were hung by their thumbs. But the officers were threatened with the same treatment. Devastated families pleaded for help from the British with civilised standards, but as PoWs, faced with unkempt brutal soldiers wielding lethal Japanese swords, they were in no position to help.[5]

Their Nippon captors demanded the formation of hand-wagon parties, where men wheeled rubble from bomb sites across the town or were ordered to chop wood for fuel in the garden and wood areas. After a city stint, Stan and Gordon were detailed to wood cutting while others continued to clear rubble. The work was hard and inevitably a language barrier existed. Soon Japanese controllers insisted PoWs learn and speak a few Japanese words. When one chap asked a question in English, the guard shouted:

'Nippongo, Nippongo!' to which the PoW quietly retorted, 'Yes; I wish you all would go, and the further the better!'[6]

*   *   *

Late in March 1942, 'Recreation on the Padang' – many games of hockey and short games of football – part of much-needed exercise and enjoyment was encouraged, albeit it was odd to see men playing field games while sporting long beards. Razor blades were soon found, and some men set to work to shave their comrades. Despite this continuous attrition, of death and working parties leaving to go up-country, there were enough 18th Division sappers in River Valley Road Camp to provide one officer – Buchanan – and seventy-two ordinary ranks for the 31 October 1942 draft to Formosa (Taiwan).[7]

As weeks turned into months, the endless diet of starchy rice lost its appeal. The tasty vegetable stew of earlier days had disappeared and rationing meant rice portions were cut. If you worked, you got 8oz for breakfast, lunch and tea. The men eked out their portions to last all day. Some shared their food if a friend was down, but most times they guarded every precious grain. Enterprising prisoners started a secret kitchen. The leader was a Swiss gastronome, purported to be head chef at the famous Raffles Hotel in Singapore. 'None of us "rankers" would have been comfortable in such an establishment in peace times, but here we were with our own Raffles chef!' The unusual aroma of eastern spices, even eggs were overwhelming, they had not experienced edible fare for weeks. Spices added to rice were alien to the British palate, but simply prepared the exotic food was delicious and made life bearable. But simplicity turned to meagre. With smaller portions and vitamin deficiencies, troops became ill due to lack of basic nutrition. Word on the camp said some civilian prisoners were chemists, previously employed by British companies in Singapore. Their research focused on the regular tropical complaint of beriberi, and results proved that Vitamin B found in rice husks was part of the dietary solution. Unfortunately, the captors were not interested and provided only rice without husks meaning ailments quickly took hold.

Health was an issue, but life in captivity was surprisingly organised and disciplined. Except for orders relating to working parties, the Japanese left Australian and British officers to manage the camps. However, they often searched prisoners' belongings for radios and devices that might alert the outside world to the bad conditions and ill-treatment. Without warning they would turn the place upside down and take anything of benefit, including books, Bibles, paper and pens. Writing was banned and all was confiscated. As a result, paper and pencils – or any surviving stationery – were discretely hidden.

In the early days the men were stoic, but cunning soon took hold. Stan chuckled into his recording device:

> *We got our own back – some did, not me personally – the Japanese troops used to love getting hold of medication and they knew about these M&B tablets* [sulphonamide tablets] *made by May & Baker which were supposed to cure everything in the army. Some of the wide boys obtained some chalk – maybe from the entertainments party – and they cut them up and made the necessary marks on them 'M&B'. I suppose they used a fine piece of wire. They fashioned this lettering on* [each] *and sold them to the Japanese who needed them to cure all sorts of diseases, one being VD. They got $1 a time for a bit of chalk tablet, which we used to consider good fun.*

*   *   *

In later years, Stan remembered some pleasant thoughts, despite the horrendous conditions, as he re-read his little diary for the recording in 1990.

One of the highlights in Changi at India Lines, in the earlier part of the PoW time, were the evenings – especially after the Dutch people arrived. They managed to bring a lot of their gear with them, and a number had guitars. We used to go up on Changi Hill, which was a big hill with a huge teak tree on top. We'd sit up there, and it was quite pleasant with the moon rising out of the sea, the balmy evening and hearing these fellows play their guitars. All we wanted was Dorothy Lamour with us, and we would've been well away!

* * *

After three months, in June 1942, postcards provided by the Japanese finally allowed prisoners to send a message home for the first time. These were completed with standard messages reflecting 'good spirits': 'My well wishes for all at home. Be there as soon as I can.'

On the other side they completed other set statements:

I'm in Changi, India Lines.

I am well.

I am working for pay.

They were asked to write that their wife or family member (name), was to be taken care of, but that seemed too final for some, like a last will and testament.

* * *

Many prisoners started to suffer from 'Black Dog' – combat depression. One of the ways they dealt with this was to relax on Changi Hill, within the permitted zone. Like Stan, they listened to music performed by other prisoners on guitars, pipes and violins. Some tunes were sombre, others classical and many reminded the men of home. The mesmerising time and sheer relaxation provided relief, if only for a short time. Even the hardest soldier enjoyed pseudo freedom, swaying and humming to melodies.

Psychologically, British administration gave the PoWs hobbies and things to think about, which helped quell the boredom and reality of worsening conditions. Concert Parties were magnificent in this respect, and lectures and religion played an integral part, lessening the pangs of permanent hunger they all felt. By now they despised coconut and rice.

Strong tropical 'Sumatra' winds often whipped up suddenly to deliver drenching rain, causing excessive humidity and perspiration. The 3ft-deep drains, intersecting the camp, always overflowed causing flatter land to flood. Rainwater subsided rapidly, but still affected the interior of their huts. The RE fixed the water systems around the camp, but this alone took a few days, so 'Sumatra' showers were sometimes the only means of bathing. It seemed a vicious circle of being continually hot and sweaty or drenched; many appeared wet all the time.

The Ulu – sounds of the jungle – both evocative and annoying, consisted of distant night-time wild dogs, shrill scratching notes of crickets, and the deep tock-tock of birds who all vied for the stage of evening jungle, matching like for like with clicking and chirping cicadas. After rain, the bullfrogs joined in with a croaking choral crescendo of snoring discord. The captives soon became accustomed to the sounds of Singapore and found the jungle buzz to be almost musical.

* * *

When Fergus Anckorn was eventually discharged from Roberts Hospital, he was reunited with his regiment in bungalows close to the hospital. Some of their number had not survived, while others were already emaciated. One had given up completely and his body was reduced to a skeleton. He stayed away from everyone and hid in a cupboard. Fergus tried to make him come round, and lightly mocked him about being ill, saying, 'It's just mild dysentery.' But the man simply whispered he was dying and wanted to be left alone. Fergus didn't see him again, but his state of hopelessness struck a chord and he vowed never to sink that low. From then on, he developed his own code for survival, as did Stan.

* * *

Under Tokyo time, one and half hours earlier than Singapore time, the island was now known as Shonan and the Japanese Army imposed a strict schedule:[8]

8.00 a.m.	Reveille
9.00 a.m.	Breakfast
1.30 p.m.	Lunchtime
2.30–6.00 p.m.	Work
6.30 p.m.	Evening Meal
9.30 p.m.	Roll Call (Tenko)
10.15 p.m.	Lights out

As the invaders occupied and took over the administration of Singapore and Malaya, the island's *Singapore Times* became *Shonan Shimbun*. The paper was to be the organ of the Greater East Asian Co-Prosperity Sphere. Printed in English and used as a war propaganda tool – it was inaccurate and one-sided – the Japanese hoped it would influence opinions of neutral citizens who were not interned or imprisoned, such as the Irish, Swedish, Swiss, Anglo Indian and Eurasian people. Copies of *Shonan Shimbun* were also issued to PoWs who gladly received the daily edition for a jolly good laugh, and as an additional supply of toilet paper![9]

* * *

From the early days, the prisoners yearned for food, but the portion of rice on their plate was often crawling with bugs. The bugs would be hiding at first, but as soon as the plate was put in the sun they appeared. The men also had to make sure no flies landed on the food as they would immediately contaminate the rice and dysentery wouldn't be far behind. Sometimes Malayan cooks had leftovers, which they called 'lagis'. 'Lagis, lagis', meant 'more, more'. This became 'leggies' to the men and some, having eaten their first portion, returned for more. But if prisoners were too late for 'leggies' they became seriously distraught, even violent.

Soon everyone learned to treat every grain of rice as his last, and this was how Fergus contained starvation. Several men started to wander aimlessly around the camp and depression began to set in from being idle, and he decided to walk with purpose, even if only to a tree a short distance away. This helped to keep his sanity, and the exercise gradually repaired his body. Before long, with a smiling disposition and interaction with other inmates about languages, music and astronomy, Fergus pulled himself through the early days. He even approached officers about setting up a theatre in Roberts Barracks. There was hope on the horizon.

Chapter 12

Six Months in – a New Order

Stan's typical day:

Us fellas had to go out every day on working parties, dawn to dusk, but working on an empty tummy was a bit much. All we had as regards rations for working people was 8oz [of rice] a day: that was breakfast, lunch and evening meal. Those who didn't go out to work, such as the limbless people who couldn't work, the sightless or those very ill with beriberi, dysentery – what have you – were only allowed 6oz a day, which wasn't good for recovering from an illness.

Many were losing their eyesight from the lack of Vitamin B₂. Some of our medics organised a type of sun visor, like a mask made out of a dead palm tree frond; a couple of slits in it helped shield the sun from a chap's eyes. They were able to get around more comfortably that way. It was amazing what was made out of the few materials we had to work with: there were toothbrushes made from bamboo and coconut fibre, needles made out of fish bones for sewing various patches on our clothing.

A lot of old steel army lockers used in army camps prior to the war, were cut up with cutting gear and a welding machine rigged into the electricity in the Changi camp, and then it was welded together again, with galvanised barbed wire, to make pots and pans for cooking. How they did that I will never know. It was very effective. The only problem was it made the tea black – there was plenty of tea, nothing else just tea and water, but anything you had to drink had to be boiled anyway, or you got cholera!

The amount of food issued to the teams at this time in addition to 8oz of rice, was 1/6oz tea, 2/3oz sugar, 1/2oz milk, 1/2oz cheese, 1/2oz vegetables, which was to make do for the whole day. If you didn't work, you had less. One of the Australian officers had a jar of tomato jam, which was to be sent to the hospital, but before it went, he scooped out some tomato pips. From these a set of tomato plants were grown, and then from there more plants were harvested in the 'market garden'.

The value of a tomato pip was not to be underrated. From one or two, more fruit could be produced to provide a valuable source of nutrients, including lycopene, and a welcome healthy addition to the men's meagre meals. They would have known little about the importance of this at the time, to them it was just a pip. Tomatoes contained 40 per cent of the daily Vitamin C they needed.[1]

*　*　*

Tins of M&V (meat and veg.) and other tinned supplies were part of the ration cargo when they first arrived in Singapore. British Army staples were sparingly mixed with local food or rice, but gradually these ran out. The prisoners had to make do with meals alien to them, 'foreign food' – most were only used to bread and butter, meat, pies, two vegetables and gravy. But prisoners from the colonies of the Dutch East Indies excelled at different rice-based recipes and their meals were laced with spice and exotic vegetables. Through their hunger, eventually British prisoners began to appreciate this diet, especially when they moved up-country.

From seeds and roots of the new type of vegetables, the prisoners grew not only tomatoes in their small gardens, but tapioca root, sweet potatoes, chillies, ginger and aubergines – black beans, ubi kayu, a cassava fruit and towgay – an asparagus tasting soya bean or beansprout paste, or its fleshy tuberous root, grated and sprinkled on their food. Amaranth, kangkong (also known as kangkory – a type of spinach), were all eaten for their rich source of vitamins – A, B_6, Riboflavin, K and C – and protein, but it stained the men's teeth green. Regular Asian foods were also introduced such as sambal, a highly seasoned condiment, gula melaka, a type of fudge made of sugar from the palm tree flower, and tempeh, a soya bean product similar to tofu.

Eventually, additional protein for their diet was found in unsavoury sources such as dogs, cats and mice, then, too awful to imagine, snakes, rats, frogs, cockroaches, grasshoppers and snails. None were palatable but necessary for survival.

From the first days of surrender, a serious lack of fresh vegetables was evident, and deficiency diseases crept in. This caused major concern fearing sickness would reach alarming heights if more balanced rations were not provided. The basic menu was: ground rice porridge, boiled rice and onion gravy, tea.

The tea was made Malayan style, weak without milk and sugar, and helped the men's teeth. It was taken at breakfast, 0930hrs. Tiffin,[2] at 1330hrs consisted of sweet, boiled rice, coconut biscuit, and tea. Supper at 1830hrs, perhaps a 'bully' and rice pasty followed by a coconut rock bun, was the daily average.

Rice was prominent. No provisions were forthcoming from the Japanese for the first two weeks and had the PoWs not brought along considerable portions of rations themselves, they would have had nothing. Eventually, they received very small quantities of frozen meat, flour, tea, tinned milk, ghee (Indian fat), salt, M&V or Irish stew in lieu of green vegetables for a while.

The officers' missed their lavish banquets but they were able to make surreptitious purchases from Malays and Chinese, which had once been saved to celebrate a special occasion. Celery soup, salmon and rice fish cakes with tomato sauce, raisin duff made from all-wheat flour, cheese on toast, papaya and cream, were deemed 'slap-up dos' and enjoyed only by invitees.

Meat rations were soon reduced. Only three and a quarter ounces – including bone and fat and expected to last three days – and 4oz of tinned onions, but the tins were 'blown' having been in an earlier fire at Bukit Timah supply depot. Supplies of tinned milk were also exhausted; the sweet milk was enjoyed in rice pudding and made porridge palatable. By May, however, there was hope of freshly grown vegetables, a godsend, since nutcake, the alternative source of Vitamin B, tasted terrible and was discovered to be cattle food. When vegetables and fruit arrived, kangkory, green papaya, cucumber and pineapple were included – and towgay, in its seed form (like small peas), could be germinated to produce small cress saplings with juicy asparagus-tasting stalks providing a good source of Vitamin B.

Weight loss of 2 stone or more was evident, but if this average kept up, there would be huge problems. By June, some excellent gula melaka was available in the canteen, but the fudge made no difference to the men's weight. New flavours such as Durian fruit became available, which grows like a conker to the size of a hard rugby ball with large spikes. The 'delectable' taste was reminiscent of garlic and onions mixed with strawberries and cream! The co-inmates declared that anyone eating the fruit should do so on the roof away from others, the odour was so bad.

Early springtime passed into summer. These were cooler months for local Malayans, recalled Brigadier Goodman. 'Prisoners continued in their working parties, but feelings of mistrust and jealousy regarding food portions grew, even though equal ration shares were strict. Morale was low due to persistent hunger.'

In contrast to many other ranks, Goodman's typical day consisted of walking around units to check if clean, and to see about any wants or needs of the PoWs; attend a conference at another area HQ, have lunch, attend a language lesson – German; dig the officers' garden, take in a lecture or play bridge, go to bed. But this lifestyle would soon cease.

The command administration of each division was not affected by Japanese interference in the early days; one hardly saw an IJA official in the camp, only a handful of brutal guards. The British officers were able to instil discipline and organisation to attempt to keep their men occupied and eliminate bad behaviour. As well as low morale from prolonged hunger, disagreements between different cultures erupted: British versus Australian, Scots versus English, Indian etc. The British had control of the kitchens, food supplies, storing and rationing, and ensured each unit received its share. The men sat in groups to eat and, before long, *Kongsi*[3] or cliques formed, and arguments ensued over coveted dining space too.

A group of officers made a communal market garden their responsibility. They spent little time working in there but stole a lot of the produce for themselves, although it was for sharing. They were called the 'Cadgers Club', but once their devious motives were discovered, they quickly disbanded. The gardens were maintained despite the erstwhile cadgers, and it was found that urinating on the garden was successful for growth. Peeing in the garden was the norm. A bucket was later supplied to collect the pee and instructions were given to everyone, including the officers, to monitor and empty the buckets the same as everyone else.

Every grain of rice was saved, even swept up from dusty floors. The debris contained maggots and rat droppings and was generally considered to be inedible. Sometimes the grain was supplemented with small portions of meat-based items such as rissole or bully-beef stew, or, at times morsels of fishcake or curry. As for pudding, tiny sweeteners like a jam-pastry, rice cake or biscuit – or perhaps a bread roll with butter – were occasionally available. Small 'extras' made mealtimes a little more palatable. Familiarity with Asian ingredients prompted the men to sample new drink concoctions as well as food. One potent drink consisted of cashew nuts, raisins, gula melaka, coconut water, apples and sugar. The men tried to make best of their lot.

In mid-July, other ranks received 13,000 tins of pineapple that were split among all formations. The Japanese captors, for no apparent reason, also presented the generals with a gift from their own unused western supplies. This consisted of stout, whisky, tinned butter and cheese. Major Beckwith-Smith then made generous gifts of six bottles of stout and one tin each of butter and cheese to his staff officers, including RASC officers, to boost morale. It was hoped extra delights would boost their weight, but he kept the whisky!

On another occasion that month, the prisoners were lucky enough to indulge in a celebratory 'tea' held after a religious occasion, where several hundreds of candidates were confirmed by the Bishop of Singapore. A special grant was issued to obtain a good variety of sandwiches – banana, cheese, kangkory, chutney, cucumber, egg, sardines and cake.

Though monotonous, the breakfast pap of rice-polishings was important roughage, washed down with a mug of raw tea. The menu was similar for lunch and slightly different in the evening, each time with something green or brown added or a thin broth of other dubious ingredients. Most men, however, were grateful for whatever food came their way, regardless of the presentation or where it came from.

Fergus had recuperated well from his injuries and joined the camp concert party as a magician. Other men had started to move up-country, but he was yet to be called and could practise his magician's dexterity, at any opportunity, to restore his injured hand to full strength. Once he practised on a Japanese officer, Commandant O'Sato. The trick was successful, and he was asked to perform in front of another higher-ranking general. As the trick involved eggs, Fergus asked the commandant for extra to improve his performance.

'How many?' asked the commandant.

'Fifty', Fergus replied.

When asked by the commandant why he needed fifty, Fergus told him, 'I need to get the trick right for the general, of course.'

He was given fifty and signed off on the haul. He practised for a while but not long after took the remaining eggs to his cookhouse where a gigantic omelette was made for his co-inmates. The ploy was repeated to obtain other props such as potatoes or tomatoes. The Japanese were highly afraid of disease and would not use the food once touched by a PoW. Fergus regularly entertained the commandant and knew as soon as he used a food item and made it 'vanish' to another part of the room, the guards wouldn't want it. The food, including tins of fish or fruit, was then taken back to his co-prisoners which helped to prevent beriberi and other diseases. One of Fergus's friends had beriberi, which resulted in deafness, immobility and blindness, but Marmite, containing valuable vitamins, seemed to be the cure. Most Red Cross mail and food parcels were hoarded by the Japanese, but occasionally, when distributed, Marmite spread was available. After four days of the spread his friend recovered. All were thankful for the Red Cross,[4] and the Marmite.

Because of disease, most rations were generally boiled and therefore tasteless, but Fergus found a way to make his more exciting. He gathered insects such as grasshoppers, then bored a hole in fresh coconut and drank the milk. When the shell was empty, he popped in the grasshoppers and sealed the hole. A few days later, he opened the hairy tomb to harvest the dead insects and fried them in oil. The insect meal was filled with protein and bearable. Tasting of coconut, grasshoppers were another path to his survival.

* * *

Administrating officers had to be resourceful to keep their troops under organised supervision, ensuring nobody upset the Japanese guards or their plans. Their Co-Prosperity Sphere scheme was being rolled out aided by their new 'guests', as prisoners were ordered to undertake many days of hard labour. All PoWs were treated abysmally, except high-ranking commanders. The IJA consistently contravened the Hague and Geneva conventions.

Under the Japanese, they felt in continuous peril. Even for the mildest swear word, guards thought they were being criticised and administered some kind of terrible punishment. Their commanders had no time for their own men either. It transpired the Kempei tai – the Japanese army police – were all trained by the German Army, almost Gestapo-like, whereas their navy was trained by the British. As a result, all Japanese soldiers and sailors drilled for cleanliness and hygiene and had their heads shaved. But the Kempei tai men grew their hair long. They were thought to be the most intelligent of all ranks and services. Some spoke other languages, so PoWs had to be cautious.

Caution was not a trait of Australian pranksters who, when fixing the Dannert wire, daringly disguised gaps in the fencing. One night a piano somehow arrived in the middle of Selarang Barracks' square. It had simply turned up right under the Japanese noses, but no one knew how. The captors couldn't admit defeat because they would lose face – a crucial element of their culture – so the piano simply stayed in the camp as if it was meant to be. Eventually it was moved to one of the concert party areas. No one was punished.

*   *   *

Horner was promoted to messing officer-in-charge and officer-in-charge of rice supplies. Every Monday and Thursday he and his team would take a truck convoy to Changi Pier to collect divisional supplies from the go-downs (warehouses). En route, via the mangroves, they passed six artillery magazines, set 100 yards back. These were supposed to be destroyed before capitulation – another example of Malaya Command's inefficiency. Horner said they were fused separately and when the first magazine was 'blown' it left a huge crater and probably hurled chunks of 20ft x 12ft reinforced concrete a quarter of a mile away. The other fuses had mostly failed, with a few minor

Stan with older brother Frank
and sister Doris, c.1919.
S.A.W. Moore Collection

Pat in the park before Stan's departure,
October 1941. *S.A.W. Moore Collection*

Driver Moore RASC- No. T/170638, early
1940. *Daisy Lawrence Archives and S.A.W. Moore
Collection*

Stanley Albert William Moore,
London, late 1940.
S.A.W. Moore Collection

Stan's RASC Unit, Droitwich, October 1941. Back row (l-r) 1. Freddie Holt, 4. Stanley Moore.
2nd row from top (l-r) 6. Sidney Cowling. Sitting (l-r) 1. Gordon Hunter. *S.A.W. Moore Collection*

Brook House, Knutsford, June 1941. Albert 'Bill' (Trigger) Weeks, 'Mac' Cothill and Stan. *S.A.W. Moore Collection*

Brook House, Knutsford, June 1941. Stan with Sidney Cowling. *S.A.W. Moore Collection*

Gunner Fergus Anckorn.
Courtesy Simon Anckorn

HMT *Andes* – Secret assignment – 'Winston's Specials'.
Photographer: Basil V. Sexton, Southampton, via records retained by David Earley

USS *Wakefield*, formerly the USS *Manhattan*.
Photographer: Gord Condie, via Haze G

Gordon and Hugh Hunter with Stan, enjoying the hospitality of Cape Town, December 1941.
S.A.W. Moore Collection

Gordon and Stan
swimming in the Indian
Ocean at Muizenberg.
S.A.W. Moore Collection

Captain R. M. Horner. 'He was the one who knew all the ropes; speedy unloading at the next destination was essential.' *Courtesy of Judith Quick, daughter of Horner's batman, Freddie Holt*

Alexandra Hospital memorial plaque.
Author – JSS

With war-like authority and 'honour' they presented to the British Army an 'Admonition of Peace' which, on 13 February 1942, advised the war 'has almost been settled already and Malay is under Nippon Power'.
Courtesy of Simon Burgess

ADMONITION.

I have the honour of presenting to you this Admonition of Peace from the standpoint of the Nippon Samurai Spirit. Nippon Navy, Army and Air Force have conquered the Phillipine Islands and Hong Kong and annihilated the British Extreme Oriental Fleet in the Southern Seas. The command of the Pacific Ocean and the Indian Ocean as well as the Aviation power in the Southern and Western Asian Continents is now under the control of the Nippon Forces. India has risen in rebellion. Thai and Malay have been subjected to Nippon without having made any remarkable resistence. The War has almost been settled already and Malay is under Nippon Power. Since the 18th century Singapore has been the starting point of the development of your country and the important juncture of the civilization of West and East. Our army cannot suffer as well as you to see this district burn to ashes by the War. Traditionally, when Nippon is at War, when she takes her Arms she always based upon the loyalty and breaking wrong and helping right and she does not and never aim at the conquest of other nations nor the expansion of her territories.

The War cause, at this time, as you are well informed, originated from this loyalty. We want to establish new order and a zone of mutual prosperity in the East Orient..You cannot deny at the bottom of your impartial hearts that it is divine will and humanity to give happiness to millions of East Orientals mourning under the exploitation and persecution. Consequently, the Nippon Army, basing upon this great loyalty, attacks without reserve those who resist them, but not only the innocent people but also the surrendered to them will be treated kindly according to their Samuraism. When I imagine the state of mind of you who have so well done your duty, isolated and without rescuer, and now surrounded by our armies how much more could I not sincerely sympathize with you. This is why I dare advise you to make peace and give you a friendly hand to co-operate for the settlement of the Oriental Peace Many thousands of wives and children of your Officers and Soldiers are heartily waiting in their native land to the coming home of the husbands and fathers and many hundreds of thousands of innocent people are also passionately wishing to avoid the calamities of War.

I expect you to considerate upon the eternal honour of British Tradition and you be persuaded by this Admonition. Upon my word I wont kill you, treat you as officers and soldiers if you come to us. But if you resist against us we will gibe swords.

(Sgd.)   NIPPON ARMY.

Singapore.
13.Feb.1942.

23

SELARANG SPECIAL ORDER No. 3 dated 4 Sep 42.

1. On 30 Aug 42, I, together with my Area Comds was summoned to the Conference House, Changi Gaol, where I was informed by th representative of Maj General Shimpei Fukuye, GOC Prisoner of War Camps Malaya, that all Prisoners of War in Changi Camp were to be given forms of promise not to escape, and that all were to be given an opportunity to sign this form.

2. By the Laws and Usages of War a prisoner of war cannot be required by the Power holding him to give his parole, and in our Army those who have become prisoners of war are not permitted to give their parole. I pointed out this position to the Japanese Authorities.

3. I informed the representative of Maj General Shimpei Fukuye that I was not prepared to sign the form, and that I did not consider that any offrs or men in the Changi Camp would be prepared to sign the form. In accordance with the orders of Japanese Authorities, all prisoners of war were given an opportunity to sign.

The result of that opportunity is well known.

4. On the 31 Aug I was informed by the Japanese Authorities that those personnel who refused to sign the certificate would be subjected to "measures of severity" and that refusal to sign would be regarded as a direct refusal to obey a regulation which the Imperial Japanese Army considered it necessary to enforce.

5. Later, on the night of the 31 Aug/1 Sep I was warned that on the 1 Sep all prisoners of war persisting in refusal to sign were to move by 1800 hrs to Selarang Barrack Square. I confirmed, both on my own behalf and in the names of the prisoners of war, our refusal to sign.

6. The move to Selarang Barrack Square was successfully accomplished on the same afternoon.

7. I and the Area Comds have been in constant conference with the Imperial Japanese Army and have endeavoured by negotiation to have the form either abolished or at least modified. All that I have been able to obtain is that which was originally a demand accompanied by threats of "measures of severity", has now been issued as an official order of the Imperial Japanese Government.

/ Over.

Holmes was summoned to Conference House in Changi Gaol by General Shimpei Fukuye GOC on 30 August 1942. He was told PoWs were to promise not to escape, and that they must sign a form. Holmes was not prepared to sign and, therefore, nor should other PoWs. On 31 August the Japanese authorities said those who refused to sign would be subjected to enforced 'measures of severity'.
S.A.W. Moore Collection

-2-

8. During the period of the occupation of the Selarang Barrack Square the conditions in which we have been placed have been under my constant consideration. These may be briefly described as such that existence therein will result in a very few days in the outbreak of epidemic and the most serious consequences to those under my Command and inevitable death to many of us now are, and the need to preserve our force intact as long as possible, and in the full conviction on that my action were the circumstances in which we are now living known to them, would meet with the approval of His Majesty's Government. I have felt it my duty to order all personnel to sign the certificate under the duress imposed by the Japanese Army.

9. I am fully convinced that His Majesty's Government only expects prisoners of war not to give parole when such parole is to be given voluntarily. This factor can in no circumstances be regarded as applicable to our present condition. The responsibility for this decision rests with me, and with me alone, and I fully accept it in ordering you to sign.

10. I wish to record in this order my deep appreciation of the excellent spirit and good discipline which all ranks have shown during the trying period.

I look to all ranks to continue in good heart, discipline and morale.

Thank you all for your loyalty and co-operation.

Sgd: E.B.HOLMES, Colonel.
Commanding British and Australian Troops,
CHANGI.

Selarang.
Sep: 4. 42.

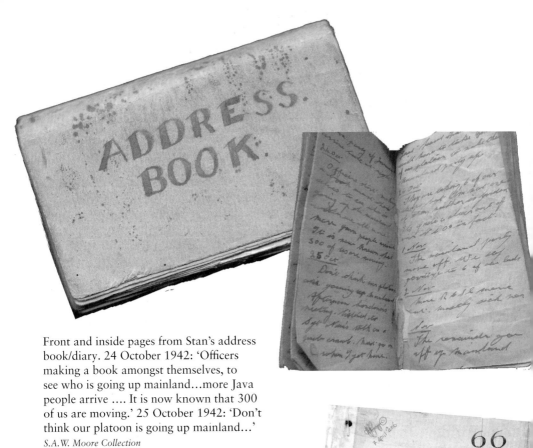

Front and inside pages from Stan's address book/diary. 24 October 1942: 'Officers making a book amongst themselves, to see who is going up mainland…more Java people arrive …. It is now known that 300 of us are moving.' 25 October 1942: 'Don't think our platoon is going up mainland…'
S.A.W. Moore Collection

Overland: RASC 18th Division 'Up Country' or 'up mainland' List, Changi.
Author – JTR Photographed at The National Archives, London.

Overland: RASC 18th Division data including Driver S. A. W. Moore.
Author – JTR Photographed at The National Archives, London.

News at last! The telegram Pat received from Stan's mother, May 1943. *Daisy Lawrence Archives*

Nearly two years had passed since they had heard directly from Stan. *Daisy Lawrence Archives*

T/170638　　DVR. S. A. W. MOORE　　R.A.S.C.

11. DECEMBER 1943

DARLING PAT-MOTHER,

AM WELL, HOPE ALL ARE THE SAME.　HAVE RECEIVED SOME LETTERS.　HAPPY 27TH. BIRTHDAY PAT. MERRY CHRISTMAS TO ALL.

LOVE,

Stan

Allied PoWs interned at Changi prison camp, Singapore, are seen giving a big cheer when Allied occupation forces arrive. The picture was transmitted by radio from Colombo via C & W. RCO 58WA 9945.v. *British Crown Copyright Reserved*

Mountbatten's address after the final act of IJA's unconditional surrender outside the Municipal Building, Singapore.
Courtesy of Gerald 'Jeff' Hoare

Mountbatten leading a cheer for the surrender of the Japanese in Singapore.
Courtesy of Gerald 'Jeff' Hoare

'Guard Your Tongue'. All were ordered to supress memories of their horrific experience.
Courtesy of CoFEPOW member Jeff Phillips

WARNING

GUARD YOUR TONGUE

YOU are free now. Anything you say in public or to the press is liable to be published throughout the whole world.

You have direct or indirect knowledge of the fate of many of your comrades who died in enemy hands as a result of brutality or neglect.

Your story, if published in the more sensational press, would cause much unnecessary unhappiness to relatives and friends.

If you had not been lucky enough to have survived and had died an unpleasant death at the hands of the Japanese, you would not have wished your family and friends to have been harrowed by lurid details of your death

That is just what will happen to the families of your comrades who did die in that way if you start talking too freely about your experience.

It is felt certain that now you know the reason for this order you will ta e pains to spare the feelings of others.

Arrangements have been made for you to tell your story to interrogating officers who will then ask you to write it down.

You are not to say anything to anyone until after you have written out your statement and handed it in.

SPE/U/2

Letter from King George VI.
S.A.W. Moore Collection

BUCKINGHAM PALACE

The Queen and I bid you a very warm welcome home.

Through all the great trials and sufferings which you have undergone at the hands of the Japanese, you and your comrades have been constantly in our thoughts. We know from the accounts we have already received how heavy those sufferings have been. We know also that these have been endured by you with the highest courage.

We mourn with you the deaths of so many of your gallant comrades.

With all our hearts, we hope that your return from captivity will bring you and your families a full measure of happiness, which you may long enjoy together.

George R.I

September 1945.

Gordon and Stan photographed in happier days. Cape Town, December 1943.
S.A.W. Moore Collection

Captain Horner's November 1945 letter of condolence to Gordon Hunter's widow, Elizabeth. She gave it to Stan in remembrance of his friend.
S.A.W. Moore Collection

No 3. Flat
1 Hesketh Crescent
Torquay
13 Nov. – 45.

Dear Mrs Hunter

I felt I must write and say how much I feel for you in the sad loss of your husband Gordon – being on H.Q. Staff myself. I saw a good deal of him at Changi, Singapore, where we both were from Feb – 1942 – April – 4 we worked together on a wood-cutting detail until he went up to Thailand. I expect by now that you will have been given details of his death, in case you haven't he died of dysentery at Songkhria Thailand on 13th August 1943 I know that no words of mine can in any way compensate you for the loss of Gordon, but believe me when I say that he upheld all the finest traditions of the British race, and his death was as much in the cause of freedom as if he had been killed in action. I feel that I have lost a personal friend with the death of Gordon in mourn with you in your loss. Yours Sincerely

Ronald N. Horner
Capt. R.A.S.C

THE MITCHAM PRISONERS OF
WAR RELATIVES ASSOCIATION

———

Chairman   Ald. J.R. Beaumont, J.P.

Treasurer   Mr. W. L. Roodhouse

Hon. Secretary   Mrs. E. Cox

Committee—Mr. E. F. Ward, Mr C. H.
Selwood, Mrs. Ridgley, Miss Culmer,
Miss Clark, Mrs. Anderson, Mrs. Smart,
Mrs. Powell

Mitcham Prisoners of War Relatives
Association

Final Celebration
7th December, 1946

BUFFET

———

Chesterfields

Sausage Rolls

Lobster Bouches   Petit Pains

Assorted Sandwiches

Fancy Cakes

Trifle   Vanilla Ice

Tea and Coffee

Reception by the Worshipful the Mayor
of Mitcham, (Ald. Mrs. E. Watson, J.P.)
and the Mayoress, (Mrs. V. Cole).

———

" Welcome Home " to our Ex-Prisoners
of War
Ald. J. R. Beaumont, J.P.
supported by
The Worshipful the Mayor

ARTISTES

Herschelle Henlere   *Entertainer*

Bobby and Elsie Smith
                Exhibition Dancers

Modernaires Dance Band

Menu from the Mitcham Prisoners of War Relatives Association, 1946. *S.A.W. Moore Collection*

2.5.95

341 Commonside East
Mitcham
Surrey CR4 1HF

Hello Christopher, your Grandpa,
this is what I got up to during
1939 - 1945 War.

I had to register for the armed services at the age of 23,
but wasn't called up until 4.4.40 when I was 24. They sent me to Herne Bay
in Kent for training as a soldier dispatch rider in the R.A.S.C. I was moved around
England with my unit for unknown reasons, East Dereham, Norwich,
Soham (Newtown St. Boswell Scotland), Droitwich, by then it was Oct 1941.
Then we proceeded overseas from Liverpool on a cruise liner "Andes" which had been
converted to carry troops, then on arrival at (Halifax Newfoundland) transferred
to SS. Wakefield crewed by American Coastguards then proceeded
on to Trinidad (West Indies), Cape Town, India, Singapore. After 2 whs
fighting the Japanese, found we were greatly outnumbered, therefore
had to surrender, and was taken prisoner over 6,000 P.O.Ws.

We were in the prison camp (Changi) working to keep ourselves
fed, growing a little food & cutting down rubber trees for fuel which was used
for cooking. Our staple diet was rice 8 oz per day if you worked 6 oz
otherwise. Other captured soldiers were sent up to Thailand to build
a railway for the Japanese, most of them died as conditions were terrible
We used to hear all kinds of rumours about the outside world, as we
had no letter from home. The one about V.E day turned out to be true.
Then we heard about the Atom Bomb, which finally finished the Japanese.
We were eventually released from the P.O.W camp & food & clothing
was brought to us by the victorious allies. (All the clothing we had
was a pair of old boots for working in a pair of wooden flip flops made from trees
root & car tyre plus a G string & a pair of old shorts for evenings.) Then we were
taken home after 4 years away from Britain.

Grandpa.

Jill please return bits & pieces.

Grandpa's 'Show-and-Tell' letter to Christopher, drafted by Grandma. C. D. Robertson

Red Cross 'souvenir' box of tags, medals and PoW mementos. *S.A.W. Moore Collection*

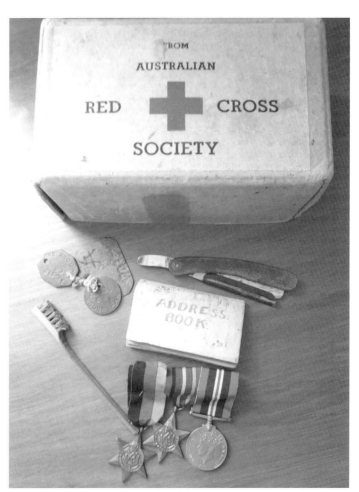

Fergus Anckorn and co-author Jill Robertson, September 2017. *Author – JTR*

STANLEY MOORE'S ADDRESS BOOK LIST

Anderson, Adam	AIF	Unknown	Australia
Budd, Ronald	Driver	T/170445	Ilford, Essex
Burgess, T	Driver	Unknown	Clapton, E5
Carter, W	Driver	T/78582	Tottenham, N15
Clarke, W D	Driver	T/181095	Wembley, Middx.
Cowling, Sidney	Driver	T/139801	Scunthorpe, Lincs.
Cothill, Geo. (Mac)	Driver	T/74398	Leonside, Co. Durham
Davies, G R	Staff Sg.	S173741	Rhymney, Cardiff
Eade, Harry H	Driver	T/164709	Southampton
Fairchild, Edward	Private	S170581	Seal, Kent
Fisher, G H	Corporal	T/188323	Wallesey, Ches.
Foulds, W B	Lance Cpl.	T/187963	Bacup, Lancs.
Gale, R J	Driver	T/176488	Lantwit Maj.,Wales
George, John Wm.	RA 85th Fld. Rg.	4539113	Newton, Leeds 9
George, Stanley A	RA Gunner	941026	Clapton, E5
Groves, Robert W M	Sgt.	4977548	Surbiton, Surrey
Hatfield, George A	Driver	T/170433	Bromley, Kent
Hickson, Clifford T	Lance Cpl.	T/168343	Shortlands, Kent
Hill, Herbert V	Private	S5780657	Dalston, E8
Holt, Freddie	Driver	T/144741	Rochdale, Lancs.
Horsman, Jack	R. Signals	2343185	Guildford, Surrey
Hudson, Sidney	Driver	T/111447	Carlisle, Cumb.
Hunter, Gordon H	Driver	T/92445	Glasgow, Scotland
Johnson, A	Driver	T/279928	Liverpool, 17
Lyster, Victor W	Driver	T/165099	Birmingham, 21
Norris, G	Driver	T/176754	Reading, Berks
Palmer, E	Driver	T/179772	London, W3
Penrose, George G	Driver	T/184906	W.Looe, Cornwall
Pitcher, Norman	Private	T/184301	Mitcham, Surrey
Roberts, Francis	Driver	T/170496	Edmonton, N18
Ross, Albert D	Driver	T/160231	Basingstoke, Hants
Shepherd, J B	Private	S2985596	St. Andrew's, Fife
Shepherd, R	AIF	Unknown	Sydney, NSW, Australia
Sherriff, Harold S	Driver	T/167262	Wallington, Surrey
Turner, W E	Driver	T/217910	W. Hampstead, NW3
Wales, Archibald E W	Private	S/29817	Kirkcaldy, Fife
Warnes, Percy C	Corporal	S/2070105	Brundall, Norfolk
Weeks, A H	Driver	T/174940	Christchurch, Bournemouth
Yarde, C W	Driver	T/176910	Taunton, Somerset

Stan's address book list
(see p.247).
S.A.W. Moore Collection – JTR

The authors with
their Daddy, 1959.
S.A.W. Moore Collection

explosions of 'sympathetic detonation', but otherwise the remaining five, and 30,000 rounds of 25-pounders, were intact.

* * *

The Japanese continued to demean British officers – recognisable only by the small star on their right breast pocket indicating their commissioned status – by continually humiliating them in front of other ranks. Senior officers were, however, permitted to keep their batmen and organise a canteen where prisoners could purchase a multitude of foodstuffs and other items using Japanese prison pay. Also referred to as an 'amenity grant', officers were given $6 a month, other ranks $3. Three food supply trucks were allowed in each week from the city, to stock the canteen. Any profit made at the facility then funded sustenance for sick prisoners, through the 'diet centre'.[5] Healthier men would also donate 25c of their pay to a kitty held by Padre Noel Duckworth of the Cambridgeshire Regiment, who bought soap and food in the city for sick PoWs.

Later, when they went up-country to work on the railway, a queue formed for the men to collect their 'pay'. It was a welcome rest, of sorts, albeit in high temperatures. This amounted to around $3 per month, with no time off. The meagre pay bought a handful of dried fish, a little coconut oil for frying, and possibly one or two bananas, rich in Vitamin E, which they believed protected against infertility – an obsessive fear that every soldier held.

Unlike the ORs, officers received sick pay. From the end of 1942, officers within standard Hague and Geneva Convention rules were paid a rate equivalent to IJA wages in local currency. But PoWs only received a fraction as amounts were withheld by the Japanese for lodging, food and clothes – commonly known as the 'rent, rice and rags deduction' – where a portion was banked for repayment after the war.[6]

* * *

In July, a rumour circulated that the main leaders of all divisions would be transferred overseas. By August it was a reality and Senior Officers Party

(SOP), including Lieutenant General Percival and Major General Beck-with-Smith with twenty-nine brigadiers, was sent to Formosa. The new order of command was now under Lieutenant Colonel E. B. Holmes, Commander of the Manchesters and Lieutenant Colonel F. G. Galleghan of the Australian forces.[7]

Stan remembered:

> *During August a ship from Africa came with Red Cross supplies in bulk, I forget how many tons it was, but it went around very sparsely for everybody, and we didn't get much from it. I think it worked out about half a tin of bully beef per person. That was a luxury! Then during this month, the Japs ordered all ranks of colonel and above to be moved off out to Japan* [the date was 17 August 1942].

Chapter 13

Divided Working Parties

In the early days of captivity, different work parties were sent to a variety of areas. Stan was detailed to work in the garden and wood party and spent many hours tapping rubber trees or cutting them down with a saw. If the trees were tapped incorrectly, they died and had to be felled. The PoWs used this vital source for cooking and heat in the winter months.

When I was in the [earlier] tree felling party, I used to work every day except Wednesdays and Sundays. Wednesdays used to be de-bugging day. Beds consisted of reinforcing rods, bent to form a frame of a bed and old telephone wire formed the legs using bent rods. There was nowhere for a bug to get far in, but crikey, when you took [the bed] out of the hut and slammed it down on the sandy soil outside, the bugs used to come out of the wire! Goodness knows how they got there; there was no real place for them to hide. We used to shake them out and they scattered onto the red-hot sand where they probably roasted to death.

Another occasion was when the working parties used to go to town and unload oil and petrol from the Japanese transporters. We used to unload mainly from lorries. A couple of ramps were put up to the lorry to roll the drums down into the necessary storage area, but unbeknown to the Japs, a pick head spike was buried in the sand and as the drum rolled down over the two planks the spike between would stick up and pierce the drum. It would then be rolled away quickly because being sandy soil it would have been noticed as it soaked into the sand. The drum then went into the storage, leaking, and eventually it would end up being empty. This was all part of the sabotage; we tried to do as much as possible without being caught.

* * *

PoWs remaining in Changi were reduced to 45,562 after working parties began to move out. This included 5,812 men who were moved to Singapore City's dock areas in April 1942 and a further 1,125 men who were later transferred to Saigon (now Ho Chi Min City).[1]

As well as invading Chinese and British Empire territories, the Japanese also coveted Vichy France shipping bases on the Malay Peninsula. The Vichy France regime, *Etat Française*, was now the governing force in lower central France, down to the Mediterranean Sea. *Zone Libre* operated under Nazi malevolent tentacles but was not occupied; instead their 'puppet' government, under Marshal Phillipe Petain, collaborated in implementing the oppressive policies of Hitler.[2]

Now in April 1942, as part of the Axis, at the command of Japanese officers, Changi PoWs were transported to Saigon, French Indo-China. Their task at the docks was to clear go-downs. The PoWs were surprised and initially relieved to see French-speaking people, hoping they might care for them in some way. Gradually, with less Japanese control, individuals from working parties deviated from the Japanese docks to the French. However, the prisoners hadn't realised the Vichy French, essentially the enemy, could have presented a huge problem. Fortunately, for them, the sympathetic citizens provided medicine, clothes and food, and in some cases important news from the outside world.

From Singapore, the Saigon contingent had been herded on to the *Nisshu Maru*, a dilapidated coal carrier, caked in unhealthy coal dust. It was one of the many 'hell ships' as they later became known. Passenger Reuben Kandler revealed, many years later, that this Saigon party of PoWs played an important part in clandestine intelligence when they were eventually able to alert British officials of mistreatment.[3]

Other hell ships would only stop en route to refuel at Saigon, sailing to Formosa and bound for Japanese labour camps in coal mines. One, the *Dainichi Maru* held 286 men in a hold under horrendous conditions, sleeping on attap mats on shale. Occasionally, the air hatches were closed for three days. They were almost mistakenly attacked by an American submarine, but, luckily, it ran out of torpedoes and ammunition. 'It is difficult to describe the horror of the voyage where men tried to live in appalling squalor, disease was rampant; rats ran across bodies.'[4]

A few hand-wagon parties also moved to Tanjong Rhu, a southern peninsula beyond Kallang airfield. Being treated reasonably well, under British Army administration, officers organised group activities, football and cricket matches, and several interesting lectures. This all helped to occupy the men's minds. Of course, the inevitable subject of food was always favourite, but in the redistribution of prisoners, many were now leaving the relative comfort of Singapore.

For the first six months at Changi, the remaining prisoners were slave labour in local places such as the garden and wood areas, or the quarry at Kallang. The shanty village was derelict and the fate of its Chinese inhabitants unknown. Captain Reginald Burton was in charge of officers from the Suffolk and Divisional Ancillary troops, such as the corps of Signals and RASC men. The divisions' hand-wagon parties amalgamated, doubling their strength, with a new commanding officer, Major Humphrey Hyde from the Manchesters. Heavy Japanese guard controlled the site, so escape was impossible.

The hand-wagon parties, HW2 and HW3, laboured in the hot quarry, isolated, with no link to the outside world. They had to shift tons of rock and cement blocks for a new runway. The scene was congenial between prisoners and guards, no boxing of ears and no cross words. One Japanese guard, Officer Kamita under General Yoshioko, even permitted a PoW to bring a gramophone with him for entertainment; they listened to his records in the dark.[5] Each night, prisoners were assembled in the village for Tenko, where even the sick and immobile were taken from their beds to ensure nobody had escaped.

The group was moved to another quarry at Pasir Panjang, where more men started to fall to dysentery, beriberi and dengue fever, including Captain Burton – who continually ached in his sick bed. He recalled Welsh MO, Dai Davis, who used the mantra, 'Stick around and drink a gallon of water a day.' The only means of communication with the rest of the PoW community was when the 'sick truck' came from Havelock Road Barracks to collect the infirm. Through this clandestine grapevine, they later heard about a serious incident at Selarang Barracks in Changi.[6]

*   *   *

Stifling weather continued. With humid insanitary conditions and poor diet, efforts to combat illness began to fail. Dysentery cases increased, and the hospital became overrun with many casualties. If one was lucky enough to survive the hospital, it still could take weeks to fully recover, and they may as well have died. Often these recuperating men could barely walk due to their injury or weight loss, which meant they were unfit to join a working party. It was upsetting especially when their full ration of 8oz of bug-ridden rice was forfeited. There was little hope for them and some succumbed to depression.

Chapter 14

Weather, Ailments, Officers Leave and Religion

The island of Singapore sits almost on the equator, 85 miles to the south. In the tropical rainforest, warm incessant downpours fell from monsoon dull grey skies, as the men watched rain cascade over attap hut roofs and temperatures rose to 32°C (90°F). The ground was muddy and hot.

Keeping cool was a problem as heatstroke and humidity sapped the men's strength to exhaustion – even before their allotted tasks. Night temperatures of 23°C (77°F), were more bearable. Singapore's pre-monsoon period had less rainfall, June–September, but as October approached, they prepared for prolonged precipitation. By March, the weather's predictability turned to heavy evening rain, strong winds and morning mists which lasted until June. It took a while to acclimatise[1] and inevitably there was sickness, including for Stan.

I suffered a series of complaints but managed to get over them, one being dengue fever, like a very bad dose of flu on the verge of malaria really. I was shipped to hospital, which was another barracks turned into a hospital [Roberts Barracks] with very little equipment and I was put on a straw mattress on the floor. All around me were fellas being sick: the smell was dreadful. Other people dying; they couldn't give you much treatment, but they kept an eye on you. I was there for two nights. By the third day I'd had enough and thought 'I don't want to die here' so I asked to be discharged and the doctor allowed me to go back to my lines – India Lines that is. I went back and managed to get over it myself. Prior to that it had been at least a fortnight without going to the toilet, all put down to shock and stress I suppose. There we are: we got through it all, thank goodness.

Another minor complaint, we suffered, was malnutrition. Lack of one of the vitamins made the scrotum break out in weeping sores [dermatitis]. The only treatment the medical officers could give us was Condage, a fluid solution, or Penang, made of a pottage. The only way to administer was with a small drop in half a coconut shell to bathe your private parts for about an hour, until it turned completely brown, but it did the trick, thankfully enough.

Discomfort and sickness affected many in the camp daily. When dysentery attacked it tore at stomach linings, making men run to the latrines several times a day. In May 1942, 1,000 cases of dysentery were recorded at the hospital, with several deaths. Some men had foot sores from the bad sanitation, causing a fungal infection which started between the toes. This was Singapore Foot – or trench foot.[2] Caused through constant dampness, the only remedy was to keep feet clean and dry to stop the fungus from spreading.

Prickly heat was caused through continuous sweating, where talcum powder was the best solution. Fergus on one occasion thought a patch of black tea leaves would help cool his feet. He assumed someone had thrown them out but as he put his feet into the black leaves, he suddenly felt a rush of sharp stings, like an electric shock, and moved away instantaneously. He had trodden on a swarm of black fire ants which injected venom into his skin. The swelling was immediate. The best cure would have been a solution of cool baking powder or ice, but in the jungle these luxury ingredients were unavailable. He suffered the pain but sought medical advice.

A vaccine was administered for cholera, but the Medical Corps ran out. Maggots, swarms of flies, general squalor and filth around the men were life-threatening, and if left to deteriorate further the prisoners were likely to be dead within a few months. Hopes for improved conditions were thwarted as the prevalence of suppurating ulcers from small scratches on legs or arms became widespread. Medics then considered amputation the only way to save lives.

* * *

Dietary remedies were found for some illnesses as camps became established, and medics devised ingenious ways of extracting vitamins from natural resources.[3] Drinks were made from tall lalang grass with feathery white heads, large red flowers from hibiscus bushes and white or purple petals rich in Vitamin C. The appearance of the green slime was unappealing – but it supplied the necessary nutrients for their ailments.

Blachang was a strange concoction for the western palate and foul-smelling. Considered a delicacy, the decaying sea creatures were pure protein, but the harvesting season was only when thousands of the tiny sea urchins hovered on the surf. They were caught, then buried in a seaweed-lined pit and covered for two months. The putrid stench when the pit was opened was almost debilitating, but if you approached with care and held your breath to accept a spoonful of flavouring to add to a handful of rice, the meal was bearable and, more importantly, nutritious.

Quinine dispensed by medics was a godsend, especially for dengue fever. The cause could be bed bugs but generally the dengue mosquito, with its distinctive striped or hooped body, was the culprit. With no nets for protection, malaria was prevalent and caused severe fevers with profuse shaking and sweating that were difficult to control.

For beriberi, heavy drinkers were often the first victims as alcohol inhibited the absorption of Vitamin B_1. Beriberi, meaning weakness, was quick to appear and came in either a wet or dry form. Wet, the worst of the two, caused swelling through water retention (oedema). It started in feet and legs and spread throughout the body. It could affect heart function and in extreme cases cause heart failure. Death was certain if left untreated. Dry beriberi damaged nerves, resulting in loss of muscle strength and eventually muscle paralysis. Initially, it led to tender and painful muscles, making it difficult to walk. Beriberi is a pellagra vitamin deficiency disease, and as cases in Changi increased the Japanese were pressed into supplying rice-polishings – husks which contained vitamin B_1. This looked like sawdust and tasted awful; the only way to swallow the pap was with decontaminated boiled water.

Cholera was more horrific, where the body rejected bodily fluids in violent explosions of vomiting and diarrhoea. If locals with the disease used the river which PoWs drank the untreated water from, it was lethal. The first priority of PoWs arriving in any new situation was always sanitation and the strong Royal Engineers immediately dug deep pits. Latrines were covered with wood wherever possible, and water was always boiled. When cholera attacks came, deterioration was rapid. A man could be well in the morning and dead before sunset. A cholera patient was often dramatically unrecognisable having rapidly lost half his weight within hours. His only chance was a saline drip. Huge efforts were made to reduce cholera cases and medics improvised with hollow bamboo needles and pieces of stethoscope tubing to make a drip. This saved many lives. If cholera was suspected, isolation huts were erected away from the main party of men. The Japanese, too, were frightened of an epidemic. Cholera was feared the most by both sides in the conflict. But with low resistance caused by hard labour and starvation, the prisoners were in the worst position as many could not fight the disease.

* * *

The SOPs above the rank of colonel left for Formosa 16–18 August 1942. Most commanders, including Becky-Smith, were transferred which brought the men's morale to another low. The news was shattering; he would be severely missed by all ranks, but now they had Lieutenant Colonel Holmes as their leader.

On the morning of 16 August, the SOPs were bussed to the city. Brigadier Goodman, as part of the 1,400 group, had plenty to carry: a pack, two haversacks, a water bottle, bedding, a suitcase, a Hong Kong basket and a kitbag. On the way, they stopped at the Conference House where the prisoners alighted and were paraded in front of an unfamiliar Japanese general. His words were short, reassuring for the future and promised they had nothing to fear; he hoped they would be comfortable in their new surroundings. The men were somewhat convinced by his statements, but not all were true. Their journey continued to the docks by lorry.

They arrived around midday and their baggage was piled in one place for fumigating with a flit gun; lighter packages were on top, but Goodman's Hong Kong basket suffered when a large box was placed on top. The SOP group was summoned and marched on to a ship where they were ordered to undress and enter a large, evil-smelling disinfectant bath. Goodman described the scene:

It was a great sight, seeing about thirty brigadiers, lieutenant and major generals all sitting in a bath together. After that we dressed again, we found that all our clothes and small items had been put into a hot chamber for fumigating. Then we were given a cup of tea, got off the ship and waited several hours on the quay.

Another waiting game ensued and at 4 or 5 p.m. they were put in lorries and taken to another part of the docks, where they were marched on to a steamer vessel and divided between the three holds allotted to them.

Goodman continued:

The congestion was appalling but we were there for the night.

About 11 p.m. food and tea were produced, which was not easy to distribute – my job. The Army Commander protested about the accommodation, which resulted in the senior party of 400 being moved about 2 p.m. the next day.

* * *

Before leaving Singapore, Beckwith-Smith sent this message to his troops:

On my departure for Japan I wish to take what may be my last chance to thank all ranks of the 18th Division for their cheerful service and loyal support on many shores and seas during the two years I have had the honour to command the Division.

I regret I have been unable to lead you to the success in battle to which your cause and sacrifice is entitled, and although I leave you with a heavy heart, I carry with me many precious memories and a sense of comradeship such as could only have been inspired by the trials and disappointments which we have shared in the last few months.

Difficult days may still be ahead, but I know that the spirit which today animates all ranks of the Division will prevail and will form the cornerstone on which one day a just and lasting peace will be found.

God grant that day may not be long delayed and that we may soon meet again.

Meanwhile GOOD LUCK, HEADS UP, KEEP SMILING.

(Sgd.) M. BECKWITH-SMITH Major General. 18th August 1942.

*   *   *

Percival complained about the condition of the first vessel and, after more delays waiting on the quay, the prisoners were crammed into one hold on a different ship, the *Tanjong Maru*, which stood off in The Roads. For two days prior, the men were put through embarrassing indignities, such as having to strip and wash at a standpipe on the dockside as there were no facilities on board. From brigadier to batmen, there was no difference in rank, everyone was treated the same.

In the hold under the decks, their two-tier bunk accommodation was hot and smelled terrible. Each area was 7ft x 2ft 6in. Goodman was at the top where the head room was about 4ft 3in to the deck plating, but due to cross girders a foot deep, head room underneath was further limited. The previous cargo carried by the ship was coal, evident from the black dust; rust-coloured water and condensation dripped down from the underside of the deck plating and leaking pipes. Two slippery and steep wooden companionways were at one end. There was little air and just an element of light from a single hatch in the hold, but when it rained the opening was closed and their only light came from a few blackout bulbs. Latrines were on deck, consisting of just four filthy compartments. On the opposite side was a grim-looking galley.

Food was sent down to them once or twice a day – rice and alien-looking vegetables in a sticky grey mess which Japanese guards called a meal. Hot water for tea-making was always on tap and useful for washing; other times a broken pipe would aid ablutions. They were trapped for days and the men grew sicker from the overriding smell and presence of human dejecta. Several senior officers were very ill, including Percival, who was struck with stomach problems. Unusually for the Japanese, he was moved to slightly better conditions in the first officers' cabin, a few days into the voyage. The ocean was smooth, but some infirm prisoners fell down the slippery companion ladders. If the weather had been worse, conditions below deck could have resulted in more injured limbs. On the evening of 22 August, they anchored off Cape St Jacques near the mouth of the Mekong River, where they stayed another two days, before setting sail again in convoy. They arrived in Formosa on 30 August. Goodman recalled:

After many orders and counter-orders, we disembarked about 8 a.m. We had spent a most unpleasant fourteen days. As we disembarked, we were disinfected by walking over a mat wet from, with what looked like pink pani [permanganate of potash], which was being sprayed over our legs with a flit gun.

They were marched to the railway station through the town on an extended route, purposely lined with school children. The train journey took forty minutes, during which they were given a loaf of bread. At Heito they were marched to another station and a light railway. In small open trucks, sitting on the floor like sardines in a tin, they travelled for another forty-five minutes. The camp facility they arrived at was finished and the officers 'fell in' to be addressed by a Japanese colonel. He told them they had 'all but captured Australia and that the British were defeated'! This of course, was untrue.[4] The prisoners survived the journey but within ten days of landing, six prisoners of the Royal Engineers died from dysentery caught on the *Tanjong Maru*: Solicitor General, C. G. Howell, Lieutenant Colonel Kennedy, Captain Walker and Lieutenants Kelmo, Dowling and Griffen.

* * *

Prisoners relied on religion from the beginning and a suitable place within Changi compound was found by Reverend E. W. B. Cordingly. In the vegetation, next to the officers' mess, he noticed a white exotic building with wide verandas on three sides featuring attap-style canopies. He described the facility as 'fairly large, hidden behind trees and shrubs that flowered profusely with purple and red petals'. At one end, a set of steps led to a domed minaret. He felt the forgotten mosque (small by city standards) ideal for a church. It was cool and light inside and permission was not difficult to obtain. The reverend and a team of soldiers soon converted the building to a new place of worship. The craftsman skills of his fellow prisoners were stunning. The building was redesigned with an altar, rails and a pulpit; all expertly handmade. Not only did they create beautiful wooden pews, but a large wooden cross was also crafted by soldier Harry Stogden.[5] The church was named after the patron saint of Great Britain, St George – who also appears on the Royal Northumberland Fusiliers service badge. St George's became the centre for all PoWs to congregate for services, discussions, debates and lectures.

A month before the senior officers departed for Formosa, the Bishop of Singapore, John Leonard Wilson, arranged for a Ceremony of Confirmation for several hundred servicemen of all ranks on 17 July at St George's Church. It was rare to confirm prisoners of war. They came from the 18th Division, 11th Indian Division, Fortress Troops and 3 Corps. Australian forces also joined the 18th Division HQ Mess of India Lines. Minister, Reverend Cordingly, padre to the Northumberland Fusiliers (who after the war became Bishop of Thetford, Norfolk), was accompanied by Bishop Wilson (formerly Bishop of Anglia prior to becoming Bishop of Singapore in 1941). They were assisted by Rev. Reginald Keith Sorby-Adams from St Andrews School, Singapore. It was a colourful affair – with the bishop in his traditional robes – accompanied by a Christian Japanese escort, four generals, ten brigadiers and the senior colonels. Many PoWs would always remember this historic occasion.

The first year of the ministry was without interruption, thanks to a Japanese Christian officer named Andrew Ogawa, but later the Japanese military felt threatened by the popularity of Christian beliefs and Bishop

Wilson, Rev. Sorby-Adams and their religious assistants were also interned at Changi.

* * *

Religion was not Stan's, or many soldiers' favoured topic prior to the war, but in their plight, solace was found at St George's, in singing hymns or meditating, allowing the religion of their culture to envelope them.

> *The church service on Sundays was always relaxing, especially when Padre Duckworth gave the sermon. He wasn't the general run of army chaplains; he was quite a comedian! He used to tell us some quite relaxing and settling talks (which weren't sermons – they were talks) and that helped too.*

With emotion, Stan's voice falters on the audio tape:

> *Sunday was a day you looked forward to in the end. But it was amazing how many that were, you know, the big and robust fellas; they seemed to be the first to 'go'. Why I'll never know.*

It is believed Stan was confirmed at the service on 17 July 1942, with other ranks, where he learned to genuflect. Thoughtfully, he explained:

> *The Royal Engineers in Changi created a beautiful cemetery for the British dead. This included a small lychgate[6]; it really was a smashing piece of work. I went to two or three funerals there. It made you think and say to yourself: 'I'm not going to end up here. I'm going to get home.'*

Chapter 15

The Selarang Incident

Many months had passed since the capitulation and clock-watching had become a diminished skill; instead PoWs used ancient methods of measuring time, by the sun, the dawn chorus and dusk's evensong. There was no need to worry about time; there were no trains or buses to catch, no dentists or doctors to visit and no appointments to be made in advance. The Medical Corps was on hand most of the time; someone was always there to help, and officers attempted to make everyone's day 'normal'.

Under Japanese guard, the camps in Singapore, and the mainland – such as Pasir Panjang and Tanjong Rhu – ran efficiently under the administration of the five British Army Headquarters. The working parties endured hard labour for hours with few breaks - 'yasume' - and then only if the guard considered it necessary. Men would often return to camp exhausted. But for the first six months the situation was somewhat free and easy where prisoners could roam and visit with each other at will. The Changi campus held the 18th Division at India Lines, Roberts and Kitchener Barracks, and the Australian 8th Army was based in Selarang Barracks, half a mile away. Together these were called the Southern Area, where certain political events led to a serious incident.

Rewinding to March 1942, the Japanese had cajoled Sikh soldiers from the British Indian Army to join the renegade Indian National Army (INA). Captain Mohan Singh, who was captured when the Japanese invaded Malaya, led the initiative with a vague promise to help dislodge the British from India. The Japanese encouraged this racial realignment of power, while others felt sympathy for the Indians, who they believed were coerced into changing sides.[1] Nevertheless, the Japanese introduced the Sikh guards. This caused consternation among the prisoners, not only because all PoWs had to salute the guards who previously ranked as privates in the British Indian Army, an insult that many found degrading, but also because the Sikh guards were traitors. In turn, it was also discovered that at night, some Sikh guards inflicted unsavoury and homosexual acts on men at the latrines. The abuse was common, and many men retaliated by complaining to their superiors, hoping to stop the attacks and acts of gross indecency. This had an enormous effect on what later became known as the Selarang Barracks Square Incident.

Seven, three-storied, off-white colonial buildings bordered the square where the Gordon Highlanders made their headquarters and packed in 800 men. Parades and drills were a usual sight in the grounds that once displayed palm trees, exotic plants and manicured lawns, but three months later the area had become unrecognisable. The original, white-painted buildings had dulled and there was no horticultural care of any type – all the beautiful trees had been felled.

The recent arrival of Major General Shimpei Fukuye, July 1942, meant IJA control was tougher. Fukuye, in his new role, demanded that four prisoners be executed. They were being held for attempting to escape and other minor crimes. Allied senior officers were ordered to observe the barbaric execution as a condition of Japanese demands. Corporal Rodney Breavington and Private Victor Gale from Australia, and two British men, Private Harold Waters of the East Surrey Regiment and Private E. Fletcher from the RASC, were shot on the beach at Changi. When the officers returned to the camp, they relayed the horrific details to the inmates, adding to their tension. Sikh guards had carried out the execution providing more evidence against them and heightening the prisoners' resistance towards their captors. A revolt was imminent – which risked certain massacre.

Anticipating the unrest, though some say fuelling it, on 30 August 1942, the Japanese ordered all Southern Area PoWs to sign a form promising not to escape. Fergus Anckorn said it was nonsense from the start. It was a ridiculous demand; they were, after all, trapped. Trying to flee across Singapore's inhospitable mangrove swamps then across the sea was impossible and erred on suicide. They felt insulted their captors needed acknowledgement of their worthless predicament and that escape was futile. Stan's captain, Horner, noted the Japanese 'screed': that each must give an 'honourable undertaking not to escape'. Fergus recalled the words:

> I, the undersigned, hereby solemnly swear on my honour, that I will not, under any circumstances, attempt to escape.

The senior officers and troops were outraged. Lieutenant Colonel Holmes and Brigadier F. G. Galleghan, Commander of AIF, addressed the problem and rejected the order with derision, but the Japanese applied more pressure. Confusion reigned on the next steps of the dispute but under senior officer recommendations all refused to sign, en-bloc.

It was the first indication of prisoner resistance and a severe risk to them; uncertainty for their safety escalated with rumour of genocide. But a slower death was threatened when Fukuye prepared to move all contagious patients from Roberts Hospital into the square. From malaria to scabies and beriberi, to dysentery and diphtheria – the overcrowded square would have been a recipe for disaster. Medics pleaded with British officers to concede to Japanese demands, but prevention was not easy. Allied High Command was incredulous: 'The order was inconceivable.' 'To comply was preposterous!' All prisoners were herded together in the confines of Selarang Square. Stan remembered:

> *On 2 September, the Japs ordered us again to sign a 'non-escape' form, which we refused. On 3 September, the fact we refused to sign this form, the Japanese ordered all PoWs in that area to move to Selarang Barracks. I don't know how many there were but there was a hell of a lot of us. We were moved into a very confined space, and I can assure you it was very uncomfortable. We were in a barracks area. I think it was five barrack blocks plus an administration block and a barrack square.*

> *The engineers turned the square into one vast latrine to cope with the various sewage needs: the sew[er] wasn't working on account of it being bombed out of existence and we were confined within the road perimeter of the barracks. The other side of the road, which circled the barrack,*

was manned by the Japs with machine guns on every corner. If you
put your foot off the kerb on to the road, a Jap ran up to you and gave
you a wallop with his rifle butt. I slept on the stairs; others were in
various toilet blocks that weren't working; we just had to make the best
of what we had.

On the day he was ordered to march out of Roberts Barracks, Fergus Anckorn felt no one knew where they were going or why. When directed into Selarang, the crowd of PoWs was told they would remain there until they signed. Every inch of the square was occupied as well as the rooftops of the barracks. The former regiments were squashed together and virtually slept on top of one another, but being British, their resolve was not broken by the demands of the Japanese and they remained up-beat.

On 3 September, Horner wrote:

Events have been moving with some considerable swiftness during the last thirty-six hours. At 2300hrs on 1 September, Colonel E. W. B. Holmes, our acting GOC since General Percival left for Formosa, was demanded by Fukuye and told that unless we signed the Parole Paper by 1500hrs on 2 September, the whole area of 17,000 troops would be concentrated in Selarang Barracks in the AIF lines. As this threat has in no way made us alter our minds, I am writing this at 1000hrs on 3 September, on the second floor of one of the blocks.

The block, where Stan and his group were, held 2,500 men when it was meant only for 300. The sight was unbelievable and resembled a bustling souk of cookhouses, makeshift canvas and wooden shacks, with latrine trenches cut through the central black asphalt. Two water trucks catered for 17,000 PoWs in one space. It was not a scene or experience anyone wanted.

Horner set up his camp bed on the balcony facing the road. It was almost comical. Trailers were piled high with kitbags, cooking utensils, everything they could carry, even livestock such as chickens and ducks. They were like fleeing evacuees, but the morale of the troops was high. However, the Japanese had orders to shoot anyone who put a foot on the roads surrounding the square. The area was guarded by Sikhs on Sentry Go – sentry duty – and everyone had to salute them. If they didn't, they'd get their faces slapped, be forced to perform press-ups or some other indignity.

Fergus thought it was a way for them to reduce their guard quota by squashing everyone into Selarang Barracks. Escape was not an option for any of them, knowing there was nowhere to conceal oneself among natives, and the hardship of jungle life up-country, the only dry route to freedom, was unthinkable. The Japanese further threatened that anyone trying to flee would be executed. Something they were adamant about. The outlook was not great.

As well as latrines, a makeshift hospital was set up under a make-do canvas, and surgeons continued with their professional skills dealing with amputations and dysentery cases. Fires were lit around the square for warmth, which meant wood was ripped from interiors of the buildings and window frames were dismantled to keep the fires burning. One dilemma was that there was not enough water for washing or shaving. Fergus recalled a man who tried to clean his teeth with water from the solitary tap on the square:

> With his mug in his hand and trying to swill his toothpaste while straddling the gully – the boundary restriction for the square – he hadn't realised the seriousness of his action when his straddling foot landed the wrong side. He was immediately shot at by a guard for drifting outside the square.

It was a barbaric penalty for accidentally stepping too far. The Sikh guard who shot him showed no remorse. Fergus didn't know if the man survived the punishment, for the one step he took too far.

The only two water points were kept for cookhouse staff, therefore skin diseases were sure to increase, through lack of hygiene. Stan reported further misery:

> *Dysentery cases were getting very, very bad while we were there and then the order came from the Japanese that if we didn't sign, they would move the rest of the* [diseased,] *disabled and injured men from the local*

hospital into our area, which would have been – well, I don't know if any of us would have lasted then.

Stan stood on the steps of the Selarang block that his unit and HQ had been squeezed into. He had a good view of the barrack square on the Padang – the old parade area. The dreadful scene was teeming with prisoners who sat upright, while others were being sick on the floor next to the latrines. Desperation was having to dash to the toilet, a race against time, bodily functions couldn't wait.

He slept on concrete stairs for three nights. It was better than being down on the Padang, despite the discomfort. Sweltering in the heat was only half of his predicament, fear was the other. Medics continued their pessimism in the spread of disease and dysentery, and general opinion increased saying, that if they had to sign to prevent unnecessary loss of life, they had better sign soon. Pride was at stake.

> There's talk of us being starved into submission. The wording on the screed cannot be changed as per an order from Tokyo and we are to sign regardless of the cost in men's lives.[2]

If they signed, it would be another humiliation; first the capitulation, then embarrassing orders to salute Sikhs and Japanese privates – and failure to do so would result in more face slapping and kicking – then the Sikh execution of the four escapees. They were under pressure for four days; it was stressful and depressing.

> *'So, therefore,'* recalled Stan, *'we signed the "non-escape" form under duress. It was signed on the 5th September about 2300hrs, in the middle of the night.'*

The lives of Colonel Holmes' men were his main consideration and signing to avoid large-scale loss of life, meant pride had to be swallowed. At 1900hrs he signed the paper. However, he extracted the order in writing from the IJA, in the full knowledge of all concerned, to stipulate this was obtained under duress. Stan recorded:

On 6th September we were ordered back to our original lines, so we had another little walk back! And the rest of the month was spent getting back to – not that you could call it – normal!

Stan and many others never would have thought they'd say, 'it's great to be back', but – after the cramped conditions of Selarang – they were. To have a shower was extremely satisfying.

Mixed emotions ensued as they returned to their barracks. Seventeen thousand PoWs in one small space was incredible, though not one to repeat. The signatures were handed in, but morale, despite defeat, was high.

Fergus's regiment was allowed on the Changi beach to clean up – like school children on an outing – it was the best place to administer personal hygiene.

'We were filthy, sweating, unwashed, some men with excrement on their legs.'

Stan was given two separate copies of the demand notification, typed slightly differently from each other, on the same day. He probably thought nobody would believe him and kept the two thin paper screeds as proof. Kept in the gusset of his Soldier's Service Paybook, never to be spoken of again until, yellowed with age, they were rediscovered seventy-two years later.[3]

*   *   *

Fergus later queried the outcome of this episode with Brigadier Galleghan. Fukuye had ordered the execution of the four men as an example of things to come if the Allied Prisoners did not obey orders, or tried to escape. The non-escape order, therefore, was declared an intimidating demonstration of power, but the brutal execution did not deter the senior officers, who refused to sign. Ultimately, however, the threat of sick men turned into the square with other ailing, but 'walking', prisoners was the turning point. Medics pleaded with senior officers, citing if men were already dropping down dead in the square from dysentery, bringing more sick men into the equation would not solve anything.

But the PoWs were steadfast. The senior officers sought a compromise by changing the wording from 'demand' to 'military order'. Although, previously, this was a stumbling block in the negotiations, the commanders managed to change a word or two.

After four days, supplies of food were low and more PoWs were falling sick. The barracks were swarming with emaciated, sunburnt bodies, while four manned Japanese guns pointed sinisterly at them. The threat of death, stench and pressure from the heat was oppressive.

With the amended words 'under duress' they signed. In imprisonment law, this confirmed the document would have no bearing on British Army decisions in the future. Lieutenant Colonel Holmes was aware of this and stood high on a chair to inform the men of their guaranteed future, if signed. With his guidance they felt morally obliged to sign and followed his advice. The alternative was a possible massacre.

* * *

Under the clock tower in Selarang Square, dejected PoWs passed multiple tables stacked with forms. Signatures were scribbled; the deed was done. Many inserted fictitious names or made signatures unrecognisable. Mickey Mouse and Donald Duck were co-prisoners too. The incident, and the Allies mutual understanding, brought them closer together. The threat of being gunned down, en masse, made each person value other people's existence, and their survival. Knowing they had achieved this feat with some form of resistance, buoyed their spirits and cemented allegiance.

Despite food shortages and squalid conditions, prison camp life was tolerable. There were no more fights, no threats of being shot, bombed, shelled or bayoneted and the atmosphere was quite relaxed. As the steady influence of emerging and resourceful leaders grew for each unit, the general response to everyone's plight was that it was not so bad. The only threat was if someone stole your food or belongings to make their lives easier. Sometimes it was survival of the craftiest!

Copy

To: – All Units, 18 Div Area.

Copy of SELARANG SPECIAL ORDER No.2 BY COLONEL E.B. HOLMES MC., is forwarded to all units for information:

1. The requirement by the Imperial Japanese Army, issued under their Order No.17 dated 31 August 42 that all ranks of the PoW Camp Changi, should be given the opportunity to sign a certificate of promise not to escape, has now been amended in a revised Imperial Japanese Army Order No 17 dated 2 Sep 42 to a definite order that all officers, NCOs and Men of the PoW Camp shall sign this undertaking.

2. I therefore now order that these certificates will be signed by all ranks and handed by Area commanders to Command Headquarters by 1100 hrs on 5 Sep 42.

3. The circumstance in which I have been compelled to issue this order will be made the subject of Selarang Special Order No 3 which will be issued later.

(sgd.) S. W. Harris

4 Sept 42   Lt. –col commanding 18th Divisional Area.

Selarang 1/A

3 Corps. S. Area, 11 Div, 18 Div, AIF., OC Hospital

Reference Selarang Special Order No 3, dated 4 Sep 42. My attention has been drawn to some concern which is being felt that there may be adverse financial consequences on individuals as the result of the signing of the non-escape certificate.

It is obviously impossible for me to give a ruling in this matter, which must rest in other hands than mine. I wish, however, all ranks to be informed that this point had my full consideration at the time of decision, and I am convinced that no such adverse consequences on pay, pension or allowances will result to any individual. It will naturally be my first endeavour also to ensure on release that the position is made clear to His Majesty's Government.

(sgd.) E.B. Holmes. Colonel;

Commanding British & Australian Troops.

CHANGI

4 Sep 42

Chapter 16

Normality? Concert Parties Recommence

The distinct lack of daily entries in Stan's diary after 'The Selarang Incident', as it became known, leaves an impression of wavering normality bordering on 'boring'. Normal, what did that mean? Perhaps there was nothing to write about until October 1942, or maybe they were settled and comfortable after the indignity of that wretched time.

The Changi University resumed, as did group activities. Lectures on music, nineteenth-century classics, human nature or social topics were taught by several officers, not just the army but by captured squadrons from Java. A new intake of RAF personnel had arrived after the Selarang episode. Thirteen of their officers were incorporated into the 18th Division mess and retold stories of a lousy time in Sumatra and Java where their heads were shaved. This made the PoWs feel lucky not to have Javanese rules imposed on them in Changi. Classes were held outside in the fresh air, which provided healing and comfort for those who made the effort to attend. Others preferred creative activities. Books had been found in numerous city buildings and houses by men on working parties and smuggled into Changi Gaol. Some PoWs had books of their own and often these were incorporated into the prison lending-library. Several PoWs tried the classes and lectures but couldn't stomach the idea of resurrecting their education. To stay occupied by reading books was hard. The novels were very English and only made them yearn more for home: home comforts, home food, home noises, home voices. 'When will we ever get out of here?' they often questioned.

* * *

Preparations for the next concert party show started with a consensus to continue the performance rehearsed before Selarang. It was due to open mid-September, but sickness had spread. The play *I Killed the Count* was postponed because of the higher threat of diphtheria spreading in close conditions. Disease could quickly mutate to greater numbers, including the accommodation units.

Depression was also prevalent, mostly due to boredom. There was little to discuss as men sat in hot shaded areas to re-read old letters, talk about home (again) or food rations. Some mess occupants decided to grow moustaches during Selarang, as they couldn't shave, but upper lip adornments disappeared when 'normal' washing facilities resumed; shaving was something to do.

I Killed the Count eventually opened on Thursday, 23 September 1942, but Horner remembered differently:

> The 3–4 days trip to Selarang did not hamper the production. The show, written by Alec Coppel, was put on at the New Windmill Theatre and I played the part of 'Mr Samuel Diamond', among a cast of thirteen. Lieutenant Mackwood of the Royal Artillery re-wrote the play from memory and created a good show; everyone pulled their weight to ensure the production went off smoothly.

Stan, Gordon and his friends watched in awe. Fergus had made friends with troops in the Dutch camp and convinced them to start their own concert party. They also had an illusionist, said to be the nephew of Houdini, known as either 'The Great Cortini', 'Cortini's Magical Eye' or 'The Professor'. After a few discussions, Fergus became his assistant, even though his injured hand needed more practice. He also continued in a group of ten performers for the 18th Division Concert Party, but with only one fully functioning hand he had to change his act. Eventually, The Great Cortini joined their troupe. With the first-class illusionist and excellent theatre facilities, Fergus was encouraged to gradually improve his proficiency while he assisted with illusions. The two put on a full magic show, where they 'sawed' people in half, and Fergus demonstrated single limited tricks. He remembered:

> One show started in a macabre tone, in keeping with our surroundings. The lights would go down and the curtains would be partially opened with The Professor standing between them. But as

you watched, he would gradually turn into a skeleton – a complete skeleton – and then he turned back into a man, bow and disappear behind the closing curtains.

The clever illusion was made possible by Royal Engineer Sapper, Ronald Searle,[1] who drew the skeleton backcloth. The former art student who sketched many Singapore scenes was determined to record the dismal prison camp episodes for posterity. Ultimately, the artistry of Searle was in great demand among the concert party community, and many cartoons of Changi and camp life were depicted through his humorous, but telling, drawings. Another feat of magical props improvisation Fergus remembered was:

A night-time scene in New York City, where the backdrop windows lit up and traffic lights flashed. There were even illuminated road signs, but most impressive were the twinkling stars. We could have been in the West End!

The resourcefulness and ingenuity of the set makers was quite incredible, considering the lack of supplies and the circumstances. Changi entertainment also gave everyone something to look forward to. It was ironic that due to the length of captivity, the shows improved and became more frequent. They were a lot of fun, and as time went on, each show became important to everyone. The concert parties made exceptional efforts to bring PoWs out from the depths of despair to another world of light-hearted imagination. Thinking about lines and scripts was a much-needed diversion from the squalor and threats they had recently endured. Several stages had been built, including the New Windmill Theatre, to remind them of home.

During the rest of September, they carried on trying to live in basic conditions, scraping together meagre meals for nutrition and survival. From a general point – after Selarang – there were quite a few people admitted to the hospital with vitamin deficiency diseases. These were on the increase despite extra medical supplies arriving. Some ate peanuts, an excellent source of Vitamin B, but still this left them tired and repeated blackouts often occurred. This happened to Horner. Ultimately his weight dropped, and he had attacks of dysentery. The responsibility of putting on shows for the men was a good distraction for him. *Gentlemen Only* at the Palladium Theatre (another troop-built stage) was a success at the end of October. But a year after leaving the shores of Britain, with illness and death, inevitably many felt very homesick.

As well as concert party shows, there was also sport. Cricket on the south Padang was where the 'rest of the world' beat the Australians by one run: 107 to 106. An exhilarating occasion.

Peaceful and heart-warming outdoor Sunday services resumed, delivered by the padre. There was even a Harvest Festival presided over by another RAF padre. The pillars, pulpit and prayer desk of the church were decorated with flowers, creeper and palm fronds, and gifts of fruit and vegetables provided a colourful display. The prisoners' abundant offerings, exceptional under the circumstances, were donated to the hospital together with wheatsheaf-shaped sourdough bread from the Changi field bakery. Aldershot ovens[2] were used to bake the loaves, rationed to one slice per person every ten days.

Major Burgess, a dietician in Malaya before capitulation, gave a lecture in October, after 1,000 hospital cases of beriberi and several deaths. Many had also been treated in India Lines for scrotal dermatitis, sore eyes, swollen tongues and feet. Lack of vitamins and good food was to blame. He was the one to recommend more rice-polishings and peanuts, plus soya beans and whitebait. However, a few days later they heard that Japanese ration levels were to be cut as additional supplies were arriving from the Red Cross. Everyone hoped this was true.

*   *   *

Joyful sounds were heard when news reached the men that Red Cross supplies were being unloaded at Keppel Harbour. The ship was the *Tatuta Maru* and prisoners were told there could be mail next time too. How they longed for word from home, even just a postcard. No communication with families for nine months was one of the hardest things they had to bear. But they heard little more about the maru and its postal cargo.

Chapter 17

Stan's Autumn 1942 – October Supplies Arrive!

The ship that brought the Red Cross supplies was finally off-loaded in October, and that's when we received our first issue of cigarettes. We received sixty-five each, so now life was a bit more tolerable. There were supposed to be more ships waiting in the docks to be unloaded, but I think that was only a rumour, because we never had any more supplies. We all had certain duties to perform even though we were PoWs, except the disabled people and those who just couldn't cope with life out there.

23 October a party of PoWs came from Java, mainly Dutch, white Dutch that is with their green uniforms.

24 October Japs started to want working parties to go up to the mainland, on a railway. We didn't know that it was a railway at the time. Various officers went, and in the end, it is now known they wanted 300 of us, but I don't think it included any of our platoon.

To keep our minds occupied, we had various talks and lectures. One officer, Sergeant Nunn, gave a talk on a pub crawl in London. He mustered all the Londoners around just to give us a talk and to give us something to think about.

Some evenings would consist of concert party gatherings. They took it in turns to attend as there were so many prisoners and enjoyed some light-hearted banter; the sound of music relieved the soul. Stan played a ukulele in a quartet, but it disbanded when men went up-country.

26 October We discovered they needed another six more blokes to make up the numbers to go up to the mainland, so six of our chaps had to go. We had to parade with our small company and those with a decent pair of boots had to give them to the fellas who were going up-country. We had to put up with whatever we could find. Most of them were NCOs.

1 November The Mainland Party moved off. We said goodbye to six of our lads.

6 November The rest of our company, all bar two of us, are sent up-country. The two being myself and one of the other fellas; an officer who has been sick.

This meant we were the only two left from our company [Coy.141], *in Singapore!*

Sketches on the Steps – Part I

The artist chose his subjects,
A tree, a bird, a ship
His paper, pens and charcoal
Held tightly at his hip.

He left many weeks ago,
Grey distant shades of war
Ambivalent, our sadness,
What was this all for?

On vessels guided,
By foreign sailing friends,
Our cruising languid evenings
Sung tunes to sunsets' end.

Sketches on the Steps,
A view from up above,
Smoking, playing, smiling,
Reading letters from a love.

PT and circuit-moves for them,
The many rank and file,
Keeps the sea-bound armies fit,
Before an unknown Isle.

Sketches on the Steps
War convoy; land on either side,
Dodge bombs and threatening sharks,
Sparkling sea of diamonds shine.

Flights of twenty-seven,
Skim the bright blue skies
Leaving dents of drastic war behind,
Midst black and burning fires.

Sketches on the Steps,
Dusks; padang, deep valley or hill,
Humid battles for sixteen nights
Pained cries; leaves frightening chill.

White Flag aborts a massacre:
Shamed troops – Capitulation!
An Army left to fight alone,
No support from home: their nation.

Sketches on the Steps
Thousands, captive in barracks square,
Must sign the non-escape clause,
our bodies – weak and bare.

Our minds: Duress is heavy
Threats, 'Add injured, ill and sick.'
Three days we stand, in thousands,
Enough! 'Tis a dirty trick.

Sketches while in Step
Marching back to normal camp
Now a better option
A roof, a mat, a lamp.

Time to bear the undertaking
All starving, ill and dashed
Return to India Lines and food
Rice: boiled or mashed!

– J.T.R.

PART II

'I regret to have to tell the House that information which has been reaching His Majesty's Government no longer leaves room for any doubt that the true state of affairs is a very different one so far as the great majority of prisoners in Japanese hands are concerned.'

Anthony Eden, Foreign Secretary

Chapter 18

Only the Lonely

'Kill all – burn all – loot all'. Historically, this evil Nippon mantra had threatened political upheaval and stability in the Far East from as early as 1937. Turmoil gripped politicians and western forces trying to bring Japan to heel. As 1938 closed, nine-tenths of Chinese railways were held by them and they continued to steal land resources by bullying the Chinese into submission with many atrocities and massacres. As the Japanese Army continued to march over China, plundering gold and other resources, they commandeered mines in Manchuria and put Chinese civilians to work. They firebombed Nankin and soon after, in September 1940, they agreed a tripartite pact with Germany and Italy.

President Roosevelt held discussions with China's national leader Chiang Kai-Shek, during March 1941, regarding use of America's Flying Tiger aircraft for two years. The next month the Japanese Foreign Minister's paranoia persuaded his government to believe the West threatened their country. At that time a four-way pact was suggested with USSR. But Japan was Russia's inherent enemy and did not agree to the plan.

Japan's aggressive behaviour in southern China that summer led to their assets being frozen by western Allies. Prevented from buying oil, a main commodity, Emperor Hirohito knew within two years Japan's supplies could be depleted. Matters deteriorated further when Prime Minister Winston Churchill met President Roosevelt on a warship, to raise the Atlantic Charter. The value of the yen fell and the necessary raw materials to feed the Japanese people were in China.

Hitler aimed to control the East as well as the West. He thought he could succeed in Europe where Napoleon had failed in 1812, but Joseph Stalin, General Secretary of the Central Committee of the Communist Party of the Soviet Union, did not believe Hitler would attack as together, they had signed a non-aggression pact in 1939. On 10 May 1941, Rudolf Hess had flown to

Scotland and landed safely hoping to intervene through the British Royal Family, the Duke of Windsor and the Duke of Hamilton, with whom it is believed he sought to discuss peace proposals.[1]

British Intelligence at Bletchley Park, through Winston Churchill, was able to alert Stalin that Germany planned to attack his country on 22 June. The sleeping beast had been disturbed. As well as the proposed attack on Russia, Germany also intended to invade Gibraltar. Britain expected a full-force invasion and the island appeared on the brink of capitulation. But with secret intelligence and the olive branch of peace handed to Stalin, both nations stood up to Hitler.

Meanwhile, German U-boats prowled the Atlantic looking for shipping targets to disrupt the delivery of food supplies to Britain. Friendly help from America protected the convoys but they would not enter the war, only minimal aid from their Merchant Navy provided Liberty cargo ships.[2] The British fought fiercely in Europe to defend the British Isles, as well as in the deserts of the Middle East to protect the borders of the Empire, from the west to the Indian continent and east along the Burma Road to China.

Before long, the Japanese became sceptical about their pact with Germany and Foreign Minister Matsuoka urged Japan to go to war with Russia against Germany. Russia refused and this brought Japan to the brink of war and Matsuoka's government formed the Japanese Co-Prosperity Sphere to wield aggressive military expansion and control.

*   *   *

By mid-October 1942, Horner's pay arrived – $20 less $5 towards messing. He felt affluent, but it was then learned the Japanese were to take over the canteen and prices would increase. The PoW's affluence immediately dissipated. Certain leniencies had been allowed before and the supply team was permitted to go with a Japanese guard to buy direct from nearby kampongs – this also ceased.

After several months of captivity, the Japanese only paid men in working parties. Now they had Malay $20 a month, but an ounce of Javanese tobacco cost Malay $22. PoWs made do with dried banana or papaya leaves instead. The smokes were reasonable, and a bit of comfort, but were like smoking brown paper. Despite little money, the general consensus was that it was a buyer's market, and if one was lucky enough to own a Bible, they'd sell the pages for a dollar or so; the thin religious text was perfect to roll your own expensive tobacco and preferable to puffing on a banana leaf.[3]

Between the last week of October and the first week of November, after the Red Cross supplies arrived, Stan pondered the demise of his army unit. Soon he would say farewell to six more from his group, who were slated for the next working party.

> *When the Japanese required more bodies to go up-country, they just used to give our administration a number and whether we had to fulfil that number. Originally, it used to be the main companies going up-country but then it finally dwindled down to HQ companies, ours being one of them. I was put on the list, to go 'up' that particular day. The following day one of our officers came around and said two people had to stay behind, with what was left of us. He asked who would stay behind and I said, I didn't mind staying and hence, I and another fellow stayed. That was just the luck of the draw ... I think.*

Out of the 141 Coy. contingent, Stan thought volunteering to remain behind meant he was missing out on the fun of the working party, who believed they were off to better conditions. But in his pragmatic way, he knew he had an important job to look after another man, a sick officer.

*   *   *

A new entertainment revue show had been programmed by Horner, for 18th Division personnel going up-country. The play bill depicted him in cartoon form, smoking his familiar pipe. He heard his new skill as compère was successful and went on to sing a song called '*Ah*' after a couple of shows,[4] giving him increased confidence in being face to face with an audience. He was on a roll, entertaining the men and officers, including special guests of honour, General Heath, 'Black Jack' GOC, AIF and Major Horrigan of the American Air Force (who had been captured in Java).

The programme for the evening was:

'Jam Session'	Jack Greenwood and His Boys
'Grimaldi'	Goodman and Elliot
'Biddy and Fanny'	Barnsley and MacDonald
'The Great Cortini'	Denis East and his Violin
'The Green Eye of the Little Yellow God'	Goodman, Mackwood, Bradshaw
'Lecture' World War 14–18	Mackwood and Bradshaw
'Ventriloqual Act'	Barnsley and MacDonald

The show was a success in the indoor auditorium, but the New Windmill Theatre was closed due to threat of spreading disease, since it was felt such a place would harbour germs.

*   *   *

Many of the senior officers were awful at pulling rank and deliberate bullying ensued. Some were trying to lend their weight to opting out of 'up-country' selection. Horner writes about one senior ranking chap: 'Bill Cowell is going up-country – he hasn't been "yessing" well enough! Hell's bells these senior officers are "bum" the whole bloody lot of them; the more I see of them the less respect I have.'

They found it difficult to shake off their higher official regimental strictness. The lists for all ranks to go up-country would redress the imbalance.

Now a 'celebrity' in the prison camp, Horner was privileged to attend other evening acts, such as two Dutch illusionists who entertained in the officers' mess: one doing sleight of hand and conjury, the other reading people's minds. It was amazing to see them in action with successful results. From this he became in charge of producing a 'Road Show' to play for both British and Dutch troops on alternate nights in a theatre set up by Cortini on the Dutch Lines. Now, as compère, he had to think of new jokes the Dutch could understand. No doubt this was where he crossed paths with Gunner Fergus Anckorn – Wizardus!

*   *   *

It was two weeks before Stan wrote in his diary again: '*On 20th November, we heard the news that 'Becky' Smith, our lieutenant general in charge of our division had died in Japan* [Formosa, occupied by Japan].'

The sad events upset the 18th Division troops and they considered whether to cancel the show. Major General Beckwith-Smith had died of dysentery.[5] He had a great capacity for relating to his men and all admired him. Everyone thought he had been given a raw deal.

With stoic resilience and stiff upper lips, the show went on as he would have wanted. About 1,500 troops were in the audience, and a few days later a formal memorial was held for 'Becky'.

The news of Beckwith-Smith's death in captivity would be the last entry in Stan's small handwritten diary. He felt distressed by the news and his own feelings of separation anxiety began to emerge. His later audio version recorded his emotions:

Being left with hardly any of my old associates I felt a bit lonely, even though in a PoW camp, but I ran across one of my old friends who I joined up with, George Hatfield. He was working on the tree felling and garden party area. So, the people who were administering asked me if I could go and work on the tree felling unit. I was allowed to go – this was under our own administration – we didn't have to ask the Japs or anything like that, just our own people in charge of us. I worked with George for nearly the final two and a half years on tree felling, going out to the various rubber plantations allocated by the Japs. They went there previously to blaze an area of trees and we went and felled the rubber trees, mainly for cooking fuel purposes. It used to be a party of about twenty other ranks and maybe four to six officers who were left behind, and we'd march out to the various plantations, carrying our gear, axes and 'chunkols' – like a spade – and [walked next to] a stripped-down lorry chassis. This consisted of a footbrake and a handbrake, a steering wheel, and one fella' sitting up on the box while twenty of us other ranks pulled the trailer on a long rope with cross bars: two aside, ten long, like a huge team of horses.

Lack of food did not help these periods of exertion, but they managed somehow. Snagging an egg or two from a local farmer was prohibited, but if they didn't supplement their meals with contraband protein, excessive tasks could be debilitating.

Some of the rubber trees had metal cups hanging on the side and when you had a bit of rubber in the bottom of the cup it congealed and looked like a fried egg. So, one lunchtime, the party's cook, a bit of a lad – an Australian fella – put this bit of rubber on a hot plate over the fire and fried it up with coconut oil and handed it to one of the Australian officers. He said it was a gift from one of the Chinese farmers, whose camp it was. He slipped it into his 'Dixie' – that was our eating implement – and he tried to cut the rubber egg and of course all of us lads were standing around watching and laughing our heads off. It was very funny.

Being in the wood and tree felling party seemed easy, even though heavy lifting was needed, but it was not without danger:

Another officer trimming the trees, was lopping a branch from a tree that had fallen on the ground. The axe glanced, bounced off and buried itself into his foot! That put him out of action for a few months. Most of the tree trimmers, after a day's work, would sit outside their hut honing their axes ready for the next day and you could bet your life some of the axes, especially with some of the Australian fellas being used to bush work, [that] they honed those axes up to a real sharp edge.

I think I was fortunate enough to be taken on in this party because it was such a small unit: just about twenty British and twenty Australians, accompanied by three officers from either side. The ranks used to do the heavy tree felling, the officers used to go around trimming the branches with axes and things like that, to trim the logs down, then you'd have another party go along and cut the logs up into handiable lengths.

Laughter with his work–detail friends made Stan's days more tolerable. They couldn't do without it and made the best of every opportunity. He always said, 'You had to laugh, otherwise you'd cry.'

> *We used to have our lighter moments, walking along singing various songs, dirty songs I suppose, calling the Japs all sorts. When you reached the part of 'Jap' you used to have to salute him and our officer would say: casha lari dari, meaning look left, eyes left or casha lari nari, eyes right. Instead, we used to say rather rude things to them, which the Jap didn't understand, he'd just bow and smile and that was how it went.*

Stan also took part in the concert party. Everyone was encouraged to undertake some type of role to help keep them occupied.

> *I was involved in the concert party for a very short while. Not in the Aussie one, only the British. A party of us organised a little string quartet; I played a ukulele. This was made from an old tennis racquet press, glued together with resin from cashew nut trees. I used to tap the tree and drain the resin off. It acted as very good glue! I used old telephone wire for the strings and really it was quite effective. The other fellas had acquired a guitar and one or two other instruments, and we made up a little group, just for an act on the stage, but it didn't last long, as one or two fellas went up-country and, therefore, we broke up.*

Stan, perhaps, was in one of Jack Greenwood's bands mentioned in the programme.

* * *

From early December, rain continued for days. It was the wettest month of the year and they experienced incredibly uncomfortable humidity. Temperatures were in the 70°C. A new open-air theatre called *Kokonut Grove* was built among the coconut trees, adjoining the mess room, complete with proscenium arch. The large audience were very enthusiastic and delighted to see an excellent professional production. Horner composed the music he wrote for a song called, *When We're Free*. He asked Sapper Searle to write the words on a stretch of canvas, for all to read. The chorus had everyone singing!

> When we're free, yes, when we're free
> Oh, how happy we shall be.
> When we see the last of Changi tree,
> Oh, what a wonderful day for you and me.

The Road Show at the Dutch Lines and the Cortini Theatre came to an end, perhaps due to an argument between Horner, Cortini and one or two of the 18th Division fellows who had been attempting a Temperamental Act, one of whom was probably Fergus. Soon after, a new hospital theatre was built, similar to the *Palladium*, for walking patients and medical staff. It was once a partially bombed operating theatre. The rewiring and stage refurbishment for the auditorium sloped down, giving the audience an excellent view.

*   *   *

Stan recalled some lighter moments:

> *We used to settle in various rubber plantations for quite some time, maybe three or four weeks. We'd get the trees felled, as ordered to do so by the Japs, and became friendly with Chinese kampong residents. A kampong was a farm, and we would camp near their wells for water. If we knew we were going to be there for a fairly long period, we would store a lot of our equipment in their well house. One day, about September time, we went to the hut to pick up our gear and found, in a huge container, six young ducklings!*
>
> *We had been giving the Chinese owners some of our rice and they were giving us vegetables, and they showed their appreciation for this by giving us the ducklings. The problem was how to get them back to the camp to fatten up for Christmas. We did it! We put them in one of the containers, put a lid on it, and sang and shouted all the way back to camp so the Jap guard escorting us couldn't hear the ducks quacking.*

Our tree felling unit was only a small party of forty and the ducks were a nice treat for Christmas. We fed them on worms we found when tree felling; put them in a tin and took them back to the camp to feed the ducks, plus any grains of rice we had to spare.

Stan learned a few words of Japanese including numbers from Korean guards counting from one-to ten: *ichi, ni, san, shi, go* – one, two, three, four, five – and other pleasantries such as *Ohayou gozaimasu* – good morning and *Konbanwa* – good evening, to keep the peace. But other words between beatings were learned the hard way, such as *Benjo* for toilet, *Yasume* – rest, and *Kurrah* – fool.

Going back to the time when we acquired our little ducklings; we fattened them up in the small background area of our billet and come Christmas time they were in quite good shape for slaughtering and cooking. That was a fabulous Christmas compared to the others. One of our fellas, a Scot from Glasgow, made up some liquor from sweet potato and gula melaka (a sweetening substance from a pine palm tree) which was heated over a fire and distilled in various ways. A bit complicated to explain how we did it, but it really turned out okay. We had the spirit analysed by one of the hospital staff and it turned out to be 90 per cent proof as a clear spirit, but we toned it down with oil of clove. Somebody, somehow, got hold of this and coloured it with burnt gula melaka. This made it a caramel colour, which gave it a brandy look. Anyway, that Christmas we had the duckling and we dished out this spirit brandy, if you'd like to call it that, using our various rubber cups (for collecting latex) as glasses. We all had a little dose of this, but it affected an officer in our party who became quite merry. He danced around the Padang with a daisy behind his ear (actually, it was a hibiscus) [clothed] *only in his 'g' string. He was really quite funny, singing, I'm a Little Prairie Flower!*[6]

By this time, we were billeted back in Selarang Barracks, much better conditions with nowhere near as many people as before. The Australian unit was billeted there too. They used to put on various shows and

*build their own theatres. It was really marvellous what they did out
of what they could scrounge. I remember one show, 'The Admirable
Crichton', a very good production. Captain Horner used to do a lot
of the production work for us, but the Australians used to put on some
really spectacular variety shows. Some of their fellas used to dress up
as well for the female parts, and it seemed to go to their heads after a
while. I think they turned a bit queer.*

* * *

Over Christmas, the 18th Division arranged an exhibition of toys made by
skilled craftsmen at the camp. They were to be gifts for the, approximately
sixty, children held at Changi Gaol, who were under civilian incarceration
with their mothers, separated from their menfolk. The amazing assortment
and clever models were a festive effort to brighten the children's day. The
AIF wanted to put on a panto for them, but the request was refused by the
Japanese. It was sad to think young children – from babies to teenagers –
endured the same awful conditions. Freshly made toys buoyed their spirits.

* * *

The months after Christmas and New Year dragged and using the 'still'
the sappers made, superb cocktails continued. Visitors to the officers' mess
were treated every Sunday. The drink was pure alcohol, now flavoured with
lime. An egg cupful was plenty! Then the discovery of heart of a palm, and
the rare opportunity of a 'Millionaire's breakfast'. The heart is cut from the
top of the tree where the fronds and coconuts grow. It was an expensive and
exquisite-tasting luxury but only because the palm tree died once the heart
was extracted.

Meanwhile, the Dutch started a restaurant, where different kinds of
fried foods were available at reasonable prices. The RASC canteen cooks
did the same and it was possible to get fried fish rissoles, chips and fried
bread for 13 cents. Small portions of 'extras' in the evening helped alleviate
hunger.

By 9 April 1943 7,000 British and AIF were listed to go up–country, and the 18th Division's HQ was included in an administrative capacity

This meant many officers were also expected to go. Consequently, Horner was left in charge of about hundred RASC personnel in Changi. At that time, the remnants of the RASC HQ were informed the camp was to close and they were to move for a time to the old 11th Indian Division block in Selarang Square. This included Stan.

*   *   *

Japan's wider plan to invade British India, again for resources, meant their forces pushed north but, as they used boats, progress was slow. The Irrawaddy River ran the length of Burma and an existing railway line ran through Burmese territory, but did not connect with Malaya. Before the war, Britain and Europe considered another railway in the area, for a faster transport system, but building a continuous track was deemed impossible. Previous routes from Thanbyuzayat to Bangkok, and Bangkok to Singapore already existed but now Japan wanted to rapidly build connections using designs for massive bridges with track straddling rivers and ravines. If completed, the railway would cover over 200 miles through difficult mountainous and jungle terrain.

The problem for the Japanese was lack of manpower, but the perfect solution became obvious with the massive number of PoWs available. A Control Bureau in Tokyo managed the captives, transferring them in great numbers, relieving the swollen Changi Gaol and surrounding barracks, and the railway extension started to be constructed. Many prisoners knew the work would be difficult, if not impossible, while others considered it an adventure.

*   *   *

Stan was sad to see his friends of all ranks go up–country. Many talked of how different it would be away from Changi. A new land with different birds and animals; travelling through the jungle, hearing new rainforest sounds. In a way it was exciting. They were told the camps en route to Bangkok and further north were better and that the air was cleaner with less humidity, less exhausting and that medical facilities were better; food would be more plentiful. They were going to a proper resort!

Over the past seven months all parties had been tagged letters 'A' to 'H' and 'L' to 'X.' Most came from Changi. Earlier groups had left in October and November 1942 from the 18th Division. However, the letters of these parties were sometimes duplicated the following year which made later research uncertain as to which dates men actually went up-country. Gordon, assigned to other working parties in the autumn, was eventually in the sixth group, force 'F', which left mid-April 1943.[7] (See p.168).

Before H Force officers departed in mid-May, they enjoyed a meal of roast chicken when all mess cockerels, except for one, were killed. After rations of just rice, vegetables and fish, the food was consumed with much appreciation. Life seemed almost bearable then – even for Stan, despite his pangs of loneliness inside that started to filter through.

Nobody realised how long the separation would last. They were nervous and exhilarated, leaving the relative comfort of what they'd called *home* since February 1942. The group was the first contingent, heading for a train that would take them through the middle of Siam to a destination called Seven Hills. Not one of choice, but at least it would be on land, and they expected the assignment to be short. They had experienced stormy seas, battled and suffered captivity and now, to their chagrin, there was still no opportunity to write to loved ones back in Britain – writing home was long overdue.

Horner had agonised over who he would have to choose to go up-country. The choice now was from 122 ORs, including three officers and those in hospital. What should he do? As the main 18th Division contingent had already left, they had anticipated this for weeks, but it was essential for working parties to get to the Selarang G & W area across the Changi Road, where his fitter men were required to work after climbing a challenging hill. Horner had learned that a further party of 3,000 was to leave and he had to assign another 50 men to F Force. After a few days, the Japanese loaned Horner's men a lorry to bring heavy items from the old area and, as he was in charge, they managed to load up a good stock of RE stores, the field bakery and water trailer, but shortly after they settled in at the G & W, rumours of further moves came. Overall, 3,444 British were to go up-country. One interpreter believed this quota would be the last for a while. Dannert wire now enclosed the command area around the Gun Park of Selarang, the G & W areas and the hospital which made this believable.

Rumour continued. The latrines became a haven to whisper to your neighbour, while sitting or squatting, to transfer the latest news and gossip and soon became labelled 'the Borehole'. Fearing cholera, Japanese guards had ordered prisoners to attend to their own personal hygiene, as they considered the area unclean and perilous. Since all guards refused to enter, a safe harbour was unwittingly provided to quietly exchange information. The rumour now was that 700 officers, and 300 men, would go overseas which seemed to be validated. Horner worried that when the next party left there would be few men to carry on essential details, such as wood-cutting and trailer parties to bring in food and distribute.

Colonel Pratley, 5th Norfolk, in command of the remaining 18th Division troops, protested that it was against the Geneva and Hague conventions to make officer PoWs work. But Horner knew all would need to work hard to bring in the wood supplies needed for cooking fuel for food, to keep the remaining prisoners alive. They were an essential operation to keep the wheels oiled – to survive.

Within fourteen days, however, Horner became part of the borehole rumour when the revised number to go up-country rose to 320, including 240 officers. He was one of 3,270 – H Force.

Leaving the confines of Changi for the intolerable conditions of the 'railway' was daunting. As part of H Force, officers would supervise the construction of a road, or a railway. They expected to return after four months. As with other departures, heavy baggage was to be left. Pre-up-country dysentery and malaria inspections were also administered. The glass-rod anal instrument used by a Japanese medical officer was now familiar, together with a pricked finger and blood smear on a glass slide.

Horner was sorry to leave his men behind; all had become close. For the last two days he continued wood party trips, pulling the trailer on a 2-mile trek, felling, loading and bringing back wood. H Force left in lorries from Selarang Square for the station on 17 May 1943 amid rumours of long marches the other end. But there was no indication from the Japanese as to how far they would travel for their up-country trip. At 1610hrs they boarded a closed box car and reached Ban Pong three and a half days later.

Most travelled in the only clothes they had, and boots were donated to those going up-country. They were ill-fitting and often belonged to a deceased soldier. Stan remembered:

> *We had to give up our boots for people going 'up-country' and had to make do with something* [else]. *So, when I was on the tree felling unit, we used to save the tap root of the rubber tree because that was the way we felled them. We pulled it out of the ground and dried the tap root off and it became very light. It was like balsa wood, and we could shape them into clogs* [or sandals]. *A little bit of old rubber tyre formed the band over the top of the clog. They were fashioned with our very sharp axes and very suitable. We used to wear what boots we could find when we were out in the rubber plantations, but when we got back, we were glad to get our boots off – what was left of them – and put on these clogs. They made a very comfortable shoe.*

Another survival effort where Stan managed with sandals he made for himself and others; they were necessary to stop foot rot.

He wasn't happy to be left behind again, but he had to stay and that was that. His mates were on the list. He was crossed off. Gordon, Mac, Sid and 'Trigger' left. One can only imagine the last night where they reminisced about the training in Droitwich, the great hours spent in Cape Town, and life in Blighty, while smoking a 'bible' cigarette between them.[8]

*   *   *

Fergus was also sent up-country. He was in trouble for arguing with a RSM, who told him: 'You're going up-country with the Japs, Anckorn, and you'll probably die.'

'I don't think so,' said Fergus. Privately, he prayed for a different prediction. The prospect of up-country was intimidating. Accounts had filtered back to Changi that conditions were not as promised.

Chapter 19

The Tree Felling and Railway Sojourn

S tan thought he'd never see his friends again, especially those in the early working parties, but tried to adjust to the situation along with his friend George Hatfield.

Another incident, while we were out on tree felling detail, was when a huge tree just wouldn't come down. Because the ground was needed for cultivating, the stumps had to be removed at the same time. Our method was to grub out all the roots under the tree, so as not to leave the stump in the ground. They needed the ground for cultivating, therefore the stump had to be removed at the same time. This particular tree just wouldn't come [down]. One of the fellas in our party, a large Welsh fellow called Taffy, had a set of leg irons (like a stirrup wrapped around the leg with a spike at the bottom) which he used to climb the tree (actually, natives used them for climbing coconut trees). He climbed up with a rope to hitch to the top and got practically there with the rope around his shoulder, but the weight of him helped bring the tree down [instead]. He had to ride the tree down from the top – quite a tall tree about 50–60ft high – right down to the ground. Luckily, he wasn't hurt.

Most working parties, on return to camp, were searched by the Japanese guard to make sure we had nothing they considered contraband. In one case, prior to this, we had a little cooking session when we got back to cook up with any little thing you could scrounge that was edible. We'd cook our own little dish on top of our usual evening meal. That was one of the things: we were always hungry! This particular time, as they lined us up to search us, one fellow had some kindling in his kit bag, and he was well and truly beaten up because he had this bit of wood. This was the mentality of the Japanese guards. If you were caught with a coconut in your kit, you had hell to pay.

It was very strange that the time we spent there a lot of lousy, horrible things happened to us, but most of the things you remembered were the happier times.

The men going up-country were a 100 per cent certain they would be working as slave labour, wherever they went. The mandatory selection process ordered was a lottery. The term 'up-country' could mean either going further north into Malaya and Thailand, or to Borneo, Taiwan and Japan, where men were transported by the maru ships to coal mines.

The new railway project was 258 miles long (415km), starting from Ban Pong, and joined the existing Bangkok railway to the Burmese border in the north.[1]

*   *   *

The journeys for each force were different. The Officers' Party, H Force, after their excruciating train ride to Ban Pong, marched through the night for 17 miles, then 15 more before boarding another train and further marching. They were given 'Mah-mee' an eastern dish of fried onions, egg, meat, tomato, suce-hoon and other unidentifiable ingredients. There was a wash house used by camp folk, including women and children. Siamese and Chinese locals had no qualms in entering the latrines to ask for your shorts or shirt. Ban Pong was a boom town emerging from rural vegetation. The expanding village, 30 miles north-west of Bangkok in old Siam, bustled with people, had rusted railway sheds jammed with old carriages and a river filled with small boats. This was part of the new country, renamed Thailand.[2] Tired, but not surprised, H Force found their sleeping quarters were flooded.

*   *   *

Fergus and his Force started their journey at Singapore station months earlier. They were raucous, and in high spirits until they saw the transport. Their conveyance was an old freight train of windowless carriages. More than thirty men were crammed into each of the narrow, steel, oblong boxes that lined the track. They stood motionless for an unbearable amount of time while Japanese guards counted and re-counted their numbers – *ichi, ni, san, shi, go*. Meanwhile, the metal carriages absorbed the intense heat of the day. It was airless and they thought they would suffocate.

The journey to Ban Pong took three days in conditions that would today be described as dangerous. The heat was oppressive, spiked only by air through a gap between the chained steel sliding doors. They moved round the carriage every so often for all to breathe fresh air by the gap, and to keep their senses in check. Bowels, however, were not in check at all. 'Benjo' was something that couldn't be held; if you were by the door you were lucky, if you weren't you had to let yourself go on the spot. The sweat and stench of bodily excretions was overpowering, but they all understood what each was going through. They were exhausted and angry but could not complain; punishment was sure to be a rifle butt across the face or a boot in the back from an armed guard, a group of whom prevented them from retaliating. Dejected, they hoped for the better camps they were promised.

The train stopped briefly at Kuala Lumpur where local coolies tried to pass up food or water. Some PoWs were lucky to be out of the range of a guard and grabbed something before the coolie was shoved aside. This was a place they should have admired, but all were too shocked to be jubilant. They were ordered to stretch their limbs outside, and locals handed out black tea and a wedge of wet rice; you could go and relieve yourself as well. After only a few minutes, the guards shouted for all to return to the train, their brief freedom ended with a scramble to 'bags' the place nearest the gap.

With renewed endurance, the men crouched in cramped conditions as the train rattled along. Sleep was difficult, a catnap was all they could manage. Other brief stops took place and light-hearted PoW gossip-whisper ensued to occasionally break the drudgery. At one stop, word from another carriage told of a chap sitting in the doorway who fell through the gap and then wandered around in the undergrowth. A Japanese guard found him and took him to a hut where he was subjected to more physical abuse. His regiment thought he would surely be killed, but an officer intervened and convinced the guards to stop the brutality by saying the man hadn't tried to escape – because he wasn't wearing boots! The guards showed some consideration on their part and brought him back.

Food continued to be atrocious. The slow, unpleasant journey took six days, along a narrow track, and at Ban Pong promises of better conditions were not fulfilled. Seven Hills was revolting; not at all the Red Cross camp they expected. Rain was heavy prior to their arrival and the mud hut floors of their sleeping accommodation were constantly flooded. Latrines consistently overflowed when it rained, and maggot infestations resulted in constant swarms of flies.

The staging post was at the start of the Thai-Burma railway, about 30 miles from Bangkok. 'Tenko' (roll call) encouraged smartness and good presentation, and the men were called to attention. They obliged as it was a way of maintaining self-esteem, no matter how undignified the conditions.

Fergus had been moved after one day to Kanburi (Kanchanaburi). Many prisoners had already discarded their personal possessions, now realising they wouldn't need them again. Items such as banjos, violins and guitars – there would be no time for merrymaking where they were going. He also heard that many had died on the marches from Kanburi to the next labour camp. Guards continued to treat prisoners like slaves, hitting them and shouting impossible orders. Lucky for Fergus he worked at the railhead or on a bridge which meant he travelled on freight wagons between camps.

Kanburi is close to Tamarkan, the site where they built the bridge across the Khwae (meaning river). In fact, two bridges were built over the Mae Khlaung and the Khwae Noi (Little Kwai), close to their confluence. One, a small service bridge made of wood; the other, upstream, was a concrete and steel construction. The wooden bridge was completed in February 1943. Fergus was there for a while but was soon moved to the stronger crossing, labouring 8 a.m. to 6 p.m.

This second structure was built high on an 'A' frame, where PoW gangs pulled on a rope with a heavy pile driver. Guards chanted '*ichi, ni, san, shi*,' until the command of '*toh*' (ten) when it had to be released. Luckily, the threatening steel-capped wooden weight fell straight on to the concrete piling which men, up to their waists in the river, held steady and level.

Hour after hour, the pattern was repeated by prisoners bowing to Japanese command. Materials were unloaded from barges, including iron track looted from railway lines after Java was invaded back in March 1942. The rails didn't match but they held the structure together. The unskilled labour force, under Japanese control, achieved an astonishing feat of incredible engineering.

It was said that conditions at Kanburi were better than other camps, but Red Cross parcels were non-existent up-country. Sixty grams of rice per a day was occasionally served with a green vegetable, but when you received yours it had to be immediately covered with your hands to prevent flies from landing on the congealed mass. Dysentery would be the next upset. Despite poor food rations and other discomfort, under the patient command of Lieutenant Colonel Philip Toosey,[3] the PoWs at Kanburi and Tamarkan attempted to keep up good spirits and military standards.

Deeper into the jungle, their next stop was the Wampo Viaduct. Here the river travelled through a limestone gorge and presented a tougher challenge as the sheer rockface plunged into the Khwae Noi. It seemed impossible to build the viaduct on the steep cliff, but 2,000 prisoners laboured perilously, blasting rock with dynamite. Injury, or death, was inevitable for some, as fuses were primed and detonated, rubble removed, wood sawn and hauled up steep embankments to support a timber-framed rail track. Time was against the Japanese and an order for speed was introduced – '*Supido*'. Now prisoners worked around the clock.

Rock removal using continuous rubble baskets was an easier task, but prisoners had to keep their minds on the job. If they slacked for too long a guard would beat them. Korean guards were the worst. They violently slapped, beat and kicked, and treated prisoners like animals, aping how Japanese officers treated them. Now PoWs were at the bottom of the pile.

Elephants were also employed to transfer huge tree trunks and logs to work areas. At one point, the Japanese thought five prisoners could do the same task, but the skeletal men could barely lift a branch, let alone a tree. It was said the elephants could stop work at 4 p.m., while humans continued working.

Wampo was a low point for many, including Fergus who was severely injured. He was told to climb to the top of the viaduct with a gallon can of boiling creosote to paint the wood. It was dangerous and he didn't like heights but was ordered to climb. He had devised for his damaged leg a rope and pulley system to get around and with this attempted to climb. The temperature was stifling at over 100 degrees, and at about 100ft, he was threatened by a guard with a pole who shouted and prodded him to climb faster. Fergus also suffered from vertigo and the ground below appeared to spin. It took more than half an hour to reach the top, where he closed his eyes and hung on, motionless. A guard at the top screamed at him to start painting, but he couldn't move and soon the guard came after him. When he reached Fergus, he grabbed the drum of hot creosote and threw the contents over him.

Fortunately, Fergus wore a brimmed hat, and the hot coal tar missed his face as he ducked away, but when the sticky liquid hit his body, he could not move. The heat penetrated and blisters formed instantly, all he could do was hold on. Creosote blisters in normal conditions, but one drop on the skin in heightened temperatures caused the burn to erupt immediately. Fergus passed out.

Prisoners below watched and acted quickly. The burns could have been fatal. They lowered him to the ground and ran to the river to wash off what they could. The Japanese saw his injuries and promptly put him on a truck to the camp hospital at Chungkai. He touched hands with his friends and uttered a heartfelt farewell: 'We'll see each other soon.' But one PoW replied, 'You won't see us again; we'll all be dead,' and three weeks later they were.

Prison labour groups were divided into forces alphabetically.[4]

A – Burma, 14 May 1942	*Celebes Maru* sails to Victoria Point, Burma.
B – Borneo, July 1942	1,500 on *Ubi Maru* to Sandakan and marched to Kuching camp no.1.
C – Japan, 28 November 1942	Kobe (Kawasaki) or Naoetsu.
D – Thailand, 14 and 18 March 1943	5,000 (divided into four groups) Ban Pong.
E – Borneo 28 March 1943	1,000 SS *de Klerk* to Sandakan.
F – Thailand, 16–18 April 1943	7,000+ Many sick, unfit or unable were still sent. This force consisted of 3,444 British, 3,600 Australian. They were entrained on closed wagon trains for five days with very little food and water. Men marched 200 miles to Burma after Ban Pong.
G – Japan, 26 April 1943	*Kyokko Maru* Moji Japan Taisho sub-camp, camps at Osaka and Kobe.
H – Thailand, 5 – 17 May 1943	3,270 (incl. 1,979 British – majority were officers) and many from recent Java intake in February.
J – Japan, 16 May 1943	to Moji and Kobe
K & L, – Thailand, June and August 1943	365 RAMC medical soldiers to work in hospitals along the railway.

Chapter 20

Communication

L ooking back, letters and cable communications to and from home were expected via the armed forces postal service and the British Red Cross. The aim was to ensure troops received comforting words from family on a regular basis, and for them to receive news from their loved ones overseas. But this became a nightmare for the prisoners of war in the Far East and their families.

Throughout their three-month voyage, and when they arrived in Singapore, the 18th Division Forces postal unit managed all troop mail on board. Theirs was an incredibly important job keeping everyone connected with mail and cables. A detailed typed account of the unit's tasks provided a diary of administration and mail count of all items passing through their hands. The eight officers in charge were corporals and lance corporals, assisted by fifteen sappers.[1]

Earlier, embarking on the SS *Oronsay* at Avonmouth between 25 October and 28 October 1941, the unit prepared and left for overseas. A ship's Postal Censor Officer was appointed, in charge of the censor stamp. All unsorted censored mail was handed to the ESO and the ship sailed at 1500hrs. When they arrived in Halifax, Nova Scotia at 1000hrs on 9 November, the unit changed to the USS *Orizaba* and transferred approximately 20,000 items, in six bags, of sorted and censored mail by the ESO. British currency was exchanged for US dollars. For seven days, troop life on board ship was also diligently recorded, such as gun instruction, lectures, competitions and climate conditions. Reaching the British West Indies and Trinidad, records showed that ten bags of approximately 30,000 sorted and censored mail items were handed to the naval postal authorities, HMS *Benbow*. Items at 68 cents per letter were dispatched by air mail. The officer-in-charge and 18th Division Security Officers visited the cable and wireless office to arrange for the troops cables to be dispatched, 'Sans Origin' – without trace of origin. Their location was always to remain secret.

The postal unit also recorded events such as the convoy's approach to Cape Town on 9 December 1941, which mentioned 'the usual crossing the line ceremony was cancelled due to strict observation for submarines – however, a printed certificate for the occasion was still awarded to all ranks. Post Office work was brisk. Further cables were accepted for dispatch in Cape Town, at 0900hrs.' Troops relied heavily on this service.

During the period 22 December to 29 December, records showed the *Orizaba* arrived at Mombasa. Cable and mail were dispatched to the civil post office and a supply of airgraph forms were obtained for all units on board. Letter, parcel, air mail, airgraph, dispatch and cable services – all rates, sans origin – were available. The unit was advised of a change in destination to Bombay by the Signals Office. Troops on board were advised to use aerograph and cable facilities, and a daily collection of mail and cables was arranged. For some it would be their last. On 26 December around 30,000 items were taken to FPOD18 (Field Post Office Division) where they were date stamped, sorted, sealed and dispatched in eleven bags to London Inland Service (IS).

On 29 December, a postal coded wire advised USS *Mount Vernon* it would sail to Malaya. After a final collection of mail on the *Orizaba*, postal workers, Corporal Gillies, Sappers Randall and Carding were dispatched to start a new postal unit, FPO22, on board the *Mount Vernon*, with the 53rd Infantry Brigade. USS *Orizaba* left for Bombay with the rest of the original postal unit on board. They arrived in Bombay on 7 January 1942 and worked with the Indian Army Postal Service, dispatching mail from troops entrained at Divisional HQ, Ahmednagar, to London. Some of the unit was sent to Deolali, attached to the 9th Royal Northumberland Fusiliers. But in Ahmednagar, the officer-in-charge was informed on 9 January that the postal address had been changed. Officers highlighted this would cause confusion and delays when they left India and that the original address should prevail. Despite the strong opposition, Divisional HQ would not amend the order.

Inspections were made by the officer-in-charge to ensure that postal stocks were properly guarded, and instructions were received on 13 January to trace any incoming mail and cables for the 18th Division. A small number of incoming letters and cables were found and subsequently delivered.

Two days later, as re-embarkation took place on the *Wakefield* and *West Point*, the postal unit was divided between the two ships together with a supply of airmail postcards. They were under orders to keep communications open, while troops pondered the danger ahead. The unit remained open until 2300hrs, accepting approximately 4,000 cables and selling all postcards to the troops. The last airmail and ordinary mail dispatches were at 1100hrs on 21 January, as the convoy sailed from Bombay to Singapore. Through the voyage the units opened daily from 0900 to 1300hrs and 1500 to 1900hrs where both ships also handled heavy sales of postal orders, to transfer money home, and EFM (Expeditionary Force Message) cables.

Arriving in Singapore, amid aerial bombardment, the reunited units immediately set up and re-opened for business in Singapore, providing direct dispatch to London IS via BAPO4 (British Army Postal Office, 4). They applied for and obtained permission from Malaya Command HQ to use airmail letter folders to England. Until then the folders were for India only. They had become soldiers' lifelines. Twenty-one thousand folders were granted from the Stationery Depot and distributed to all 18th Division units. Arrangements were then made to reprint a further 200,000.

By the end of January, Singapore was in a state of siege, the causeway had been blown 'destroying connection with the mainland', as recorded in the postal unit's account. The corporal received instructions for future working methods. FPOs 20 and 21 were opened on land at the 54th and 55th Infantry Brigade HQs, and another at the Advanced Division HQ. At this time, Malayan stamps were issued and copies of the Unit War Diary, with all necessary forms, were handed over to GHQ, 2nd Echelon. Between 3 and 7 February a small amount of postal order cash, in multiple currencies, was transferred to the Command Paymaster at Sime Road where final cash accounts were reconciled and forwarded to the Assistant Director Army Postal Service (ADAPS) Middle East Forces (MEF), Cairo. A circular FPO service for delivery and collection of incoming and outgoing mail and cables was instituted daily.

Two vehicles had to be loaned as the unit's postal service vehicles did not arrive in Singapore, and supervision of all Indian Postal Service FPOs took place in the Bukit Timah area. The men, after the sergeant major's inspection were 'all found to be working excellently under extreme conditions'. The quantity of outgoing cables was high. It was further noted 'Japanese forces landed on 5 February. On 7 February Tanglin Barracks were heavily bombed. FPO Div. 18 was not hit; no casualties.'

Operations continued as normally as possible to 9 February when, on 10 February, instructions were given by 18th Division headquarters to vacate the barracks as frontline fighting drew closer. The unit fled with their equipment as the barracks came under heavy mortar fire. After several near misses, full evacuation was completed, without casualties. The 18th Division, including the postal unit, moved to a rubber plantation off the Tampines Road, at Payar Lebar, where instructions were received to destroy all forms and records. On 11 February, they were ordered to move again in an air raid and relocated to Newton Road, but the postal unit no longer functioned.

A Japanese raid also bombed the Rear Division HQ at 30 Newton Road and one man, Lance Corporal Rogers, was wounded in his left leg and abdomen. His injuries were not serious, but another, Sapper Logan was conveyed to hospital. He was hit in the left hand and later his forefinger was amputated. At 1430hrs that day, instructions were received from the camp commandant to move postal unit personnel to Colliers Quay. Three bags of ordinary mail and two bags of airmail were flown out through Singapore's civil post office, to Batavia, Java, but this would be the last as, under heavy air raids on 14 February, orders were given by Malaya Command HQ to destroy all incoming and outgoing mail. These instructions were followed by dumping all mailbags into the sea.

On 15 February, the Return Letter Office at the British Army Post Office was destroyed. By 1830hrs, news of the capitulation had been received with orders to lay down arms. Secret papers, postal codes, stocks of postal orders and stamps were burnt by the officer-in-charge. Date stamps, sealing presses, scales and all useful Post Office equipment were transported to the port and sunk. But the postal workers had tried valiantly to dispatch troops' mail right to the end.[2]

* * *

After capitulation, plenty of correspondence was sent by loved ones, but the Japanese failed to adhere to war conventions, and hoarded mail to and from Singapore. The last communications many families of the 18th Division received were from South Africa or India; not all letters and telegrams made it out of Singapore.

Stan's telegram was transmitted from Post Office 165 Singapore on 2 February 1942, addressed to Pat in Kenlor Road, Tooting, SW17. He wrote four sentences:

> *'Letter and Telegram received many thanks. Very happy to hear from you dearest. Am fit and well. You are more than ever in my thoughts at this time.'*

An officer had given Stan an airmail folder which he thought would arrive faster than a standard letter, but it was the last letter he wrote before the capitulation, which Pat did not receive for two months; his last letter of freedom where he glossed over the life-threatening terrors and preferred to be matter of fact, telling his fiancée about his army friend and his washing hanging on the line. He hoped the war would 'end soon and he could get back home'.

Stan wrote this at Payar Labar. Most soldiers had no wish to cause alarm at home and made their situation sound okay. But ceasefire, capture or death were all on the horizon. For security, some soldiers' letters were destroyed before the capitulation, but Stan's impartial airmail folder survived. News of survivors after capitulation was non-existent and this, his last communication, was one Pat clung to, not knowing if he was dead or alive.

Mail from England stopped, and Stan had no way of knowing how much his family knew, or the anguish they suffered. To them he was 'missing in action'. Family and friends of many tried a multitude of ways to obtain information. Pat's brother, who was in the RAF, used his resources in the Middle East and sent her a telegram on 7 May 1942: 'In touch with Cairo about Stan. Take Time. Will wire or signal immediately. Don't Worry. Keep Smiling. Harry Lawrence.'

His message pre-dated any official news and advice to families regarding the Singapore operation and the missing troops. Many months passed as relatives' desperation increased. Official reports from the War Office, all information and news from the Far East, was blocked.

A lengthy TEN months after capitulation, the same questions were being asked. But some news was trickling through. British journalist Garry Allighan, on 31 December 1942, published another article: *No __Official__ News is Good News.* Forty-seven-year-old Allighan had a popular daily column, *Question Time in the Mess,* which had become a centre point for many families searching for information about their loved ones.

'*Reported missing*' are the two words which are keeping thousands of service men's families poised tremulously on the watershed that divides hope from fear.'

Via the War Office, he consolidated information where the greatest number of reported missing was in Singapore, Malaya and Java. He wrote:

> Far easier for a man to have been cut off from his own comrades, but to have escaped the enemy, than for worse to have befallen him. Those two facts must satisfy, for the time being, the hundreds of wives and mothers who have written, asking me to print the names of their husbands and sons 'reported missing' in the Far East in the hope that some comrade may have definite news of them.

Allighan had names of missing men – too many to include in his report. Instead, his advice was to write to the War Office Casualty Branch, Bluecoat School, Liverpool or the RAF Records C7 section in Gloucestershire, to ensure no (bad) news was yet in hand. For the North African campaign, he had revealed names of casualties adding, 'almost invariably received by these (War) offices within four days of their notification to Records in Cairo'. He assumed a similar system was available for Malaya.

A serviceman's wife had written: 'There must be thousands like myself hoping and praying for news. I have never given up hope because that is precisely the enemy's aim.'

Allighan reported:

> I am informed by the Casualties Branch of the War Office that the position respecting British prisoners of war in Malaya is now a little more encouraging, and next of kin are being informed immediately names are received in this country. No list of prisoners has yet been received from Java and, while there is nothing to indicate that they are not being well looked after, the War Office hope soon to be in possession of their names.

He attempted to provide answers for many questions. One mother asked: 'How could he be "presumed dead" when the public were not being given any names?' Allighan offered:

> Nothing had been received from Tokyo, and the private effects of airmen cannot be officially released until death has occurred once conclusive evidence is received. If such evidence is not received within six months of the date on which the airman was reported missing, the Air Ministry will presume death for official purposes. In some cases, circumstance may make the period slightly longer than six months.

Lack of communication from the Japanese left families in Britain not only in emotional turmoil but also in financial need. Where were their soldiers? What was happening? Why can't they be freed? Trying to obtain government answers to their pleading questions created havoc for many. Finally, in January 1943, more reports filtered through. But it was still several months before official news of Stan reached his mother.

* * *

In Singapore, mail from home was collected by the UK Red Cross and religious orders in Catholic countries before reaching Malaya – some went via Russia. But this was irregular, as many men had not received word from home since they left England at the end of October 1941. Conversely, mail sent by captives to Britain was often received two years out of date. One explanation for the failure was due to German bombings of mail carriers, as in the case of a British Overseas Airways Corporation (BOAC) flying boat in July 1943. Over 30,000 items of troops' correspondence plummeted into the Atlantic off the coast of Ireland. It was deemed 'lost at sea'.[3]

One can imagine the acute worry of families having to wait for news with no communication from their soldier. Eventually, PoWs were permitted to send a small pro-forma postcard, but most families did not know their whereabouts until end December 1942, despite a clandestine means of broadcast messaging developed in the Middle East at the beginning of 1942.

The PoWs and families were all victims of mail confiscation and confusion by the Japanese. On 22 January 1943, a request was made to allow more facilities for writing home, but the Japanese refused.

Changi inmates were exuberant in March 1943 – a consignment of mail arrived! The receipt of news brought a different perspective – it was a huge development, but hard to believe the mail had taken eight months to arrive, most had been written in July 1942. The same month, the prisoners received disturbing rumours their reply postcards never left Changi Gaol.

Meanwhile, officers realised wireless messages were reaching folks at home as cloaked references to clandestine broadcasts were made. Brave signalmen risked their lives in rigging up secret radio signal systems. But, in June, a frustrated Horner wrote in his diary, from up-country. 'The canaries rarely sing up here, which is maddening.'

When batches of letters arrived in November 1943, Horner received six! However, they were dated September and October 1942, more than a year had passed. Knowing that only two paltry postcards might be received by their families, the prisoners' clandestine radio messages were even more important, no matter how short.

Other captives told of several bags of letters being delivered to Changi. But a couple of PoWs were caught stealing at the docks and as well as being beaten and punished, the Japanese burnt all the bags of letters.[4] Punishment for all. They were more than two years old; it was inconceivable a delivery of letters would take that long. Most agreed that ancient messengers on horses were faster!

*   *   *

Colonel Toosey of the 135th Regiment, up-country, distributed pre-formatted postcards enabling prisoners to at least say they were alive. Their fabricated words were limited and had to be written in pencil, but still each short message was vetted or censored by the Japanese. Nobody could mention their work, their bad treatment, where they were captured or any detail of their incarceration – only that they were well. The Japanese couldn't lose face.

Some risked a hidden message, such as Fergus whose shorthand squiggles and dots appeared as scratch marks. The censors didn't notice and when the postcard arrived in 1943 his mother, Beatrice, dismissed it as fake.

'That's not his signature,' she said.

Distraught she went to bed, convinced her son was killed in action.

Ten minutes later she screamed, 'He's alive!' Subliminally, she had recognised the imbedded message of an 'st' loop and the upward stroke for 'l' – 'still', with consonant strokes for 'k' 'n' 'b' 'r'. She was a proficient secretary and Fergus's father, Gordon, had been a journalist, inspiring him to learn shorthand and typing in London. The course had paid off because now she recognised Fergus's scratch marks as Pitman's New Era Shorthand. Miraculous relief overwhelmed his parents as they continued to translate the short message, 'Kanburi,' and that he *was* 'still smiling!'

Journalists badgered authorities for 'news of our boys?' It was said that 24-hour radio monitoring services in neutral countries were being maintained to translate Japanese broadcasts. Prisoner lists were read occasionally, and relatives were informed.

Postal authorities confirmed letters could take six months, via a Murmansk convoy or the Mediterranean through neutral Russia, the nearest country to Japan. However, thousands had already reached Tokyo and would be sent to PoW camps. Thirty-two thousand letters from camps in Japan, Formosa, Hong Kong, Shanghai, Korea, Siam and Malaya had reached Britain, but 27,000 were lost in the Eire plane crash. Of the greater loss, frustrated journalists asked: 'Why are we only just beginning to hear?'[5]

The postal official said the Japanese had undertaken to open a mail service in June 1942, but they did not until January 1943. They ignored Hague and Geneva Convention rules. Officials concluded that families should hope and keep on writing, 'He is most likely safe and well,' was the blanket reply.

* * *

Some families unwittingly received news from the British government via amateur spies, according to PoW and radar operator, Reuben Kandler, who met one in French Indo-China. He was known as 'Sparks'.

Kandler had trained in coastal radar – a rapidly developing top-secret technology – and left the UK from Liverpool on the *Dominion Monarch*, September 1941. As a young radar operator, he also encountered U-boat threats, a trip to Cape Town and electric storms across the Indian Ocean. He knew little about events in Asia, except for shocking Japanese atrocities against China, known as 'the Rape of Nanking'.

He was based at Military HQ Fort Canning and Changi barracks from November 1941. However, when Japanese forces attacked down the Malay Peninsula, the Changi Naval Base became strategically vital and Reuben and his team were dispatched to southern Malaya. Their task was to warn of approaching enemy aircraft, sightings of which they transmitted to Allied gun positions. As Japanese bombing raids increased during January 1942, the only transmission facility on the peninsula was in jeopardy and they were ordered back to the island. But by the end of January, Changi Naval Base was also in danger as Japanese forces surged forward.

With Churchill's agreement, it was determined this strategic British resource should not fall under enemy control and the base was demolished by the army, who wrecked fuel tanks, cranes, workshops and the power station. Reuben and his group were moved to Anson Road football stadium by Keppel Harbour to keep sea lanes open for escaping civilians. After the long battle, on 15 February he was ordered to destroy all secret documents and technical equipment on command of General Percival: the official war signal for imminent surrender.

After capture, he was detained in gaol then put on the *Nisshu Maru*, a dilapidated hell ship coal carrier, to Saigon,[6] as one of the first parties of 1,125 PoWs sent as dock workers. There, Reuben and his fellow PoWs secretly interacted with Sparks (aka Emile Lienard), in the French Indo-China capital, known as the 'Paris of the Orient'.

Lienard, from northern France, was an expert on electricity and water supply systems and the Japanese relied heavily on his knowledge. Consequently, he was granted free rein of the city. During his day-to-day tasks around the prisoners' dockyard compound, he realised he could help them, but he had to take care, as his life was at risk. He started documenting European PoWs and by May 1942, had a roll of 700 names and addresses of

British prisoners and their next of kin. The list was secretly transferred to London's War Office in the lining of a coat.

Between PoWs, Sparks' cunning and a spy network, three microscopic photos were formed and sewn into the hem of a fur coat worn by a Swiss diplomat's wife. The couple could travel freely during the war to neutral Switzerland, where the microfilm was intercepted, enlarged, and secretly sent to London, possibly in microdot form.[7] By September 1942, the information was confirmed and letters were sent to the many families whose loved ones appeared on the list, revealing only that they were held captive in Japanese hands. The news was harsh, but they were alive. The prisoners' location remained secret to avoid repercussions, and to keep the spy network open.

* * *

Stan was not part of the dockworkers' party, but it took more than fifteen months for his mother to know he was safe. Emma Moore heard that her son was in a Malayan camp. Three other ex-Tooting Co-op colleagues of Stan's were also mentioned in the *Mitcham News & Mercury* article she published: George Appleton, Charlie Brooks and Stan Fitsch. All had survived the seventeen-day battle. Their good news and information gave hope to others, as more civilian reports trickled through. But it was bitter-sweet as their sons were captives – prisoners of war under the Imperial Japanese.

Stan's mother also notified Pat, his fiancée, in a telegram to her workplace. It simply said, 'Stan Safe.'[8]

Chapter 21

Summer 1943 – Stan's Humiliation

Thinking of his family at home and his determination to survive, Stan continued to avoid punishment by keeping his head down, but he was not exempt.

The Japanese guards, or in our case Korean, were very unpredictable if you had occasion to talk with them. You'd maybe have a joke one day – the next day you could have the same joke and they'd whack you around the face. It was like a real hard punch, so you didn't quite know how to take them. If you had any sense, you kept a low profile.

On one occasion when I was still considered a dispatch rider, but I only had a pushbike instead of a motorbike, I had to ride from one camp to another, in the same division, to deliver various documents. Still under our administration, I had to ride through an area of no-man's land which was guarded, in this case, by a Sikh. I delivered the necessary to HQ, to our colonel, and on the way back I just nodded to the Sikh guard. He shouted at me to get off my bike and I had to bow to him. It was one of the most humiliating things I had to do while I was there. Anyway, I got on my bike and rode off saying so and so to you! Many of us came upon these incidents. It was one of those things you had to live with I'm afraid, if you can call it living.

The Korean and Sikh guards had to be saluted despite their pecking order being way below the Japanese guards. Retaliation was brutal; a hard slap to the face or worse a punch; a rifle butt in the core, or a boot.

'We'd find out soon enough if we forgot to salute, or just didn't see them coming.'

Japan had occupied Korea for more than thirty years and Korean men were recruited into the Japanese military, but not trusted as good soldiers. However, they still became prison guards. The Koreans had been kicked around for years and now they handed out the same treatment to PoWs. There was no understanding or empathy.

Their 'salute' was a forward bow from the waist. The stiff greeting in Eastern circles was long established but for Westerners it was now an expectation to show respect to their captors, and every guard wanted to humiliate PoWs. But a guard who did not receive the obligatory bow was worse. Their mishap was followed by a ferocious kicking and beating. Most PoWs had an experience of this nature.[1]

A veteran Korean guard later said: 'the Japanese soldier and the pigeon are at the bottom of the heap' indicating the Korean soldiers were ill-treated by their own hierarchy. Consequently, this treatment filtered to the lowest level who were, in their eyes, the prisoners, unworthy of civil treatment.[2]

* * *

As well as observing brutal beatings, and the physique of others, Stan's hunger was rarely assuaged; he too was losing weight.

The main topic of conversation when we were in the prison camp was food: what we were going to eat when we got home and the first thing we'd eat. When it came around to evening mealtime, we lined up to collect our spoonful of rice, and possibly fried rice – shaped like a Cornish pasty, with nothing in it or maybe a bit of fish, you never knew. Perhaps a watery vegetable soup made from kangkong like grass. It filled you up for an hour but after that you were bloomin' hungry again.

Those who survived walked about like skeletons. Some of the prisoners who couldn't go out to work, such as disabled people with no limbs – that sort of thing – used to keep a garden patch going. Of course, I don't know where they scrounged the seeds or plants from, but obviously they did, it was one of the main things of a PoW's life, to scrounge what you could. They had their own little garden, tomatoes and things like that and of course you needed manure, and all the urine that was passed was saved and put on the company garden. On one occasion a fellow stole a bucket of urine for his own garden. He was caught and punished for it, not by the Japanese but by our own administration.

Survival was the main thing. You even, more or less, had to nail down your own belongings or they would be stolen by some of the other inmates. I was fortunate I had no belongings at all, so I couldn't be robbed.

Stan laughed.

*   *   *

Stan learned ingenious ways to recycle and utilise scraps. It was a way of life, and like the sandals he made for himself and others, 'industries' in useful commodities started to spring up.

Europeans who had lived and worked in Asia, before Malaya fell to the Japanese, came from volunteer forces. A long tradition existed in the British Empire, stemming from the Crimean and Boer wars, which encouraged low-paid employment for the experience of a different culture and to learn a new language. They were doctors, religious ministers, commercial executives, miners and planters on rubber plantations. North-west Malaysia had grown rich from the tin that lured colonial mining companies, which in turn attracted banks and bureaucrats. Now, as prisoners they engaged with locals in their own language, through wire fences, and gained sympathy for their plight.

One was John Clemetson, a captain of Federated Malay States Volunteer Force (FMSVF), and a former employee of Kinta Electrical Distribution Company, a subsidiary of British GEC, Ipoh. When Malaya was invaded, Clemetson's wife and young son left on one of the last vessels heading for Freemantle, Western Australia, leaving him behind to begin life in captivity. He was keen to find an activity to keep himself and troops busy while offering some practical benefit, and soon started a repair and shoemaking group. Prisoners' feet were particularly vulnerable from the foot rot, when cuts to the feet of malnourished or sick men were difficult to heal. Minor injuries often led to life-threatening ulcers.

Clemetson's team used scraps of leather, bits of old boots, belts, lino, kit bags and tyres to patch footwear. Wooden clogs were also made, and Changi Gaol's corridors echoed with the sound of clip-clopping feet. This aided those with failing eyesight, as they began to recognise who approached by certain footfalls.

Planters had extensive knowledge about the lifecycle of a rubber tree and Duncan Paterson, also FMSVF from Ipoh, was asked to find supplies of rubber. In peace times the commodity price in world markets was managed, now the lack of supply was affecting world trade. It was a concern, but there was nothing they could do. Instead, they shared their practical knowledge to help prison life.

Before capitulation, rubber supplies were formed in large sheets, now these were hoarded by the Japanese and inaccessible. The PoWs set about using their rubber tapping skills but could only manage half a pint each day. Clearly the trees in Changi were unsuitable for large amounts of latex. They added other substances to their meagre collection – anything they could find – soot, sand, sawdust, hair clippings and coconut fibres were used to make footwear. It was painstaking, but after five months they discovered that red laterite clay, which is soft when dug up, hardened on contact with the atmosphere and mixed with latex became an effective coagulant and filler. With this new advance in the captive's footwear, the group presented a rubber sole to Lieutenant Colonel E.B. Holmes, who agreed they could continue. The first 'factory' in an old building in Changi Village opened in October 1942. However, that soon collapsed, and they moved to another workshop built with debris from the first. It became known as Changi Industries Inc. All staff – thirteen 'tappers' and ten other workers – were volunteers classed as 'unable or unfit to work' on Japanese construction projects and were not sent 'up-country'.

They used latex for other items such as covers for old cricket balls and pliable rubber to repair or make new pairs of false teeth. Badly disfigured profiles (from beatings) were reset, and life became bearable as PoWs looked better and found they could eat food properly. Other experiments involved bad eggs to make boot polish and soap from palm oil. In 1944, the Japanese agreed to give John Clemetson and Changi Industries the hoarded rubber sheets to produce durable shoes. By the end of the war, they had made a total of 21,736 shoes and repaired – with their own concoction of latex – nearly 21,000. The quality of work was so good that Japanese guards brought their own footwear to be repaired.[3]

While the FMSVF was commendable in prison camps, military officers, in hindsight, thought such expertise should have been shared earlier, when the Japanese invasion started. By blending abilities into one force – local intelligence, geographical knowledge and important language skills – they would have been at the heart of the CRE and CRA defence battalions as they went into battle. With their experience, guidance and know-how, the outcome might have been entirely different for Changi, the original camp.[4]

Boots were confiscated if the prisoners no longer worked on the railway, causing them to suffer more from trench foot. Doctors advised the use of rags as bandages, first soaking them in fat from the cookhouse to become waterproof, to prevent water from penetrating their sores. The men then walked on their heels with toes pointing up, aided by two bamboo sticks.

*　*　*

Kanburi wasn't as bad as the other camps in Thailand. The further north along the railway route, the worse the food and conditions became.[5] Food and work went together; the more you worked the more you were fed – if you couldn't work, you received little sustenance. The conditions were abominable; dysentery, diphtheria and malaria were the main cause of illness. Fifty to sixty thousand PoW troops were in the country and they were dying at the rate of six to eight each day. H Force had vaccinations, but not all troops received these.

The officers moved on to another station, Tarsao, and by the afternoon had orders to march to Tonchan, then they were dumped in a field. They camped al fresco, trying to sleep amid the threat of snakes, scorpions and ants. Sleep was difficult but they rested. The next morning, they cleared jungle undergrowth and erected tents.

Horner was allocated to 'working fatigues', carting and felling trees in the jungle. This was not what they were told – as officers, they were supposed to supervise. The monsoon arrived and for three days it rained. With eighteen men in one small tent, the road under water and ankle-deep in mud, it was almost impossible to keep dry. Their routine was: Breakfast 0730; Parade 0800; work until 1230 or 1300 for lunch; 1500 work, supper at 1900, parade and roll call at 2000hrs. Wearing uncomfortable wet clothes all day until roll call just added to the misery.

They were at their lowest ebb, with some ready to give up. Dutch prisoners gave in quickly, their death rate was higher. Suffering from scrapes and injuries in terrible conditions, disease, sweat and mud for twelve hours every day affected their inner resolve. It was a downward spiral. There was no evacuation of the sick or contagious who walked around with dysentery or other diseases. The PoWs had to put up with continuous swamp conditions from the rain. A small stream ran through their camp – it was the only place to wash minimal clothing and themselves.

Then disaster happened with an outbreak of cholera in Tarsao camp upstream; a Japanese and three British were affected. Tarsao contained a collection of huts, overseen by brutal Japanese NCOs.[6] Three coolie camps surrounded theirs, where deadly cholera had already affected fifty Tamil coolies who had used the contaminated stream. PoWs were prohibited from bathing or going elsewhere, and cholera struck swiftly with no leniency. It didn't take officers long to realise that F Force's constant marching was, in effect, to cull unwanted prisoners. Their numbers were fading fast.

Another party officer, Colonel Knights, of 4th Royal Norfolks, reached camp Tarsao in advance of ill-fated F Force to build a better camp. He hadn't said what was to come, to keep up their failing spirits. The officers' party proceeded in the rain in darkness, through threatening, almost impenetrable, jungle. They negotiated slimy potholes and ridges and held hands in a human chain; if one person fell, the line halted until he was on his feet again. This angered the Japanese guards, but then British solidarity reigned.

> We stopped at Tonchan (139km) south for 'yasume'. Hot sweet tea was given to us by camp gunners. Several camps in this area were well built with almost luxurious quarters for Japanese engineers. They had beds with raffia matting. IJA uniforms were worn by engineers who were waited on by Korean servants; Tamils in one camp, British gunners in another.

The camps varied but inevitably the weather of the south-west monsoon period April–October played a large part. Knights' group did not stay long at Tarsao. The next day they travelled further from civilian life, until they reached the structure being built in the distance – the Wampo Viaduct. Here workers died from many illnesses, including malaria which lead to blackwater fever. Some fell into the gorge after they were beaten with sticks by the guards – brutally attacked and left to roll into the ravine – murdered. The viaduct was mostly built by Australian PoWs, but their blood was on the hands of its developers, the engineers. For every railway sleeper laid, a prisoner would die.[7]

* * *

As part of a rural convoy, with pigs on a rustic cart, Fergus's creosote-injured body was placed on a low-loader and taken to Chungkai hospital camp.

His burns started to heal once he was transferred to a hospital hut. His blisters were drained, and powder applied to help repair the skin. Within two weeks he was ready to work, but now he was allocated to British Medical Officers. He worked in the Ulcer Hut with nasty infections caused by a mere scratch or cut that had turned septic. If the wounds were not cleaned quickly, bacteria would eat the skin, fat and muscle. Some limbs were amputated because of this; the pain was considered preferable to alternative suffering or certain death. Chungkai's operating theatre was made of bamboo and mosquito netting, and surgeons such as Senior Medical Officer Colonel (Weary) Dunlop and Captain Jacob Markowitz performed operations.[8]

Next, Fergus had the sobering task of preparing corpses for burial. In a small 10ft x 8ft hut, he felt he could escape the rain. It was one of Fergus's methods of self-preservation, despite the harrowing job of sewing bodies into sacks for burial. The hut was always dry, even when the rest of Chungkai was flooded. The people he put into sacks had suffered from malaria or malnutrition. In his opinion, he managed to avoid malaria by making his own preventative tent – a primitive bivouac. Before his job in the morgue, he found a blanket which he'd sewn into a sleeping bag with a buttoned flap at the top. Despite getting uncomfortably hot and sweaty, he believed his resourcefulness protected him from mosquitos and their bites.

After sewing burial sacks, Fergus mended clothes for others. He patched and repaired, and soon his needlework skills started to earn him a little cash. It was during this time he came across an old friend from home, Dutchman Frans Bakker, once his sister's erstwhile suitor. The friends set up a mending and washing service and helped each other whenever one was ill. Their friendship was good, and they were great business partners.

Fergus's hand had recovered. He was now known for his magic by the guards at Chungkai. Tomimoto, a new friendly guard and a magician himself appreciated his skills to his detriment. They had exchanged different tricks and cigarettes or food, but Tomimoto had fraternised with the enemy. Drunk guards shouted at him, and he tried to reason, but they brutally attacked him with a bayonet. The next day, another guard told Fergus that Tomimoto was dead; killed because he had spoken to a prisoner to discuss magic. The warning was heeded by all prisoners.

*   *   *

The concert party performed again in Chungkai. Everyone looked forward to the productions. Men would write a small note with their name to put on a mat in the theatre. There were no chairs, but if it had been 'booked in advance' the space reservation was respected by all concerned. The audience numbered 300–400. The front row was kept for amputee prisoners.

During one show, a snake got into the back of the concert hut causing panic. People at the front thought the Japanese had come to kill them and scrambled to escape, clambering over each other in the rush. The performers called for calm, but several died. The Red Caps (the captive British Royal Army's military police) came to clear up the next day, removing bodies and collecting the nine sacks of left clothing. In Fergus's opinion, the heavy-set Red Caps military police PoWs were fed far better than anyone else and liked to throw their weight about, rather like the Gestapo.

Shortly after, a mound was built at Chungkai for the audience to watch performances. The concert party put together a full orchestra, but Fergus was shipped out again before another performance. His sojourn at Chungkai ended abruptly when he found himself in a large group of prisoners on metal train trucks going back down the line. This time beyond Ban Pong to Non (Nong) Pladuk, again under the command of Lieutenant Colonel Philip Toosey, who had been in charge at Kanburi and the bridges over the Khwaes.

* * *

In July 1943, nine prisoners succeeded in an escape from Songkurai camp, along with an Indian fisherman. They cut a path beyond the cholera crematorium, where the Japanese guards would never go and travelled 4 kilometres each day hoping to reach the west coast of Burma. The escape party diminished, however, when one died within a month, and four others by mid-August, leaving four officers and the fisherman. The diminished group met two Burmese hunters, who took them to a Burmese kampong. It is possible the head of the village reported them for monetary reward, as the four PoWs were arrested on 21 August and taken to Japanese headquarters at Ye. The Indian fisherman, Nur Mahommed, was taken out of the group and possibly exonerated, but details of his demise do not exist.

On 5 September, the prisoners went to Moulmein under Kempei tai Police guard. They were handcuffed in pairs and returned to camp and used as examples not to escape. After brutal interrogation at Songkurai, the four were slated for execution. But a court martial held at Raffles in Singapore gave them eight to nine years' hard labour. The men who died were Brown, *Feathers, Wilkie, Robinson and Jones. The four survivors were Machado, Anker, Bradley and Moffatt. James Bradley, years later told his story and went on to receive the MBE.[9]

Chapter 22

Autumn 1943 and the Year Ahead

Death continued to drastically reduce all PoW work forces but debilitating *supido* (speedo) did not end until 19 October 1943. The 'impossible' achievement was monumental in its time. As Japan celebrated completion of the Siam–Burma railway, their engineers were congratulated, but surviving prisoners showed little jubilance for this bitter-sweet moment. They no longer slaved under untenable conditions, but disease, bad treatment and losing friends was a cruel waste of life. They had nothing to celebrate. Their predicament far from home was unbelievable. As the inaugural train, festooned with coloured bunting and carrying Japanese generals, steamed through Burma, from Kanchanaburi to Thanbyuzayat on 23 October, British troops could only think of those same fateful October days when they left Liverpool docks, two years before.

As they left Songkurai, the British troops looked back at the vast wooden structure where they had slavishly toiled. Its span seemed to fill the horizon across the Khwae, bank to bank. Prayers for their future and for those who lost their lives were said as they stoically embarked on yet another stage of uncertainty. The sacrifice of men who died in the brutal campaign of enforced hard labour and the onset of life-threatening diseases, was uppermost in their minds. Cholera was everywhere and blamed on coolies' unhygienic methods, as they moved from camp to camp. PoWs had to lay and work beside them, and the disease quickly took its victims; some went to bed well, vomited in the night and died the following evening, but slowly the losses started to decline.

*　　*　　*

Stan witnessed the return of survivors during the winter months of 1943:

A number of parties started drifting back to Changi, from up-country in their one or two-hundreds, and they were in a hell of a state,

including our old sergeant major, who came back looking like a tramp!
It was very unusual for him and it took about a week before he was out
on parade with all his spit and polish again. Talk about never say die!

Many were part of Force H6 who left Stan's unit May 1943, the latter *officers'*
march.[1] With no news of prior first-hand accounts, he was astounded by their
arduous ordeal. Prisoners from all nationalities, and civilian coolies, were
ordered to trek for miles to undertake dangerous and inhumane work. The so-
called move to a better 'resort' had been a horrendous nightmare as they were
forced to march between camps to construct the railway. The Death Camps, as
they were known, were controlled by inscrutable two-faced guards who showed
traits of savagery and irrational anger. If a prisoner was killed by a guard, the
same guard would lay flowers on the prisoner's grave. It was then Stan also
heard a shocking account of men being beheaded simply for using a radio.

*   *   *

The practice of obtaining information through clandestine methods relieved
prisoners' boredom. Proficient signals officers had set about making secret
radios from the most basic of means – perhaps an unlikely relic of schoolboy
comics, such as *Boy's Own*, where fundamental instructions on construction
of crystal radio sets and earphones was useful. Copper wires, tubes and
batteries were obtained to make a receiver when prisoners, ordered to work on
vehicles, used every opportunity to collect essential parts. Reliable selected
men convened in the dead of night in a remote area – normally the latrines –
where the secret radio was hidden. Two or three men silently listened to the
news, or whatever they could tune into. One PoW was always on lookout
duty for guards, but fearing cholera, the guards never went there. A small
number of officers oversaw, and confidently helped deter any suspicions of
hidden devices from the Japanese. Unfortunately, however, their cover was
not always successful, and the senior officer took the blame. He and his group
of operators were taken for punishment but often never returned.

Radio sets were disguised from the Japanese in many ways: inside walls
or under beds, inside bunkbed framework, walking sticks, broom heads and
poles, or buried in tins underground. A stethoscope contraption was used

to listen in. Word was sometimes on 'the pipe' or by 'the old lady', but 'the canaries are singing' was the usual surreptitious whisper around the camp. When working parties were transported by rail some radios even made it to those areas, one 'in a tin of bully beef'.

A makeshift coffee tin was also used for a primitive crystal set. Broadcasts from New Delhi's 'All India Radio' could be heard via the 4in x 9in tin with a false top. If opened, it appeared to contain groundnuts. The device remained hidden for a year, but its owner was eventually caught. He was beaten, made to stand to attention in 100 degrees heat for two days then repeatedly ordered to swing a sledgehammer on to a block of wood. As news of the discovery and his punishment percolated through, others were defiant and undeterred. Officers and nominated listeners simply became more vigilant and careful in their interception and delivery of news. Nothing could be discussed out loud. If Japanese guards had the slightest whiff of captives exchanging outside information, they immediately suspected an illicit source. Even if based on a poor translation, a hunt would ensue to find the secret radio. Ultimately, a period of two weeks was considered safe to leak news; they said they'd heard it from a local farmer, or a Singaporean. Secrecy was hard to maintain, especially when alarming reports came through such as the raid on Dieppe, the year before, where many died. Short reports of truthful news on 'the griff', were enough to keep the men hopeful for a positive outcome. They never wrote anything down.

However, traitors were in their midst. This came mainly because of the vital secrecy of senior officers and their select group of radio builders and trusted listeners – not always from the same hut. Other prisoners were suspicious of their clandestine activities in the dead of night, when diluted radio reports were passed to only those 'in the know' to keep new information from the enemy. It was a mystery as to who spilled the beans. Was it a bribed prisoner? Senior officers were very aware of guard searches and swiftly alerted their teams to deftly convince the Japanese command there were no hidden devices.

* * *

Those who returned were almost glad to be back in the constant treadmill of Changi repetitiveness. Stan was glad not to have experienced such degradation and hoped his friends would also soon return. Hunger and hopelessness for their plight meant he tried not to think too much of the future, maintaining a goal to reach by the end of each day. This was a natural coping mechanism for some; brain numbness was safe and less suicidal.

One could say the menial orders of Japanese officers helped expand the numbness, despite seeming ridiculous. One such order insisted prisoners catch twenty flies each per day. The absurd instruction was just another insult to their self-esteem. The flies were counted and delivered to a Japanese officer by a lieutenant colonel. Guards validated this by declaring that flies spread dysentery, but an order from Tokyo for better hygiene and modern chemical controls was the reality. The island's government needed to tackle the death rate, for everyone's sake, but scientific controls were not materialising.

Stan observed:

It was hard for locals to find anything to eat. Our cookhouse was near the perimeter fence where a drain ran out to the other side and the natives could get down in the gully. When our cookhouse chaps would do the necessary washing up of cooking utensils, a certain amount of rice grains would be washed down through the open drains and out towards the sea. But the natives used to congregate outside and collect the grains of rice [and any other scraps] *to add to their diet.*

It was hard to see their suffering, perhaps more than the prisoners. In October 1943, reports were received of 1,700 deaths in F Force – many were 18th Division which had consisted of 7,000 men. In H Force there were over 800 deaths out of 3,400; proportionally this was a sad match. Adding to the woes, up-country, rations could not be delivered as the Khwae Noi was dry and barges could not get through.[2]

At a major turning point in the war, Stan noted:

Through the grapevine we learned the Italians had thrown in the towel. Strangely enough, at that particular time there was one of their submarines in Keppel Harbour. It had been stripped out of all its internal unnecessary bits and pieces, like armaments, and was loaded with raw rubber from Malaya. Of course, when the Italians packed it in, the Japs took the crew off and put on their own and sent the submarine crew to our camp. It was rather strange to see these fellows arrive, all in their brilliant dhoby whites and we, all looking such a scruffy mob. But we didn't give them much sympathy, I am afraid.

The Italian PoWs were quarantined at Sime Road. At first the other prisoners were not allowed near them, but eventually the officers were turned loose within the confines of Changi. They'd had a choice and joined the Allies when they obeyed their sovereign, instead of Hitler, Mussolini or Tojo. It took a while to accept they had switched, but mistrust broke down quickly. Most were shy and behaved with prudence. To their credit, none of the Italian submarine crew avoided imprisonment by opting to fight with the Japanese. For some PoWs, it was astonishing to think that rival factions could be convivial, but most British at Sime Road accepted the Italian officers as part of an Allied PoW brotherhood. They happily accepted the newcomers and even enjoyed jokes and glamorous tales of their time in Paris, a few months earlier, including frivolous private photographs.[3]

Part of H Force had returned to Sime Road Camp, and comparative luxury, by 26 November. The gruelling journey took five days with the men, once again, tightly packed in closed-goods trucks. The lucky ones found a charpoy (camp bed), a joy after months of chungs (bamboo slats) or just hard ground. Skin conditions – scabies – improved, and minor doses of malaria were tackled with quinine.

The men returning all had awful stories to tell. Horner had gone as far as camp Konkuita, tree felling. At one point in a limestone cutting, in scorching temperatures from 1030hrs to 1600hrs, the heat and glare from the stone was unbearable. He'd lost count of the times his body had been beaten for taking a rest; his left leg had swollen like a balloon due to long periods of standing and walking with tropical ulcers. As captain with responsibility and examples to set, he was stoic but tired and retained a gracious attitude, despite learning that officers of H Force would not receive pay for two months.

'It won't last forever and one day we'll sit back and laugh about it', a phrase they used to bolster their hopes in anticipation of a better life.

Stan watched as more bedraggled men returned. One wrote:

> At Sime Road it was surprising to see HQ personnel were actually
> the fittest of the F & H Force survivors. They had been sent in
> advance to the camp and after only four days of civilisation the
> change was amazing. These officers were so clean and well-shaven;
> they had polished footwear, clean slacks, shorts and shirts, and
> shiny badges of rank.[4]

As commanders emerged from the railway truck journey, it was hard for them
to hand over the last men in their groups. Their 'charges' were in tatters with
dirty, overgrown beards and long hair. Most of the returning men were sent to a
dry, well-lit wooden hut, where the officers apologised for sparse conditions. But
the men cared less; this was luxury compared to what they'd endured. Bedrolls
were thrown on to concrete floors and they slept at length. It was probably the
best sleep of their lives. Overwhelming relief helped in putting memories of
the railway far behind – it was unlikely they would ever return to the jungle's
humidity, the odour of human decay and servile feelings of hopelessness. The
last decent washing facility for the men had been at Ban Pong in April. Now a
welcome shave, shower and wash of clothes – to remove bugs, lice and dirt from
everywhere – left them refreshed; their matted hair was shaved, and their new
polished appearance made past months seem like a bad dream.

But it was real. Their days had been laden with disease and illness such
as blackwater fever,[5] pellagra[6] and trench foot.

The saddest news for Stan came in December 1943 from returning PoWs,
when he heard that his best friend Gordon was dead.

They said Gordon died at Songkurai in August (d.o.d. 13 August 1943)
while working on the bridge over the Khwae, from dysentry. Stan was
devastated to lose him. Reflections of happier times in Knutsford UK,
their voyage, Cape Town and the beach at Muizenberg in South Africa –
swimming, chocolate, strawberries and cream – were uppermost in his mind.
Captain Horner also later lamented his death. Stan's other pal, Sid Cowling,
succumbed in October. Both had been part of F Force.

* * *

By January, the remainder of H Force had returned from Thailand. The death toll in the officers' group reached 885. F Force was still in the process of returning either to Bangkok or another camp in Singapore, but the reported figure of more than 3,300 casualties was shocking. Deaths from cholera, beriberi, malnutrition and starvation were eight to twelve per day. Many of Stan's friends in the ill-fated 18th Division were part of this high proportion. The 18th Division Provost Company (British Army military police) sent seventy men on F and H Force parties – but only six survived. In addition to disease, some prisoners were ordered to fight each other to the death.[7]

* * *

In March 1944, Fergus was at Non Pladuk, though not part of F Force. This camp was at the start of the railway line, where large marshalling yards, called Hashimotos, had been created for supplies from Malaya and Bangkok to be sorted and sent to Burma. Colonel Toosey was there, now an Allied Commanding Officer; he had arrived a few weeks before. What became known as the 'Toosey effect' was now apparent at this camp: mail started to arrive and with it came long-overdue joy. Fergus's letters pre-dated those he received in Chungkai and he realised then that news of their first days in Singapore, leading up to captivity, had only been received during 1943 – eighteen months after they left England and fifteen months since they were captured – families at home didn't know what had happened to them for months. But as more letters arrived, home-spun wartime news made Fergus and other prisoners feel confident that victory was in sight.

With new assurances came increases in exercise, including games of football and basketball, all supported by Toosey. The camp also had a small theatre and Fergus hoped to meet his concert party pals, but only one was at Non Pladuk: Denis East the Philharmonic violinist. He had suffered the pain of a tropical ulcer on his wrist and, like Fergus, almost lost his hand. Other members of the concert party were in F Force and hadn't returned. The exact increase in death figures of both F and H Forces would be determined.

Chapter 23

State of Affairs

The degradation of prisoners and their living conditions continued; most were oblivious to the sparse information their relatives received of their plight. Despite huge efforts, families received little news. Reports from other countries were unreliable until the British Foreign Secretary, Anthony Eden, in January 1944, read a formal statement to the House of Commons, almost two years after their capture:[1]

> I fear I have grave news to give to the House. Members will be aware that a large number of postcards and letters have recently been received in this country from prisoners in the Far East and that these almost uniformly suggest that the writers are being treated well and are in good health. I regret to have to tell the House that information which has been reaching His Majesty's Government no longer leaves room for any doubt that the true state of affairs is a very different one so far as the great majority of prisoners in Japanese hands are concerned.

For some time, intelligence information had reached His Majesty's Government concerning conditions for Far East detainees in Japanese hands, but as this was distressing news, and likely to cause immense distress to the families involved, the government felt bound to investigate for factual evidence and, therefore, delayed public announcements.

Its reliable sources revealed that many thousands of prisoners from the British Commonwealth were unwillingly compelled to live in jungle conditions without adequate shelter, clothing, food or medical attention. Eden further declared that men were forced to work building roads and a railway and that their health, under the tropical conditions, was rapidly deteriorating; a high percentage were seriously ill, and thousands had already died. One eyewitness from a camp in Siam reported: 'I saw many prisoners clearly. They were skin and bone, unshaven and with long matted hair. They were half naked.'

The same witness reported they had no hats or shoes, and Eden reminded the ministers that in a tropical climate, where the neighbouring country is virtually uninhabited, there were few local resources to provide medical or other material relief.

Stan's family thought he was still alive and a prisoner of war, but they did not know his location or the conditions of his captivity. Eden's speech was just as devastating to them as thousands of other families. Not only were their men imprisoned but reports of reasonable conditions were untrue. Eden's message was broadcast around the globe to strong reaction from western-world governments. Messages of support condemned the Japanese nation, and they began to lose face. Consequently, the Imperial Japanese Army started to amend its disgraceful tactics.

* * *

Conditions improved over the next two months. Modest clothing was supplied – a new loin cloth and basic valuable footwear, especially for those suffering with trench foot, but some felt they should have more – a pair of shorts or a shirt perhaps. Basic hygiene measures, inoculations and resources for the sick improved and the Japanese commandant requested a few prisoners to write an essay of their experience. He hoped to reverse recent bad publicity in a radio broadcast. Several accounts were submitted but only one, by Captain Faraday, was released, starting:

> I had never had the pleasure or otherwise of meeting Japanese people until I was posted to Singapore. There I discovered that they were the most excellent barbers and first-class photographers too.

The Japanese seemed happy with the rest of his essay. Faraday had faintly praised them, and the PoWs' lot, without revealing their degrading and inhumane treatment. But in this he had masked references to fifth columnist spies prior to the invasion. This was enough to indicate to Allied military intelligence a way to obtain the truth using their own spy network. The fifth columnist activists – mainly Malay civilians – had taken many pictures of Singapore military installations without suspicion, while barber spies gathered information through local gossip as British Army soldiers had their hair cut. Now, ironically, the spy roles were reversed.

* * *

Throughout, the Moore and Lawrence families continued to believe Stan was still alive and pulled together to keep each other informed. He was unaware that Pat now worked for the Foreign Office and diligently collected newspaper cuttings from all over Britain relating to Far East prisoners of war. Through her advisory sources she had already contacted the Vatican War Enquiry Department. Pat was not Catholic but felt she must utilise the service and sent her first enquiry to the Sister's office, in Cavendish Square, London W1, whose initial reply was: 'So far we have received very little news of prisoners in the Far East.'

But they offered help by forwarding Stan's name and army details to the Vatican.

'If news is available, you will be at once informed.'

Pat had joined the throngs of many other women and families searching for their men in the Far East. Would there be divine intervention? A second letter came from the nuns, 2 June 1943, advising Pat to send a message of fewer than 125 words, indicating her fiancé's name, rank, number and camp, along with her own address details. They would forward this on for her. A comforting salutary close from Mother Mary Joan (Sec.), of 'God Bless You', gave Pat a glimmer of hope, but she heard nothing more for months.

In December, however, there was hope. In Changi, Stan and his fellow captives could send correspondence with the prospect of it reaching their families. Stan dictated a few lines for a postcard, on 11 December 1943, to Kenlor Road, Pat's home address. He had no reason to send it elsewhere. Astonishingly, it arrived in reasonable time - under two weeks - and Pat's sister, Ciss Collingridge, swiftly sent a telegram to relay the brief message to her workplace at PO Box 111, Bletchley, Bucks. By Christmas Eve, Pat and Emma Moore had at last received their first personal words from Stan in captivity:

Darling Pat-Mother. Am well, hope all are the same. Have received some letters.

Happy 27th Birthday Pat, Merry Christmas to all …

The postcard, received before Anthony Eden's speech, said nothing about the prisoners' poor living conditions or the degradation they suffered, but after learning the grave news in Eden's speech they could only assume he remained well. The general public still felt the government did nothing and it would be another gruelling seven months before more news reached Pat, through a letter written by her mother in July 1944:

Another postcard from Stan, but I wasn't surprised as Mrs Moore [a neighbour with the same surname] in our road, had received one from her Bill. I had the card dropped round to Mrs Moore [Stan's mother] by the children. [Pam, Tricia and Ron Collingridge – Pat's young nieces and nephew who were evacuated the next day].[2]

A second card from Stan was another happy missive and the families hoped for others. Then further correspondence arrived in August 1944. But it was Stan's first telegram arriving eighteen months late having been cabled 2 February 1942 – prior to capitulation!

*   *   *

By 10 October, Pat had found another route to find Stan. Her wartime Foreign Office position at Bletchley Park led her to the All India Radio Message Service, BANTONY, SIMLA. The officer-in-charge acknowledged receipt of her letter and advised that her message to Stan would be broadcast from Delhi to Malaya, 16 November 1944.

On 11 October, a newspaper announced: '*Jap-held Prisoners to Cable Relatives. Red Cross Will Pay.*'

This broadcasting service had connections with British Intelligence; it would have been shrewd of Pat to make use of her wartime employment.[3]

Chapter 24

Word on the Wire

A s we have seen, PoW Reuben Kandler and 'Sparks' took risks to ensure records were kept regarding communications and men's safety. The lists of hundreds, whether embarking on a ship, detail duty, a work party or a concert party, was used for some to record the whereabouts of many, and to maintain administrative order. When Reuben was transferred to Kinsaiyok in 1943, after *supido* finished in October, he discovered there was no longer a list of the Saigon battalion. The 1,123 soldiers who travelled there in the grim coal hold of a Japanese maru disappeared either through redistribution – some were sent to Hanoi – or death. Kandler commented on this to his superior, Captain MacDonald. The next day, the officer gave him something he could use: an inexpensive, brown, hardcover notebook.

He started to record all the names of prisoners who had died through ill-treatment and ill health, while also retaining his original list. Sadly, the list of the fallen grew, as sergeant majors from each battalion provided information for annotation. The secret lists were well hidden, and officers came to trust Kandler since none had the time nor the tools to collect names themselves. As the campaign continued, the list was in danger of being discovered until, on one occasion, a zealous and often inebriated Japanese administration official – who loved to stamp documents – was distracted by Reuben's fellow prisoners. The original list was slipped under his nose, and he unwittingly applied the official stamp, which meant the list was now exempt of suspicion. It was a true mark of genius and guts. Another handwritten copy of the list was made later but subsequently burnt. The original survived.[1]

Kandler was one of the longest survivors at Kinsaiyok, a camp where sick men regularly passed through en route to hospital camps at Chungkai or Tarsao. Before boarding another train, the sick talked to other Kinsaiyok prisoners and, in turn, Reuben. Patients' names and those who had died, including men from Songkurai, were collected. Word-of-mouth was the only way the ghastly news and conditions could be gathered. As men from F and H Forces came to Kinsaiyok, they arrived on their last legs, evidence of extreme ill-treatment, hunger and starvation. Their weakened and injured frames resembled skeletons, but their names were immediately updated or added to the list. Kandler played an integral part in recording this history by compiling and maintaining these important nominal rolls. Many families would be none the wiser if it were not for his diligence and his bravery.[2]

* * *

Bird in Hand was the last production held at Sime Road Camp in April before they had to move. A party of barnstormers sang many numbers from all the old shows. It was a good rollicking time which helped them let off steam; they were quite at home at 'Sime'.

But, after a delay of five days, on 5 May 1944 Stan's unit swapped their Sime Road accommodation with civilian internees. The move back to the confining walls of Changi Gaol was not welcome. The internees, mostly women and children, were to have the slightly better conditions. On the day of the changeover, a rope and sheet screen was erected to prevent male prisoners, or male internees, from seeing female internees. It was bizarre, because of course they did, but it was probably the first time in two years that the men had glimpsed western women. Stan resigned himself to the change.

We were sent down to Changi Gaol itself. Our particular unit was put into the solitary confinement area, where cells were arranged in a horseshoe fashion. Normally they held one prisoner during peace time, but in this case, they put three of us to a cell. Luckily, they never closed the door! The cell consisted of one concrete block, the size of a single bed. In the corner was a squat type lavatory, so with three of us in the cell, it was a toss-up as to who had the centre concrete slab. Our little group took it in turns, no mattress mind you, and a pillow made up of your own change of clothes.

Other Ranks and officers were housed in wooden huts outside the main building, numbering approximately 5,000, while another 5,000 were squashed into the gaol that usually held no more than 600. He recalled with empathy:

> *The British party were one side of the horseshoe courtyard and the Australians were on the other, so we could see and barrack each other, on and off. Close by was another area where people, chaps who had lost their minds, were housed and you could hear them screaming and shouting, which was pretty grim.*

The rest of the year was spent carrying out work-party duties, day in day out. But British troops' concert parties continued to be organised, and theatre productions were numerous, some combined with the AIF concert group. Kicking footballs, batting balls or playing darts helped to pass the evenings.

September saw the opening of the Changi Gaol Playhouse in one of the courtyards. Food was in short supply and hunger persisted. The grovelling and bartering of personal effects for an iota of luxury, such as blachang to flavour the bland rice, was widespread.

And while the PoWs enjoyed their theatre, the British government cheered when they heard the news that a Red Cross request had been accepted by the Japanese. A ten-word cablegram was permitted, excluding address and signature, to prisoners' next of kin and would be sent via Geneva.

'The Japanese have undertaken to forward as soon as possible by airmail. The success of the whole scheme will depend on their willingness to implement their undertaking.'

Minister of State, Richard Law, hoped the service would start at once, but as most prisoners were in occupied territories, all depended on cables channelled through Tokyo.

Excitement also erupted on Guy Fawkes Night,[3] 5 November, when British troops heard Allied bomber planes fly over Singapore. Their firecracker resonance created gleeful jubilance around the gaol which spread like wildfire. A rumour followed that release would be next month – the prisoners couldn't believe it. Now the sound of forty-five planes and ack-ack guns was thrilling. Was it the beginning of the end?

Showers of leaflets were dropped from Allied planes the next morning. In a dire warning, the Japanese general ordered for prisoners to be shot if they picked one up. A day later, reports came of bombs dropped on Seletar, north of Changi. Civilians were among the 1,500 casualties and two ships were sunk, one contained vital rice.

Anticipation of freedom in November was exciting. Allied attacks were erratic and Japanese administration introduced air-raid drills. If anyone was found outside their hut or the gaol during an alarm, they would be shot. This meant the latrines were out of bounds.

Gunner Fergus Anckorn did his best to stay alive in 1944 at Non Pladuk, he continued to work and entertain, surviving on whatever extra food he could find. The railway close to this camp, however, was another target for Allied bombers as they attempted to gain control of Thailand. When planes roared over, PoWs realised they needed to alert the pilots that not only Japanese Army battalions were below, but they were there too. With haste, using their football pitch lines, they cleverly painted a huge white sign emphasising the letters P, O and W within the angles and prayed the sign's visibility kept them alive.

*   *   *

December was quieter at Changi, and disappointing. They were still prisoners and the end seemed even further away. The atmosphere had changed. There were no more raids and communication was lacking. A morale boost was needed.

Promises of more shows were tannoyed around the camp: A Command Performance and a panto '*M&B 693*' – a reference to the fake May & Baker chalk tablets they manufactured in the early days. On Christmas Day, a sermon was given by 'Ducky', Padre Duckworth, and senior officers visited RASC men in gaol or hospital. A successful comedy, *Twinkletoes*, was performed at the Playhouse, and the audience sang along joyfully at the end, hoping this would be their last Christmas in captivity. It was their fourth away from home, their third as prisoners. The good news, however, was that shows were also broadcast to Great Britain and PoWs hoped their loved ones could tune in. Perhaps the air raids and permission to broadcast at Christmas were related, to ensure the Nippons did not lose face.

The prisoners also asked what the point was of keeping them confined now that the railway was finished. Were they slaves? Bartering fodder?

Still in a state of war without combat aggression these men were a useful commodity for future co–prosperity–sphere plans but, if set free, troops could reform to commence a new battle – a foolish move on any enemy's part.

*   *   *

During the Allied bombing raids, Stan made other attempts to communicate with his family and Pat but didn't know if his messages were being heard. On 24 December 1944, Ronald Horner was delighted at the thought of further communication when he wrote: 'Broadcast not taken place yet – all British personnel are allowed to send wireless messages (twenty-five words) home. Whako!'

Others noted 'the Red Cross took three years to set this up', but were excited to be able to cable twenty-five words. These references were dated a week after Stan sent his broadcast.

*   *   *

On 17 December 1944, a message from Stan had been radioed via a 'report broadcast from Singapore' to Pat at Kenlor Road. However, it's route via the War Office was laborious and did not reach her until eight weeks later. The message came in the form of a letter from a Colonel at i/c RASC Records in Hastings, southern England, dated 8 Feb 45:

Dear Madam, T/170638 Dvr. Moore S.A.W. *Received letters, radio messages, dated November. Glad to hear Frank's news. Keep smiling and look after yourself for my sake. Myself well. Hope you all same. Fondest love,* Stan.

The colonel's letter requested that the broadcast report was not mentioned when she replied.[4]

Pat's mother read the message to her by telephone and then forwarded the letter to her work address at Box 111 (B45) Bletchley, Bucks. This small amount of news was huge! And an immense relief to Pat, and Stan's parents. The same day, 11 February, she wasted no time in drafting a cautious reply. How much should she reveal of Stan's words? This was probably the only chance for him to broadcast a message. Was the source valid? There was no other evidence of other messages. Illicit radio contact had serious implications if caught, and she thought Stan almost certainly would have no direct means to secret wireless apparatus.

*   *   *

St. Andrew's Malay School

Without realising, Stan was only months away from the end of his PoW period. His routine continued with the captors' usual demands, until one day there was a different task to undertake.

> *The Japs apparently needed a working party to go to a warehouse to sort out some Red Cross parcels. It was March 1945 – I suppose I was lucky being one of the sixty people chosen to go down to the town, to help deal with this. We arrived and found it wasn't a warehouse, it was a huge Malay school[5] and all the classrooms were stacked to the ceiling with Red Cross parcels that had been sent in, but never received – until now (six months prior to being released).*

> *We had a hell of a job sorting this out. It was in a state, mice infested. Vermin had been living in it and various broken tins had sent the rest bad. We had to sort it out. You can imagine, with temperatures being 80 degrees all day and all night, it was a pretty formidable task. Anyway, we got most of this stuff organised. With sixty of us we got it down to a fairly fine art, so the Japanese thought there were too many of us and sent some back to Changi. I was rather fortunate to be kept back along with an officer, and two or three sergeants.*

With a handful of other ranks, Stan's group was reduced to twelve and left to do the final sorting. He thought the task was more pleasant than being in Changi Gaol. However, there came a time when his, and the rest of the party's hair grew too long to be hygienic.

> *Our commander, Major Jensen – a general in the Indian Army*[6] *– managed to find hair-cutting equipment in one of the Red Cross parcels. How he did that I don't know. He asked for a volunteer to do the necessary hair cutting. I said I had cut my dad's hair before joining the army and he said, 'Right, you're the bloke.'*

> *I did the necessary on his hair and quite enjoyed it. I think – as it turned out – I did quite a good job, even though I say so myself. Of course, the rest of the fellas immediately lined up and we went through all eleven of us. I don't know who cut mine, but I was done eventually. I had clippers and a pair of scissors and made a razor out of wood and a blade; this did the job. I was satisfied with it….*

He was proud of his useful task, but his skill did not stop there.

> *One day, the Japanese brought in three pigs to be slaughtered. They were herded in by a party of Indian prisoners, but they wouldn't butcher them because it was against their religion, so they asked us to do it.*

In his mind, Stan was immediately transported back to happier days at Tooting Co-op and the meat department:

> *I volunteered to do the butchering along with a real butcher from Lancashire. We decided to quarter the pigs up, score them first; get all the hair off the big old-barbed head, then butchered them up. We had our cookhouse in the same building as the Japanese guards at the school and they had a huge kawali. This is like a large wok pan set on stones over an open fire. We had a similar arrangement for ours. Once the pigs were quartered, we cut off all the fatty bits and put them in the Japanese pot; all the nice lean bits went in ours. I don't know how the Japs enjoyed it, but I know we enjoyed ours!*

Their days of working in a small autonomous group, albeit still under guard, was a refreshing period of light relief. They were more relaxed and at times acted like mischievous schoolboys. With restricted conditions for over three years, they now looked for entertainment, but with little immediate concern for their safety. Stan continued:

> While still at the Malay school, I and two other fellas knew of a big room under lock and key which we knew contained officers' army equipment. Very delicate stuff: flowered blankets, socks, boots and all sorts of things. So, one night we thought we'd raid it to see what we could get out. It was risky, but we made an attempt. While we were climbing down a wall into this room, and down the stairs, the Japanese guard appeared, but he didn't see us! At the balcony he stopped and had his smoke – the guards wore these rubber slippers; you couldn't hear them coming. We froze.

Their lives were in mortal danger; their attempt to pilfer was almost scuppered.

> He would have seen us had he turned around, but he finished his cigarette and walked off. I've never been so scared in all my life! We carried on and were successful. The booty we risked our souls for was distributed among our working party.

> We were in the school sorting for quite a few months. We had finished various areas, so the Japs gave us a little job of erecting a detention area for Japanese Army defaulters. It was a good task and we made a thorough job of it, really secure, so the so-and-so's couldn't get out! The defaulters were fellas who had gone absent without leave or caused some sort of misdemeanour for which they were punished. They were put in the tiny cells we made, and we were glad to do it!

Stan and his group were pleased to give them a dose of their own medicine, at last.

* * *

The converted Sime Road Camp was mainly for British and European interned civilians, including Lady Daisy Thomas, wife of Shenton Thomas, former Straits Settlements governor. Skilled civilians and electrical engineers were also held not only as internees but as workers. Armbands differentiated them as 'civilian enemy while at work'. Men and women were divided, including families where young children – brothers and sisters – were separated. Some were based at River Valley Camp.

They built a chapel in the compound, among the huts with palm-leafed roofs, and religious services at St David's Church helped to occupy their long days. They also had to be resourceful, growing vegetables and making their own camp repairs, as the Japanese had first pickings of their Red Cross food parcels from home, leaving little for internees.

Older children secretly sat exams for the Cambridge School Certificate, a system organised by R. Cheeseman, former Deputy Director for Education in the Straits Settlements. Six students passed and obtained the Certificate.[7] Women painted and embroidered mementoes, including sewing stories of their incarceration into their work. Pencilled drawings became tapestries oversewn with discarded threads, such as the portrayal of St David's Chapel, delicately stitched in secret under moonlight.

The separation of men and women was devastating for families, but covert ways to communicate with each other were adopted wherever possible. A brief glance or passing touch during Tenko, for example, was all that could be risked. If seen by a guard, the result was certain punishment, but fortunately, there was always bin day. Pre-planned, a wife would offer a coded wink or a stroke of her hair to indicate it was her turn to do the bin tomorrow. Her partner was told, and each side would endeavour to bring the couple together for a few fleeting seconds while the rubbish was disposed of. The smallest display of affection was all they could show, but it helped. They lived in fear of being discovered – but there was always a waiting list for 'bin day'.

Chapter 25

The Last Months

Victory in Europe was widely celebrated on 8 May 1945. Ecstatic crowds thronged the streets of London in spontaneous jubilance and held 'typically British' street parties using pooled rations. Children were excited, joyfulness was infectious. But for those who lost loved ones, or those who didn't know where their men were – reported missing in the Far East or held prisoner – sadness was uppermost. With mixed emotions and uncertain moods, it was difficult to celebrate. Churchill's short speech on the crackling radio at 3 p.m. did not fill them with hope either. The VE Day speech was given from the balcony of the Ministry of Health overlooking Whitehall, his gruff but eloquent words resounded:

> Yesterday morning at 2:41 a.m. at Headquarters, General Jodl, the Representative of the High German Command and Grand Admiral Dönitz, the Designated Head of the German State, signed the Act of Unconditional Surrender of all German land, sea and air forces in Europe to the Allied Expeditionary Forces and simultaneously to the Soviet High Command. Today is Victory in Europe Day. Hostilities will end officially at one minute after midnight tonight.

He concluded minutes later:

> We may allow ourselves a brief period of rejoicing, but let us not forget for a moment, the toil and efforts that lie ahead. We must now devote all our strength and resources to the completion of our task both at home and abroad.

The task took another three months before signs of peace arrived in the Far East. But in the July general election, Churchill lost his premiership.

While thousands of dejected men returned from the battlefields of Europe and Africa it seemed the great man was good for war but not for peace.

The Overdue Surrender

Around that time, the demeanour of Japanese guards altered. The first sign for some prisoners was a bonfire in the camp square, where their captors hurried to burn documents and files. Prisoners, such as Reuben Kandler, thought of Fort Canning three years before, when they too burnt intelligence notebooks with a look of panic and defeat in their eyes. PoWs knew something was about to happen. Stan recounted:

We had a Malay volunteer fella in our party, at the Malay school, who was an interpreter; he used to chat to the sergeant's batman in this place and he mentioned something about a bomb, which we knew nothing about. We'd just heard rumours about Americans attacking the Japanese position pretty well. Anyway, he said to us look towards 4 August and everything was going to happen for us. How he knew I'll never know. A year or so back, we used to get various rumours of American successes and things like that, but we classed them just as rumours – borehole rumours because it was the only quiet place where the Japs wouldn't go near, to listen to what you were saying.

Stan laughed.

One imagines the mystery of the 4 August rumour was intriguing and helped boost their spirits, because even with the sorted and dispersed Red Cross supplies their morale remained low. In the last days of July 1945, a further party of emaciated Dutchmen arrived at Changi from Sambawan. Sixty more souls who might not survive through hunger, or worse. Organisers, including Horner, were concerned that extra mouths to feed would rapidly reduce supplies and everyone's survival. The PoWs daily food intake was now less than 20oz each.

*　*　*

Fergus Anckorn was at the Ubon camp then, on the French Indo-China border. Japanese guards had ordered prisoners to build airfield runways, but in a complete turn-around, they were ordered to dig trenches across them to prevent enemy planes from landing. Shortly after, prisoners were ordered to dig more trenches around the airfield. This project appeared to be a 10m x 10m mass grave to the PoWs and Fergus feared for his lack of identity after losing his dog tags, three years earlier, when his truck was destroyed in February 1942. But a Dutch friend made him another tag from the top of a mess tin, where his name and number were meticulously engraved. Now he could rest in the knowledge that his body would at least be identified.

In an attempt to keep up morale, ambitious concert parties – with revolving stages and a mock four-engine bomber, complete with actors inside – took place. There was a vast amount of talent on hand and prisoners sang along with gusto, evoking memories from home; words they'd sung many times such as *Out of The Blue Came Sunshine* and *Home*.

When shadows fall and dreams whisper days ending

My thoughts are ever wending. Home.

* * *

Meanwhile, at Changi, prisoners heard powerful-sounding planes high in the sky. Lockheed Lightnings? They wondered. Days later Horner recorded, 'a Short Sunderland and a Liberator flew over, and the Lightnings, this time much lower to take a good look.' He also noted that a depressed Korean guard had shot himself on 26 July.

On 4 August, Horner and his men working on the wood-trailer party saw seven Lightnings pass over. They soon returned flying at 3,000–4,000ft and blasted the airfield. A Japanese Zero interfered and went down with smoke pouring from its tail; was this what Stan's Malay interpreter meant? Was he a knowledgeable spy?

Over the next few days, more allied aircraft flew over Changi, but revenge tactics for the allied attacks were now being used by the IJA. 'The 'Nips' offered 'Food for Watches'. If anyone still owned a watch, they could receive food and an IOU for the watch to be repaid after the war – the prisoners thought that this smacked of being sold their own rations. Then electric heaters in the officers' area were also confiscated for two weeks due to a time infringement by Dutch officers. Things were becoming petty and desperate, and perpetual hunger was debilitating. How long could they continue? Why were these planes flying over?

*   *   *

At the Ubon camp, Fergus met with other Dutch PoWs twice a month in a French-speaking circle. The group were news bearers who exchanged information in an arrangement with locals during a secret out-of-camp hillside rendezvous. It was risky, since breaking back into camp was harder than breaking out. One night, locals revealed news of a *'bombe atomique'*. Fergus took a stand saying he was taking too much of a risk for such 'cock and bull' stories, as in his view, the idea of a small bomb destroying a big town was unbelievable and unreliable.

But he was mistaken. Allied atomic bombs had been dropped on the Japanese cities of Hiroshima and Nagasaki on 6 and 9 August, with devastating results. Fergus and his army comrades would learn more much later.

Over... It's Over!

An early announcement came at breakfast time. Was it true? No more hunger or waiting in queues, or ragged clothes. No more sore feet, beatings, degrading conditions or life-threatening abuse. Was it really over? Or another false alarm? The working parties still carried on with daily wood-trailer duty, as Japanese guards were oblivious to the news on 11 August. Over the next two days, the PoWs began to think it was another ploy to shoot them. But on return from the working parties a great hubbub of chatter came from the huts as unexpected sirens sounded and Japanese fighters took off in a hurry. Then they realized most guards had left.

'War has finished!' came another astonished shout on 15 August, in Fergus's camp, but he was already celebrating with Dutch rice coffee.

Chapter 26

Freedom

'When the balloon finally went up and the Japanese had surrendered, we were ordered to get the entire Red Cross stock out of the school on to lorries to distribute the parcels around various camps on the island', recalled Stan. *'I don't think I worked as hard as I ever did that time'*.

The parcels were more of the Japanese hoarded stock. Approximately 47,000 packages from the Sime Road issue of 1944 were also added to the expanding Changi campus. How many lives could have been saved if this been distributed a year before?

A lot of the British Red Cross parcels were wrapped in a type of sacking, impregnated with arsenic powder to keep the vermin off,[1] so they didn't get into the parcels. Of course, [laughs] we had to handle them in this state. You'd have thought we were the yellow peril, not the Japanese, when we'd finished loading – we were covered with the stuff! Anyway, it washed off eventually. After we completely cleared the school, we were sent back to Changi Gaol. There they told me that when the final surrender came, a plane had flown over and dropped a medical orderly plus a second lieutenant of the medics, and he took over the whole of the gaol for the time being.

Funnily enough when we were released, or the Japs had capitulated, an officer came to our little party and took us into the room and said help yourself to what you want! We needn't have taken the risk at all! I had two good blankets of Japanese origin. I think I still have them.

But the joy of freedom was dissipated by the slowness in finalising the surrender. It was three weeks before the official ceremony took place. Stan remembered:

We were issued with much better rations. I don't know how they got hold of them;[2] tins of M&V [meat and vegetable]. We were given one of the tall tins, one per man at one a time and of course, the fact we were deprived of food for so long, our stomachs couldn't manage a whole tin; we just ate what we could. There were people that thought they could eat more and there were one or two – a couple apparently – who just ate and ate, and their stomachs burst. They couldn't take anymore. They died.

A few days before the Japanese surrendered, a fellow went missing; they thought he'd tried to escape, but no. One day they went to the latrine area and there was a lid partly open; they wondered why and opened it and there was the body of this fellow still in the borehole, he dived down headfirst; committed suicide, poor devil.

There were other fellows who had attempted to escape previously. They were tortured by the Japanese with Chinese drip torture[3] and finally went mad. They were brought back to a solitary confinement cell, near us. We were fortunate enough to have showers rigged up in the latter part of our confinement, but every time, as soon as the water was turned on, these fellows would scream their heads off. It was pitiful to listen to.

They had trained their minds for so long to never look towards tomorrow, and now tomorrow stretched before them. Their future! The emotional grip of freedom was suddenly absurdly inhibiting.

*   *   *

Details of the horrific carnage of Allied atom bombs dropped on the Japanese cities of Hiroshima and Nagasaki were not common knowledge, but they ended the war, saving tens of thousands of lives – civilians, as well as prisoners of war. Without this action, the conflict would have continued for many months longer and PoWs would have starved to death. But the surrender of Japan was more than a signing of an agreement of terms, which included freeing all prisoners of war and the Allies taking back control, it was a change in world politics.

As Allied planes flew over the freed troops, they were stricken but delighted to receive clothes, cigarettes and other supplies.

Each day, the size of consignments grew. It was exciting for the men, who were bereft of attention and luxury for so long. But safety soon became an issue when prisoners scrambled to the landing place of a 'drop'. In one camp, a supply package missed the mark and fell directly on to a bamboo hut, killing the occupants. They had been told to run there for safety. To die in freedom was a devastating blow after years of captivity.

Drops included bundles of newspapers, including *News of the World*. Men were shocked by the drastic changes, as unfamiliar names stared up at them from black print. The prime minister was no longer Winston Churchill; Clement Attlee was head of the British government after a general election in July. The reports often seemed insignificant or alien, but they were weeks old, and there was a marked absence of news regarding the thousands of Far East Allied soldiers who fought and became prisoners of war. They were forgotten men. Their victorious homeland seemed to think there was only one war, and that was in Europe.

*   *   *

Men felt weak and worried about the coming days and some needed convincing this was not a phoney twilight zone. Positive reports for the freed men at Changi were needed. Good times marked by birthdays with feasts of make-do food and 'Doovers' – a quarter of breakfast pap, tapioca flour and blachang – made their evening meal more substantial.

Horner and other officers were annoyed at the delay of the official surrender and 'infernal lack of order'. Indecision dragged on and promise of a surrender agreement delayed until the arrival of the 'Lord Louis circus' – Commodore Mountbatten, Chief of Combined Operations, who had recently been promoted. Surrender was now becoming an anti-climax, and the days of a slow-motion 'victory' were just another degrading chapter. But the tables had turned.

Within the hiatus, rumour said a ceasefire had been ordered by Mountbatten, but fatigues and working parties were to continue as usual, with the same activity from guards. A plane flying too high to be identified was spotted. Did this mean something? The next day, working parties ended and parties living outside the Changi area were told to return, although there was no official notification of the end. It was a farce.

In the first thirty-six hours, anticipation of freedom seemed premature once more; tensions increased. They prayed there would be no hitches. Mountbatten's fleet was at least 'on standby; their release would not be delayed too long'. Tokyo commanders had to accept the Allies' terms of surrender.

Finally, news came that the IJA had agreed. All was strangely peaceful, the night search lights shone and at midnight on 14/15 August, an official broadcast announced the surrender of Japan, exactly three and a half years after the Fall of Singapore. The safety of Emperor Hirohito had been negotiated via Geneva, and he was persuaded by his ministers to speak to the Japanese population from the *Royal Rescript*.[4]

The omnipresent Japanese flag, which prisoners had nicknamed the 'poached egg', still flew over the gaol at 0900hrs early that morning. More Red Cross supplies were promised. The end was in sight.

Working parties returned to Singapore by 19 August and Japanese soldiers were disarmed of their full equipment en route. Medical and Red Cross supplies arrived and were issued at the rate of twenty-one parcels per day instead of twenty-one every two weeks. It all seemed too good to be true. A week passed after the unconditional surrender. 'Waiting patiently', was the mantra which helped to avoid rising tempers. It was difficult but all men did their utmost. Nine lorry loads of supplies arrived, including packs of Chesterfields (a popular brand of cigarettes at the time) giving each prisoner twelve days' worth of smokes – twelve more days they didn't want.

The fate of thirteen American pilots and B29 bomber crews taken from the jail at Outram Road by Japanese military was unknown, but it was said they were executed in reprisal for the Allied bombing of Japan. The remaining prisoners of Outram had their sentences rescinded and were free. Later that evening, a moving service of condolence and thanksgiving was conducted by Eric 'Bish' Cordingly in Changi, for the deceased and all survivors.

Meanwhile, tit-for-tat punishment spread. Amid reports of Allied pilots shot down by the Japanese, Malay Civil Service personnel were removed, including the former Federal Secretary who was decapitated, for their concealment of forbidden radios. Two American marines, imprisoned in Changi at capitulation, said to be disguised as Euro-Asians, also disappeared. It is uncertain who they were, what they did or if they survived. As the Japanese were disarmed, the Chinese applied retribution for their bad treatment and horrific massacres such as at Sook Ching, but this was confined to Sikh Indian guards, where fifty to sixty were executed with rifles and machine guns.

*   *   *

Men could send a cable now. Only five words, but it was enough. Locals sang, shouted and cheered. The working party from Blakang Mati returned and old friends, such as Freddie Holt - Stan's pal and Horner's former batman - hoped to reunite. Neither had seen Freddie since 1942 after his working party was assigned to the island off the shores of Keppel Harbour. The men were delighted to meet again.

After years of deplorable treatment, Japanese soldiers delivered fresh pork, fish, wheat flour, eggs and clothes in a belated show of generosity; they couldn't lose face. Did they think their captives had such short memories? Most of the excess food was donated to the hospital.

On 23 August, Count Hisaichi Terauchi, marshal in charge of the Southern Region,[5] officially ordered the ceasefire with effect from midnight and personally surrendered to Lord Admiral Mountbatten. ORs were given a new shirt, a vest, shorts, a G string, towel and boots – frustratingly, all size 8 and under – for 10,000 men. It was another attempt at generosity but there was so much it was impossible to sort. Did they really think this would help them? After so much suffering it only made the case against them worse. The Japanese had supplies, all along.

Roll calls ended, but burials continued, including the two unfortunate men who ate too much and literally exploded. Their patience had worn thin, but measured portions for a few more days would have saved their lives.

Radio access was provided, and news flowed freely. Further Red Cross supplies came with the fresh fish and meat. New blankets afforded comfort at last after years of sleeping on rags, rice sacks or nothing at all.

*   *   *

A British bugle sounded over the camp two days later. Reveille had not been heard for years. Everybody stopped to listen as the musical notes sliced through the morning silence.

For breakfast they received towgay with 10 ounces of butter per day (extraordinary!) – but they were careful not to upset their delicate stomachs. Allied planes would soon drop more supplies.

The concert party made a tremendous effort to put on a show for hospital patients, where an audience of nearly 3,000 liberated men sung in glorious unison. However, their health was still difficult to control, despite the improved conditions. Some faces and legs began to swell and medical officers saw beriberi increasing. Two British medical captains, two lieutenants, two orderlies and more medical supplies arrived from the British base at Trincomalee, Colombo, Ceylon.[6]

Towards the end of August, newspapers and transmitters were dropped by planes, and Liberators and Mosquitos dropped vast amounts of tinned food, but still it took a while for the men to absorb the fact their days of hunger were over.

Chapter 27

Waiting to Leave

'Now we're back at Changi Gaol,' Stan recalled, 'with a certain amount of freedom.'

Our administration allowed us down to Singapore City from whatever time you went until midnight. So, two or three of us went from my little crowd, and we came across a few sailors in the bar. They'd come off the cruiser HMS Sheffield. They said, 'Why don't you come aboard and have something to eat?' We thought we could go for that one – all that grub! We had a smashing meal, and they gave us soap and toothpaste which we hadn't seen for three and a half years. After that they said, 'Why don't you stay the night?' Which we did; we laid a bed on the deck – just rolled out hammocks and got back into Changi Gaol again the following morning after hitching a lift.

This went on for almost a month while we were waiting for our ship. With the bit of freedom we had, some of the lads – the fact they had been deprived of women for so long – couldn't resist the temptation of the prostitutes downtown. One fellow – I won't mention his name – went with one of the women that the Japs had been with, and he had to later undergo medical inspection prior to arrival in Colombo, Ceylon (now Sri Lanka), on our way home. He was diagnosed as having VD, so the poor bloke had to be taken off at Colombo for treatment; we had to leave him behind. I don't know how or when he got home. I suppose he did eventually, but this was hardly the sort of thing you wanted to do, when all you wanted was to get home to see your loved ones.

But not all was plain sailing, as delay after delay kept Stan and friends on the island.

What annoyed us most was the fact the American PoWs were flown out very quickly, in fact they left after about a week and travelled directly back to America. Plus, the Australians were shipped out quickly too. Us poor old British were there waiting for our ship to come in. Anyway, eventually it arrived.

The long wait took its toll on the men, not least for the mentally depressed and the sick but for the boisterous, tempted by the women downtown.

Gradually the number of days reduced to when Stan's group could board a ship and they reflected on the worst time of their lives. The saddest part of course, was the friends they had lost.

* * *

The signing of the Instrument of Surrender - the agreement that defined the victors' sovereign rights - took place on 2 September 1945. America's General Douglas MacArthur had officially accepted Japan's surrender aboard USS *Missouri* in Tokyo Bay. In Singapore, the men listened to the ceremony via broadcast. MacArthur's mission was to oversee demobilisation of the Japanese military and commence restoration of displaced troops and war-torn areas. It was appropriate that Percival stood beside MacArthur at the signing. A euphoric moment ... though some were sceptical about all Japanese keeping their side of the accord.

At Changi Gaol, British, American and Dutch flags were to be 'broken' at midday, high on the prison tower; freedom was assured from that point. But unfortunately, the flag poles were not erected in time.

A trumpet fanfare eventually heralded the raising of the Changi flags on 3 September. It was an impressive and moving moment. Colonel Holmes for the British Empire performed the ceremony with Lieutenant Colonel van de Hoogenbad for NEI (Netherlands East Indies) and Lieutenant Miles Barrett of the US Marines.

The liberating forces were well received apart from one disconcerting observation on their part – the PoWs smelt. They concluded the main reason for this was due to their ingestion of local oil and foods over three years, which had permeated their bodies and changed the composition of their body odour. But that was soon forgotten as more food parcels and sweet-smelling toiletries were parachuted in by the 99 and 356 squadrons RAF and RAAF from the Cocos Islands. As they returned to their European version of human beings – they had after all lived like animals – the men felt comfortable and civilised at last.

*   *   *

Now they watched from beaches when a report of a ship was on the horizon, and early in September the hospital ship HMS *Cleopatra* and HMS *Sussex*, pulled into Keppel Harbour, as their brass band played *Sussex By the Sea*.[1]

On board was Signals Operator Gerald 'Jeff' Hoare, a young British naval volunteer recruit from signals intelligence, who had sailed from Trincomalee, Colombo, for the clean-up and to help repatriate PoWs. 'Those poor men,' he later said, having witnessed their degradation and suffering. The navy also took artefacts from war-torn Changi Gaol, including part of a concrete wall with wooden shutters that was shipped back to Gosport, England.[2]

In a final surrender ceremony aboard HMS *Sussex* on 5 September, the delegation of General Sir Robert Mansergh, Rear Admiral Cedric Holland and Lieutenant General Christison met and accepted the Japanese Singapore Garrison Surrender from Vice-Admiral Fukutomi and Imperial Japanese Army General Itagaki. Act 1 of the Allies 'Operation Tiderace', a plan set in force to recapture Singapore, was finally complete.[3]

Singapore was festooned with flags and cheering crowds as officers from Recovery Allied Prisoners of War Internees (RAPWI – the men joked 'Retain All PoWs Indefinitely'), re-established communications at the Cathay Building. Carried by the enthusiasm of civilians, the visits of RAPWI personnel and Red Cross nurses moved and elated the former detainees. But underlying the celebrations there was still no sign of transport home unless you were sick. It appeared the fitter PoWs of the 18th Division would be last to leave. The promises of Lord Louis were fading, until Lady Edwina Mountbatten visited the camp on 10 September and made a charismatic, uplifting, broadcast via the camp radio. She was the first free British woman they'd heard for years. With words of sympathy and comfort, she gave her support. However, the moment was fleeting as the men, justifiably, only wanted to go home to their own wives and families.

The uncertainty of the Japanese not fully surrendering created tension and became real when PoWs discovered that British officers had been scheduled to work on tunnels at Kranji. They probably would have been shot and left to die in the mass grave they had dug themselves. The plan was uncovered by Colonel Stewart who had documentary evidence from guerrilla factions in the area. Everyone at that point realised how lucky they were to be alive.

Surrendering and getting home seemed to take an age. Two days later at the city centre Municipal Building, the IJA signed another Instrument of Surrender to Allied Forces on 12 September. An audience of army and naval personnel, cadets and civilians watched from the grass Padang in front of City Hall as British officers appeared on the pillared colonnade in ceremonial white uniforms. The Allied victors presented in sharp contrast to the dullness of the Japanese Gensui's brown and booted attire. Photographers' flashlights popped, as the solemn party of officials came into view. Newly promoted Lord Mountbatten, Supreme Allied Commander of South-East Asia Command, addressed the crowd as officers dressed in army khaki mingled with the brighter colours of American and Australian personnel descended the twenty grey-stone steps to the Padang for a Victory Parade. It _WAS_ truly over. Jeff Hoare recorded Lord Mountbatten and this important moment in history on his camera.[4]

* * *

There was still no news for Stan regarding embarkation. He'd had jovial visits to the city, meals shared with Chinese families and random invitations to Australian parties, but now it was 20 September. The remaining AIF might go the next day, but nobody knew for sure. They were getting a raw deal, almost living under the same Japanese conditions. With no money and the city 13 miles away, it was equally confining. But soon their homeward vessel was announced: HMT _Sobieski_, a Polish ship, and by 28 September Stan was back on the ocean.[5]

On board there would have been talk of the official surrender to General Douglas MacArthur. He appeared to be the hero and they heard details of the hard-fought battles and success of US campaigns in the Pacific, the defeats at Bataan and Corregidor, and that Filipino forces played a crucial role in vital surveillance for aggressive American and Allied counterattacks after Pearl Harbor.[6] MacArthur had defended the Philippines as governor in 1937 and was recalled in 1941 as Commander United States Army Forces in the Far East following the Japanese invasion. He escaped Corregidor with his family and was appointed as Supreme Commander of Allied Forces in the Southwest Pacific; meanwhile, American and Filipino forces were forced to withdraw to Bataan where they held out until their eventual surrender in May 1942.

Allied naval forces had fought the Battle of the Coral Sea that month, and in June 1942 the Battle of Midway. A lengthy period of fierce fighting took place to recapture Guadalcanal, 7 August–9 February 1943, then another month-long fight in Guam from 8 August 1944 resulted in victory. MacArthur returned to the Philippines in October 1944 and that December was promoted to Army General, commanding all armed forces in the Pacific. The battle for Okinawa began April 1945 and, after another tough battle, his forces triumphed on 22 June 1945. His campaign to defeat the Imperial Japanese Army finally prevailed, but the Atom Bomb in August eclipsed his success.

* * *

Fergus was not party to the official celebrations as he was still in Ubon, Thailand. Food and medical supplies had been dropped for the troops and Colonel Toosey urged them not to eat and drink too much, 'as dire consequences would ensue'. But as before, some gorged on the food until their emaciated bodies could take no more and they died after surrender; a situation that would have been avoided if they had heeded advice.

His Royal Artillery 118th Field Regiment was nearly 700 strong when it arrived in Singapore. On departure, records show 287 died; approximately 420 survived. Fergus left Ubon by lorry: destination Bangkok. The camp gates opened, and the road ahead was lined with Japanese guards. Some bowed in traditional style as the trucks sped through, some even waved.

Their journey to the railway was via a wide river crossing where small canoes ferried men across, six to a boat. There were hopes of an RAF airlift to Rangoon, but Ubon's runway was said to be mined, preventing planes from landing. Fergus's group eventually arrived at a Bangkok aerodrome, where

Dakota planes left every few minutes with troops to whisk them to safety. The plane he was in carried newspapers, and headlines from the outside world raised their spirits and tempered their mixed emotions. The sympathetic pilot thought Fergus and his fellow troops would enjoy a breathtaking flight over the railway they built. Over Kanburi and Tamarkan, Fergus could see Chungkai and Wampo Viaduct. He was both sad and amazed.

'Mile after mile, bridge after bridge, the whole area spread out below us. It was incredible to see, but also horrific to think how our slave labour built this.'

The passengers were silent. Everyone knew what it was like down there – when they were lost to the world. They were the lucky ones who survived the confines of brutality, disease, starvation and death. Now, as they flew over the graveyard, each silently remembered the many friends they left behind; their bodies buried among the palms, flora and fauna of Thailand's jungle.

'Rest in Peace,' they murmured.

It was a beautiful and peaceful scene, but its serenity disguised the horrors. Some wiped a tear; others shut their eyes to eliminate the nightmare.

If Stan had taken the same route, similar sentiments would have been felt, remembering his best friends Gordon Hunter, Bill 'Trigger' Weeks and Sid Cowling. Such vibrant young men, left behind in a grave below, and sadly immortalized forever in their twenties.

* * *

Fergus flew to Rangoon. The noise of the low-flying Dakota scattered herds of buffalo; another scene etched into their memories as they crossed verdant landscape towards freedom. The plane was met by members of the Womens' Auxilliary Service Burma, WAS(B) known as 'WAS-bees'. Fergus was assigned to Insein Road camp – laughably pronounced *insane* – where he slept in a bell tent with different mixes of rank. The group was held there for a month for 'fattening up', but that was not what they wanted, they just wanted to go home. He enjoyed the delights of Rangoon in his new uniform, and eventually heard the good news that he would be on the SS *Orbita*[7] – home, the final journey.

Chapter 28

Homeward Bound

Former high commanders began to return as Singapore and Malaya became secure. Now the hierarchy saw the damage for themselves. The Mountbattens' brief stopover was soon followed by a visit from General William Slim.[1]

The PoWs eventually discovered their release was secured not only by atom bombs dropped on Japan by the US military in a secret Allied operation, but also in hard-fought Pacific battles. By the summer of 1945, Allied forces had reclaimed Borneo, Java and Sumatra, while British forces from India fought southward for the Malay Peninsula. The battles of Kohima, Irrawaddy and Imphal, and the Foo Fighter skirmishes in the Chindits, were also successful but with thousands of casualties. Pro-active planning had also called for a stronger resistance against the Japanese, and General Slim's 14th Army began to advance and attack through the peninsula to Singapore.

However, the interception of the US atom bombs, dropped on 6 and 9 August stopped everything. Undeniably, it was devastating, but not before time, as PoWs later learned they were to be exterminated. The IJA's chilling annihilation was planned for 23 August; tens of thousands were to be massacred and thrown into mass graves. When President Truman's strategic atom bombs were dropped, Japan surrendered within a week.

General Slim's men would have been two months too late, as they were estimated to arrive 23 October 1945.[2]

US action helped free the long-suffering men who were in danger of starvation. It was a grand plan that took time to implement and succeed; longer than McArthur[3] envisaged, as Japanese forces were defiant. The two British ships carrying naval personnel from Kenya and Colombo, were HMS *Cleopatra and* HMS *Sussex*. They, in turn, would help prisoners regain their strength and dignity, as well as clear the destruction. Signals operator Jeff Hoare[4] recalled of Changi: 'It smelt like the devil.'

*   *

Fresh 'jungle greens' were issued in Singapore and at other camps. Finally, with decent clothes, the men began to feel free and human again. Trucks arrived every few days to collect the PoWs in preparation for their journey home. The promised ships arrived at the port and in most cases, the free men were assigned to a hired military transport ship (HMT). In the two-day period of 26 and 27 September, Stan was finally selected for a vessel. He was happier now, but it had been six long weeks since the surrender:

The one I was aboard was the Sobieski, a Polish ship. We set sail the end of September for the UK. We went via [Ceylon and] *the Suez Canal and the Mediterranean.*

When they called in at Colombo, there was a terrific welcome. A Scottish band met them on the jetty and, strangely enough, Colonel Ferguson Roberts, who Stan knew from his training in England years before, also greeted them.

In Suez, at Port Taufiq, the men were further kitted out with winter long johns, thicker uniforms and cream army socks. The troops were amazed by the size of the canal cut through the sandy terrain. For many, this was their first experience of the Middle East, spiced aromas and vivid colours, amid a cacophony of maritime sounds in an array of activity; they were grateful for the shorter route, instead of via the Cape of Good Hope. Home was on the horizon.

After the ship's captain carefully navigated the Suez Canal, avoiding other vessels, they glided through calm waters of the Mediterranean. For most of the voyage they bathed in glorious sunshine observing rocky outcrops of the distant islands, Sicily and Malta, and Tunisia's headland. A short lay-over in Gibraltar received mail from the British Fort, the last port of call before entering the great Atlantic. They also received warming navy rum – one serving every day – 'it was wonderful!' The climate became colder as they followed ancient naval routes of the Portuguese and skirted close to the recently liberated Channel Islands off the coast of France. Home was in sight. Just a few more hours. Excitement and anticipation grew. What would it be like? Was it the same? Does she still love me? Over three years had been wasted.

> *We carried on to England and arrived just outside Liverpool Harbour, where we were told we couldn't dock until the tide had come up …*

Stan laughed at the irony.

> *There was a bar apparently across the harbour and the tide was too low for our ship to go through and of course, we were sweating.*

It was Tuesday, 23 October 1945. They waited anxiously, but still had to wait to disembark at the port.

> *We arrived at Liverpool* [later that night] *and on to the jetties the following morning we were met by the Women's Voluntary Service and were coached to a big school, where the WVS women were given the job of sewing our various campaign ribbons on to our new tunics that we'd been issued with. We slept the night there. The following morning I boarded* [a specially commissioned] *train to London.*

To prevent them from speaking of their awful experience, a warning notice was handed to each man: *'Guard Your Tongue'*.[5] Stan shoved his in his pocket.

Their voyage had prepared them in a small way for rehabilitation, but the overwhelming feeling of false order in England was unexpected. The culture shock was astounding. After living in such primitive conditions for so long the sight of organised traffic and people smartly dressed – walking arm in arm – was too much. There were no beggars or guards. Had there been a war? Of course, they all knew there had been, the bomb sites of Liverpool were proof, but everyone seemed relaxed. British stoicism, stiff upper lip? Perhaps Stan had forgotten his native culture.

Typical England, it began to rain as the troops reached the busy railway station. The rushing crowds of people were somewhat alarming, but gradually they laughed off their nervousness and settled, absorbing familiar sights.

Little had changed since 1941.The public waved to them through wrought iron barriers as they, with army precision, were permitted to board first. The solid metal railway coach with eight seats per compartment had stuffed-horsehair seats of dark green mottled velour. The comfort was welcome and quite different for some after their last train journey. Just a few more hours, they were told, to London and 'the smoke'.

Stan eased his kit bag from his shoulder and stuffed it into the brass hammock shelf above the seat. His army issue rucksack was under his arm acting as an arm rest. He was lucky to have a window seat for fresh air, the blinds were pulled down. Some sat on their kit bags in the corridor. His breathing synchronised to the sound of the soft rattle of the train as it departed and increased speed along the tracks leaving Liverpool. Wrapped in his great coat, his emaciated body relaxed and before long he was snoring softly as they travelled south.

When he awoke, he chatted quietly to another soldier and smoked the Senior Service cigarette offered. The two ex-prisoners swapped their war stories careful not to wake others. Stan ate the cold NAAFI bacon roll he'd saved from breakfast, but he was thirsty. They had little in the way of sustenance for the long journey – disappointing after all they had been through, but at least they were nearly 'home'.

They trundled along the tracks to the east side of London, a circuitous route perhaps. They had veered away from Euston or St Pancras, instead passing through Highbury, Islington and Dalston stations to Bethnal Green then, finally, Liverpool Street. The men were shocked to glimpse bomb-damaged buildings through gaps in the blinds – evidence of wartime misery.

Guardsmen guided in the train with their flags, as they pulled alongside the platform. Civil servant officials armed with clipboards awaited. The clatter of carriage doors opened for the public to alight first, while the steam whistle blew, but there was no welcoming fanfare.

The dismayed soldiers thought the government didn't want the public to see them, they had been hidden for the whole journey; they were an embarrassment due to the capitulation and because of their emaciated appearance. The thought of being an outcast grated on Stan, but he was glad to be back in London.

We were met at Liverpool Street station by various voluntary conveyances: taxis, cars, you name it, they were there, including – as I later discovered – my brother-in-law-to-be, Harry, who couldn't make contact, owing to the various people controlling the arrival of us troops.

The WVS was on hand again, at numerous portable tables with refreshments – corned beef sandwiches, tea or water. He opted for London water. How could he have forgotten that taste?

Eventually, we were finally moved to an area where there were people calling out 'anybody for this and that?'

Somebody called out: 'Anybody for Balham and Streatham?'

'Yes, over here. I'm for Streatham.'

It was close enough. Stan said goodbye to his army pals and promised to keep in touch.

I got into a particular [volunteer] car, with all my luggage issued enroute from Singapore, and was soon on my way home to Mum and my fiancée.

The continued sight of the devastation in his capital city was shocking, far more than in Liverpool the day before. They crossed the Thames at London Bridge and drove through unrecognisable bombed and broken areas of his childhood – Borough, Elephant and Castle and Kennington. It was Thursday, 25 October 1945. Lost in his thoughts, he pulled the tiny address book from his breast pocket. The faded entries revisited his ordeal as, against the names of those who did not survive, he wrote in black ink with his new-issue fountain pen: 'Dead'. There were eight, including Gordon. He flipped to the back where he'd started his diary – 26 October 1941. He was 24 when he left. Now at 28 he reflected on the four years exactly that he'd been away.

Such a long time to be gone, but he was almost home.

*   *

Fergus and the former PoWs were well cared for by nurses on board the *SS Orbita* as it crossed the Bay of Bengal. They stopped in Colombo and then at Port Tewfik (Port Taufiq), at the southern end of the Suez Canal. From there they sent messages home. The telegram message pads were pre-formatted, a quick fix for message selection, but there was an innate desire to hang on to the pad and pencil – just in case they might be useful – a survival 'need' from days in captivity with few possessions. It was unavoidable; several others copied him.

Fergus' journey home was later than Stan's, and they prepared for colder northern weather and were taken to an army warehouse for warmer clothes. An empty kit bag was handed to each as they were directed to individual piles of army garments. Packing them into the bag they were told they could spend two minutes adding more from the store – whatever they wanted. No records were kept as most just grabbed anything. Fergus chose a potato peeler!

Compared to the silent arrival of HMT *Sobieski*, Fergus's experience was different at Liverpool docks on 9 November 1945. There was a huge welcome with loud fog horns sounding in all directions as they approached the Merseyside port, but by nightfall the noise had dwindled. At disembarkation there was nobody to greet them as they walked down the gangplank, almost as if their arrival was secret. They were split into different groups and sent to a reception hall, where a general greeted them, and announced that no one could leave. This was their accommodation for the night. They were given a meal and received back-pay to October 1941. However, they were told to look after the cutlery, as it would be all they would get, and to bring it back for breakfast in the morning. Such frugality jarred with the troops, especially after what they'd gone through. Fergus kept his.

Following Stan's routine two weeks before, their fresh uniforms had campaign medals attached and the men boarded a train reserved for troops. On board, all doors were locked, and blinds pulled down for the entire journey to London. Why didn't anybody want to see these returning troops? Were they a disgrace as part of the biggest capitulation in British military history? If so, the disgrace wasn't expected to continue on home soil. They were stunned.

Imprisoned (again) in compartments akin to rice trains, everyone sat quietly wrapped in their thoughts. Soon they would see familiar faces and hear about their survival in the war-torn streets of London – hear about death, illness and then victory over Europe. Would they tell their families of their experiences of danger and deprivation? Could they? Would others understand what they had been through at the hands of the Japanese – uncivilised conditions, hardship and brutality?

Fergus's train arrived at Paddington station via another circuitous route, and the doors were unlocked, but only after civilians in the other carriages alighted. The troops could not immediately leave the station but, eventually, were guided to lines of waiting cars and lorries with destinations plastered on their windscreens. Fergus chose a lorry going to Charing Cross station. For the first time he could see the devastation of war-torn London. He barely recognised the streets and city landmarks, but then he realised his driver was going in the wrong direction. Fortunately, his faint memory was able to redirect him. Soon they arrived on the station's concourse and straight away he spotted his brother and sister-in-law with their daughter Valerie – and Lucille, his fiancée.

Sketches on the Steps – Part II

Sketches under Palms
The peaceful tranquil dusk
Thousands of ailing 'slaves' now
'Go up-country.' Told they must.

Build high wooden bridges,
Early starts to 'pyramids' aloft,
Finish late, gross torture,
Attap floors ne'er seemed so soft.

Sketches on the Bridge
Men weary, sick and squalid
They 'die' to live another day,
Pray; hear their fading bid.

Instead: 'Increase the ailing thousands!'
Souls decreasing by the hour
'Supido' in the monsoon heat
Depletes Frangipani flower.

Sketches in metal boxcars
Huddled, scorched, confined
Decaying transportation,
Trek through jungle slime,

Exhausted working parties
Leave kwae bridges far behind,
Less those fallen by the wayside,
Death for them was kind.

Sketches on the Pathways
Displaced and weary bands,
At Sime Road hunger pangs dissolve,
As we return to safer hands.

Then – white uniforms, smart,
Inmates from seized Italian sub!
They saw our foul and dirty huts,
Were hard to avoid and scrub.

Sketches on the Move
Squeezed to airless cells we're cast
Four to eighteen square feet.
For some, this is home at last.

Then, under Japanese Ideal,
The dreaded Co-prosperity-sphere,
Though prayers, one summer morning,
An answer did appear.

Sketches on that August Day
Whispers: 'Aren't atoms normally small?'
A great impact, a radiation flash!
Enola, Bockscar – US planes did it all.

From flying Liberators,
Leaflets peacefully flow,
Like confetti they drift and skim the air,
'We're glad you're here!' we crow.

Mighty powers on ships at sea
Agree a vital surrender pact,
Soured years of desolation:
'Why'd it take so long to act?'

Sketches freely on the steps
Imagined, before we sail,
These damn ships are so late
Will civility prevail?

Crowds fill the Mersey quay,
Lean to extend a wave –
As smiling Scousers welcome,
And thoughts of home, we crave.

Sketches from a British Train
Blinds down, hidden from the day.
There is no flag-waving welcome.
'Guard Your tongue'. But we want to say!

Our minds are numb, and bodies broken
Nightmare sweats and midnight screams,
But home's fresh air has woken
To the hopefulness of dreams.

Blamed and forgotten troops, we are
Fattened up in lands a yonder
Disguised our skeletons of cruel defeat
So that Victory in Europe goes not asunder

Sketches on the Steps
Brings the horror to the masses
A realisation that something like this
Is bad, as internment and gasses

For survivors: compensation fiercely fought,
Fifty years and maybe longer, then
Millennium year, a final sum (less tax!),
A thousand pounds ... times ten.

Sketches out of step,
Can't transpose, justify or tell,
Exactly why the British Government
Left these souls, when Singapore fell.

Jill T. Robertson

Aftermath

In the volunteer's car, Stan pulled the government notice from his pocket. All PoWs received one as they stepped on to British soil:

Guard Your Tongue

You are free. Anything you say in public or to the press is liable to be published throughout the whole world. If your story is published in the sensational press, it could cause unnecessary unhappiness to relatives and friends...

This was an order, a warning – they were not to repeat anything about their horrific experience, but an interrogation officer would be available to record their confidential story if needed.

Weary and war-torn, men returned in fractured units; remnants of 1941's young and fit brigades. There was no public inquiry as to why thousands of men intended for service in the Middle East had changed course to the Far East and been ordered to surrender within a fortnight of arrival. It would be decades before Stan knew the truth about the mortal danger they were in, and General Slim's 14th Army's plan to recapture Singapore.

* * *

Stan's driver took him to the top of Mitcham Road. He thought it odd that not a single friend or relative met him at the station. He walked the rest of the way noticing traffic was busier than before, as he passed familiar streets – Greyswood, Southcroft, Seely, Vectis and Links – under the railway bridge, turned right on Ashbourne then second left into Edenvale Road. He congratulated himself for remembering the way; number 32 – home.

He tried the front door. It was locked, but he tapped loudly on the windowpane, supposing his familiar rat-a-tat-tat knock might still be recognised. He waited for what seemed an age staring at the step. Finally, he turned away, to think of another plan as he didn't have a key. Then suddenly the door opened and there stood his mother, wide-eyed, in disbelief.

With open arms she gathered him in, laughing and crying not wanting to let go. Her enveloping hug was just what he wanted and few words were needed through their laughter and tears.

Emma Moore couldn't believe it was him. At last. She saw her son was tanned, much slimmer and smart in his uniform, but under his greatcoat the khaki fabric hung loose. She could feel his protruding bones and looked again at his thin face. They both knew why, but no words were spoken for a few seconds. She cupped his face in her hands as he removed his army cap. His once thick black hair had gone leaving only thinning Brylcreemed strands over a shiny bronzed scalp. She bit her lip. So many questions, so many years. 'Let's go inside.'

Silently, she helped him carry his kit into the sitting room, where he took off his coat and sat down. He was expected, as Pat's brother was due to meet him at the station, but Stan didn't know Harry would be there and must have missed him. He explained his journey from Liverpool to London and the volunteer's car and his mother wanted to hear about the last three years, but it was too much. Stan kept quiet, remembering the notice 'Guard Your Tongue'.

Instead, she made tea. Stan was tired and his hands shook as he sipped the hot milky drink with two sugars from the familiar china cup and saucer. A cream-coloured envelope lay on the small table in front of him. 'It's for you,' said his mother.

Surprised, he put down the teacup and picked up the letter, noticing the embossed Royal Crest. Inside was a single sheet from King George VI. A hero's welcome home. They both struggled to speak; but Stan knew his mother was proud. Moments later, his father returned from his allotment and was equally overwhelmed with joy to see his son alive.

His parents understood his reticence to speak of his ordeal. Stan processed his thoughts; it felt strange to be in England after months of captivity – free and back to civilisation. He asked about Pat. His mother said she would send a message. There would be another time to tell his story to others, for now he wanted a relaxing bath and a comfortable bed. His nightmare 'adventure' lasting three and a half years was behind him.

Stan was asleep when Harry arrived. He was flustered because of the poor communication but glad to hear Stan was safe. The misunderstanding was upsetting for both, but Stan made sure of the most important rendezvous a few hours later when he was reunited with Pat and, in that moment, three and a half years of deprivation seemed to vanish in an instant.

THE END

Epilogue

'Vanish in an instant', how could that be? Three and half years of fear and degrading conditions, missing family, the death of many friends under atrocious conditions. But Stan Moore looked to the future, harbouring only memories of which he preferred not to speak. Outwardly he was a jolly person with a happy disposition, and able to deal with anything thrown at him.

Valerie Anckorn captured the day Fergus came home:

The first memory I had of my Uncle Fergus, was on the day he and his fellow Japanese prisoners of war were returned in army lorries from Liverpool to Charing Cross station in London for collection by their relatives at the end of World War II. It was November 1945.

My parents and I waited and waited – I was about 7 at that time. The station was dark and dismal with soot-coloured walls. Many lorries drove into the murky station forecourt filled with thin, grinning soldiers in their khaki uniforms, all so happy to be nearly home. But no sight of Fergus. After what seemed like searching forever for his familiar face, there he eventually was, gaunt, but with such a cheeky smile – emaciated, thin as a rake.

We took the homeward-bound train, passed innumerable bombed-out houses with gaping walls that revealed ravaged bedrooms, and tattered curtains on the breeze. Nature had begun to take over: buddleia bushes with their purple flowers growing on high-up broken walls and pink willowherb covering piles of fallen bricks, brightening up bomb-blast exteriors. Twenty minutes of 'clickity-clack' on the steam-train and soon Dunton Green station appeared where the rest of the Anckorn Family waited on the platform for Fergus, with huge grins on their faces.[1]

Fergus began to come to terms with being home but suffered mental exhaustion a few weeks later, when his memory failed. On a return journey to central London, Fergus couldn't remember why he was there. His surroundings felt familiar – he knew he was back in England – but he realised he needed help. Finding a traditional red telephone box, he flicked through the A–Z telephone directories for a long time, until he came across an advertisement for his father's employer, DC Thomson. He rang the number and asked for his father by his first name, Wilfred, which he'd managed to extract from his memory. The switchboard operator connected him.

'It's Ferg, Dad.'

They were supposed to meet for lunch. His father had waited more than an hour. Fergus said he was at a station and his father suggested Charing Cross, which Fergus confirmed, but he had completely forgotten where he was going and why. When found, there was no analysis, only silence during the homeward train journey, nothing more was said. No questions, no explanations, just a father's intrinsic acceptance of the help required for his son's recovery from his wartime ordeal.

Valerie remembered:

> Fergus retired to his bedroom and wouldn't come out for weeks having, in his own words, 'gone a bit peculiar' – no psychiatric help in those days for the after-effects of the trauma of war and incarceration. I was told specifically never to mention the Japanese. However, he eventually recovered and could talk about his experiences.

His niece remembered his skills fondly, he had crafted her some authentic wooden shoes:

> ...blocks of oblong wood with toe thongs for the village fete Chinese fancy dress, straight after the war.

She won first prize!

> I delighted in Uncle coming to our house. He and my father, Gordon
> Anckorn, were competitive siblings, attempting to outdo each other
> on the lawn by back-flipping around the perimeters. They would
> also walk on their hands and do all sorts of gymnastics. I was a silent
> and awed little spectator.

They were both members of The Magic Circle and performed clever and
astonishing conjuring tricks. Valerie believed they were wizards.

On 26 January 1946, Fergus married Lucille and they honeymooned
in Scotland at Melrose, where he had been posted in 1941. They had two
children, Deborah and Simon.

After the war, he was re-employed by Marley Tiles for six years and later
became an office manager at a Brasted timber yard, then at Redland Bricks.
While there, he applied for an evening part-time teaching position in French
and Pitman's shorthand at West Kent College, Tonbridge. This enabled him
to embark on a successful new career for the rest of his working life.

When Valerie was 18, she joined one of Fergus's classes to spruce up her
secretarial skills.

> Fergus had learned shorthand early on in order to be a journalist like
> his father – a food earner for him in the PoW camp, as he could write
> down the phonetic 'sounds' the guards uttered and run across the
> camp to read them back to the recipient. He wouldn't have known
> what he was repeating, but he was understood. Food was his reward.

> His classes were a delight. He always had a dry sense of humour and
> deadly wit (that probably helped keep up his spirits when in captivity).
> He was always a hero in my eyes and so damned handsome to boot!

*   *   *

Stan, on 'Y' List, was assigned to 333 Company in Hounslow, a few weeks
after returning home, to complete the rest of his army service. It wasn't until

May 1946 that he was released from Royal Army Service Corps duties and that his colonel spoke of his exemplary military conduct via a testimonial attached to his RASC 'Soldiers Release Book Class A':

> Driver Moore has been a PoW in Japanese hands for over three and a half years, which unfortunately precludes the provision of a full estimate of his capabilities. Prior to capture he was employed as a driver and carried out his duties very satisfactorily. He is honest and of sober habits and is recommended for civilian employment corresponding to his former military employment.

Gordon Hunter did not receive a letter from the king or a testimonial from a colonel, but that month, Stan received a letter from Gordon's widow, Elizabeth Hunter, in which was enclosed an original note of condolence regarding the death of her husband. The letter, dated 13 November 1945, was from his officer in the Changi wood-cutting party – *R. M. Horner. Capt. RASC.*

Stan had been deprived of a good friend, but Lizzie Hunter had lost her husband. The rawness of a war widow was heart-wrenching, but Captain Horner's duty to write to bereaved relatives of his fallen men portrayed Gordon as a serving soldier of whom she could be proud. Lizzie's further contact with Stan helped dilute their emotions at a difficult time, sharing acts of kindness and compassion for their loss. Stan kept Horner's letter safely among his wartime possessions for the rest of his life.

Pat and Stan made plans to marry on 29 June 1946, at St Nicholas's Church, Tooting, SW17. He wore his de-mob suit and Pat wore a new pale blue dress that matched her eyes. A wedding telegram dryly observed, 'From one captivity to another!' They sped off on Stan's motorbike and sidecar to honeymoon on the Isle of Wight, off England's southern coast. At the end of 1946, they were both invited to a welcome home party for prisoners of war by Mitcham relatives of the PoWs' Association, where 'Chesterfields and sausage rolls' were on the menu – an unusual combination.

In April 1947, Stan completed a carpentry course under the rehabilitation programme offered at Waddon in Croydon. There he improved skills he'd learned in Changi and worked as a cabinet maker at Marco's in Streatham.

He tucked the war years behind him and looked to the future. He knew he was lucky to be alive.

After eight years of marriage, Pat and Stan built their own house, had twin girls and upgraded his motorbike combination to a car. First, a black Ford, then a blue model E93A with orange indicators that flipped out at the side, and a front-opening windscreen. Stan was happy for the most part; always whistling and dancing while he performed household tasks or worked in the garden each weekend. Summer family outings to watch cricket in a sleepy Surrey village was not boring to him. All he wanted was peace.

'Not remembering' became a choice but might not have erased the horrors he experienced. Details lay undivulged for decades. Some of the worst stories seeped out from 'up-country' workers, which left men such as Stan, who stayed in or near Changi, feeling guilty because they had not suffered in the same way. Deleting mechanisms were employed but anger bubbled deep inside. The government warning, galvanising the instruction never to speak of their experience in the Far East, was uppermost.

Years faded the feelings of victims of the Japanese and Korean guards, expunging, perhaps, the memories of those who had been there. But hidden in the heart and soul of many who passed through the camps in the Far East and Japan, an intrinsic and everlasting scorn and hatred remained. Flashbacks of the brutality, starvation, depravity, psychological malnutrition, murder and torture terrorised these people, far beyond the comprehension of any civilians or future generations.

As time evolved, British Legion clubs around the country became places where they could gather and laugh about the funnier side of their ordeal. This led them to wonder, and appreciate, how on earth they had survived; but their light-heartedness only disguised heavy truths and, often, the burden of their nightmares stayed with them for the rest of their lives.

*   *   *

Our dad was a cheerful, mild-mannered man who loved to cook soup from abundant home-grown vegetables, brew beer, ferment wine, or turn his hand to almost any craft. As a trained cabinet maker and shopfitter for thirty years, he learned many techniques and used his Changi recycling skills to create something out of nothing. Our families' houses were full of Stan-made wooden furniture and other creations, some from old rubber tyres repurposed as garden plant pots or, even unwanted flip-flops to replace the soles of our worn-out shoes. The carpentry profession was strenuous and did not pay well then, however, and he would not rest after a day's work because he needed to be occupied, a solid trait that had helped him through captivity.

He left Marco's and worked in the south of England with his employer, Len Whatley, on several shopfitting projects. One time, on 21 July 1965, they survived the vortex of a rare British tornado while driving along the A3 close to Wisley, Surrey. Their Bedford Transit van was engulfed by a swirl of roaring wind, leaves and debris, resembling a crazed flock of birds, when a large tree smashed through the windscreen. They both survived, suffering only shock and Stan's grazed knuckles when he froze as he gripped the steering wheel.

He later moved to a larger firm in Tonbridge, Kent, where he built insulated freezer units for cold storage rooms such as J. Sainsbury. Assignments were far but he always came home as our mother suffered from depression. Pat (Daisy) was on a prescribed mixture of drugs which Dad had to make sure were taken correctly to maintain her mental stability. Her propensity to be called 'Pat' was dropped in the mid-sixties to avoid confusion since she was also known as 'Lawrie' to her Co-op and Bletchley Park friends. Her wartime years in the Foreign Office had taken a toll on her too and, as a consequence of her intelligence work, she never wanted to speak about the war, or travel far, for fear of attack or sinking ships. Instead, Dad arranged short coach excursions in England and Europe, usually accompanied by relatives or friends. However, when he arranged a flight to Singapore to re-tread his steps as a PoW, and for him to show her the origin of his Red Cross box of mementoes and where he spent three and a half years of his life, she conceded. In the mid-1960s he gave up smoking to save for a trip to Singapore and Thailand – the ultimate pilgrimage. Friends, family and neighbours were astounded he wanted to return to the country of his incarceration! In the 1980s it was a trip of a life-time and nothing would stop him.

* * *

Growing up, we listened to the BBC's *Two-way Family Favourites* presented by Cliff Michelmore and his wife, Jean Metcalf. They played music for British forces posted overseas (BFPO), but the requests meant nothing to us then. One place was Kowloon, Hong Kong. The radio show aired for many years after the Japanese massacre and imprisonment of the medical professionals. Now, knowing the Second World War atrocities in the Far East, we see why this programme was so important; the tragedy was still fresh in many folks' memories. The programme continued until 1980.

Stan was a remarkable man. Warm, mild mannered, polite and considerate, with a cheeky sense of humour, charming to be around. He was always happy to lend anyone a hand using his skills and, while he troubled over spelling and some maths, he was expert with a 'Stanley' tape measure applying acute precision in all his woodwork. When we, his daughters, had art projects at school he was delighted to educate with sketching and drawing. Nothing was too much trouble. If our bicycles or cars needed attention, he would fix them. He helped other relatives with significant carpentry projects: a bespoke hatch, cabinets or a front porch. Pottering around his garage, greenhouse or garden, was his joy – it was immaculate. Our parents courted an uncomplicated life, for reasons we now understand. 'Anything for an easy life' was his mantra.

When he discovered years later that the Japanese emperor had ordered surviving captives in *every camp* to be exterminated in August 1945, Stan had the upsetting realisation that his life, as he knew it, might not have existed.

Now we all know why.

Authors' Notes

In 1999, after decades of campaigning for compensation from the government, FEPOWs won entitlement, via the Royal British Legion, to ex-gratia payment. Previously, they had been offered derisory amounts of £30.00 and £70.00, but only when led by the RBL, who backed ex-PoWs, such as Ernest Warwick – the sapper who helped the old Chinese lady in 1942, and who was punished by being tethered to a tree in a coffin for days – did they achieve acceptable recompense. Campaigners knew the Government waited for the majority of PoWs to die but in 2000, the Millenium ex-gratia payment £10,000 (less tax) was eventually offered. Those still alive took it.[1] The deliberate 55-year delay ensured the government had less to pay out.

If it wasn't for *The One Show* and meeting Fergus, we might still only have a partial account of our Moore prisoner of war story – written sparsely in a small pocket diary and elaborated on a set of Philips cassettes. We are thankful for his story and that of others who provided visual insights into the experiences our father endured.

Jill learned through several conversations with Fergus that, among his many legacies, he ensured a commemorative tree was planted in 2000 at the National Memorial Arboretum, Alrewas, Staffordshire. The plaque reads:

In memory of
The many hundreds of the 118th Field Regiment,
Royal Artillery who died as slaves of the Japanese.

Fergus forgave Japanese leaders for the torture and ill-treatment of prisoners of war, knowing that we all have just one life and to bear a grudge is futile. Stan and Captain Horner were not so forgiving.

On 22 September 2017, Fergus performed what was to be his last '*Conversation With …*' evening, moderated by his author and good friend, Peter Fyans. From the small stage at Hurstpierpoint Assembly Hall, they spoke of his time in Changi and up-country in Thailand. A surprise appearance by Magic Circle magician and winner of *Britain's Got Talent* – Richard Jones – enthused Fergus's appreciative audience in West Sussex. Further magic followed and in a flourish of showmanship Fergus officially announced he had passed on his magician secrets especially for his renowned 'egg trick' to Richard, his successor. Six months later, 22 March 2018, the great Wizardus passed away.

*   *   *

From our father's memories, mementoes, the tapes and the letter regarding Gordon Hunter, we knew he too served with Captain Horner. We discovered a wealth of his wartime history, but regret missed opportunities to delve deeper with him personally, on many aspects: was he a member of Jack Greenwood's Nit Wits? Through CoFEPOW, Jill contacted Horner's youngest daughter, Sally McQuaid, author of *Singapore Diary: The Hidden Journal of Captain R. M. Horner.* This diary was also a vital source of information and with a small group of family and friends, we invited Sally and her son Anthony, to unveil a commemorative plaque in honour of our parents. The black slate memorial, installed in the front porch at our house in Mitcham on 31 May 2014, fondly recognises Driver Stanley A. W. Moore, our mother Daisy Evelyn Lawrence (Pat) – for their respective wartime service in Singapore and at Bletchley Park – and honours the lives of all Second World War heroes. It was an emotional occasion, especially when we discovered our fathers, who both lived full and healthy lives, died the same year – 2001. It was sad they never met again.

A few months before our mother died, in January 2006, Jill came across Dad's faded diary again in some of Daisy's mementoes and instantly remembering, she decided to take ownership of this wartime treasure. Daisy, knowing of Stan's 1990 recorded story that Jan had asked her father to dictate on her Philips cassette tape, was happy that his story (their story) would one day be transcribed and perhaps published. The transcription of the diary recommenced in 2013 – it was bitter-sweet – Dad had lost many army friends, but our parents' relationship had stood the test of time, despite their individual wartime battles. They were, after all, grateful to be alive.

In March 2016, Jill opened her front door and in stepped Judith Quick, the daughter of Freddie Holt, Captain Horner's Batman – another route to more information. She also had the formal 18th Division company photograph (which Jill was able to tell her was taken in Droitwich). On the back were names of some of the men in Stan's tiny address book. We examined other photos that she brought and compared celluloid scenes in the grounds of Brook House, Knutsford where our fathers were posted for training in June 1941. Here was proof that Stan and Freddie stood shoulder to shoulder with Sid, Mac and Trigger, and we hope to locate the other thirty-nine men in the 'Address Book', especially for Gordon Hunter's story and his widow, Elizabeth Steele-Hunter, who later remarried to become Mrs Hunter-Montgomerie, living in Glasgow. See *Address Book List* in the photo plates section.

Meeting so many descendants of FEPOW brings tangible feelings of family and good fortune to perpetuate the memory and this never-to-be-repeated sad episode of history.

* * *

Researchers, Meg Parkes and Geoff Gill, from the Liverpool School of Tropical Medicine, have compiled many studies on tropical diseases aided by the diminishing band of Far East PoW survivors. Parkes states the diseases are not easily eradicated and that ex-PoWs suffer recurrences for many years. For instance, malnutrition, with an irritating symptom of tingling feet, damages the nerves. Their studies on tropical wartime malnutrition, even recently on one 90-year-old person, still saw worm infections.

The loss of limbs was widespread, not only for those in combat but also for those with malnutrition and other diseases. Temporary prosthetics were made by creative Far East medics under extensive and challenging conditions. But their amputee supports could bend at the knee and ankle and were well made. They defied the odds to make life bearable. In the 1980s, a surviving amputee with a camp-made prosthesis suffered severe ulcers and a new device was made for him in Britain. However, he found it uncomfortable and returned to the old version – which he used until it fell apart. The original was made from bamboo and a rucksack![2]

Tens of thousands died. Land, money, greed, religion, power? What was it all for? Freedom? But freedom is rarely free, and memories of war and hurt only linger for survivors. Some told their stories; others cannot – their horror too painful. Man's war is not a game. It is murder. Security with diplomacy is preferable and one continues to hope lessons are learned, especially for future generations now that strong empathetic women leaders endeavour to address the imbalance of male-dominated oppression and physical conflict.

The Imperial Japanese nation may have lost the battles for resources to attain their co-prosperity sphere, but as the USA were prominent in patching up a war-torn world, they also involved Japan in a new world regeneration. The Japanese may have lost the aggressive war but in the end were successful in their technological and economic battles.

'Seventy-one years ago, on a bright cloudless morning, death fell from the sky and the world was changed…,' began President Barak Obama on 27 May 2016, in a conciliatory step to acknowledging America's part in war horrors. Japan had apologised before, several times, for the conduct of its Imperial armies.

President Obama's emotional apology for America's atomic bomb attack on Japan was made at the Hiroshima Peace Memorial in the presence of President Shinzo Abe.[3] He asked the world to take stock, learn from past aggressions and heed what type of mankind we have become. Our human race – a family at war? Is nuclear defence protection? Could it happen again? Our world remains fragile from lack of diplomacy, too many weapons, too many greedy people, restrictive trade tariffs, divisions and global warming. The memory of such tragedy should never fade.

Appendix

As the men arrived home, the reality of how they had been freed gradually became known and they discovered how enemy tactics affected the lives of troops and civilians during their three-year incarceration. But some operational secrets and strategies were not released for many years.

Liverpool Docks

This operation, known as Western Approaches HQ, worked with British Intelligence. Another place of wartime secrets, its identity was not revealed until several decades after the war. Through their work, the German ship *Bismarck* was sunk in May 1941. Nicknamed 'The Fortress', Western Approaches employed 400 staff who searched for threatening German vessels and U-boats in the Atlantic. The secret Map Room contributed to the safety of convoys and ultimately victory in the Second World War. Reports on enemy message intercepts were processed there daily to ensure merchant ships crossing the Atlantic had 24-hour protection as they brought precious supply cargos to and from Britain. This protection also extended to the lives of troops transported abroad including Winston's Special convoy in October 1941. *Liverpool Museum Rumford Street, Exchange Flags, Liverpool L2 8SZ.*

Hainan

Japanese forces assembled for the invasion in 1941 on Hainan Island and in French Indo-China. Troop build-up was noticed by the Allies and challenged, but Japan advised this related to China operations. When the Japanese invaded, they had over 200 tanks. In addition, they had over 500 combat aircraft. Commonwealth troops were equipped with the Lanchester

6x4 Armoured Car, Marmon-Herrington Armoured Car, Universal Carrier and only twenty-three obsolete Mk VIB light tanks (in the 100th Light Tank Squadron of the Indian Army), none of which were sufficiently armed for armoured warfare. They had just over 250 combat aircraft, but half of these were destroyed inside the first few days of combat. *En.Wikipedia.org/wiki/ malayan campaign.*

Internees – Singapore

Final roll call August 1945 for British Sime Road Internees camp was:

	British UK	British Eurasian	British Jew
Men	2167	305	222
Women	393	299	170
Children	58	154	90

Other nationalities included: American 14 men, 9 women; Australian 143 men, 31 women, 11 children; South African: 8 men, 1 woman; New Zealanders: 50 men, 3 women; Netherlands: 65 men, 28 women; Chilean: 2 men; Iraq: 57 men, 47 women, 7 children. Many smaller groups of adults from India, Spain, Belgium, Greece, Egypt, Norway, Brazil, Rumania, Armenia, Southern Ireland, Iran, Russia, Denmark, Poland, Czechoslovakia, China and about nine other undetermined nationalities. The total 'bottom line' of the Roll was: 3,159 Men; 1,023 Women; 328 Children (with a mere 3 missing from camp). *Changi Sime Road Camp Internees. Final Roll August 1945.*

https://specialcollections-blog.lib.cam.ac.uk/?p=11086

Bibliography References

Atcherley, Harold, *Prisoner of Japan* (Memoirs Publishing 2012)

Burton, Lieutenant General Reginald, *The Railway of Hell* (Pen & Sword Books 2002)

Cordingly, Louise, *Echoes of Captivity* (High Winds Publishing 2020)

Farndale, General Sir Martin, KCB, *The Far East Theatre 1941–46* (Brassey's, Royal Artillery Institution 2000)

Felton, Mark, *The Coolie Generals* (Pen & Sword Books 2008)

Fyans, Peter, *Captivity, Slavery and Survival as a Far East PoW – The Conjurer on the Kwai* (Pen & Sword Books 2011)

Gillies, Midge, *The Barbed-Wire University* (Aurum Press 2011)

Kandler, Richard, *The Prisoner List* (Morsworth Publishing 2010)

McQuaid, Sally, *Singapore Diary, The Hidden Journal of Captain R M Horner* (Spellmount Ltd 2007)

Slimming, Jan, *Codebreaker Girls A Secret Life at Bletchley Park* (Pen & Sword 2021)

Thompson, Peter, *The Battle for Singapore: The true story of Britain's greatest military disaster.* (Piatkus 2006)

Urquhart, Alistair, *The Forgotten Highlander* (Little Brown Book Group 2011)

Abbreviations

AA	Anti-Aircraft
ABDACOM	American British Dutch Australian Command
ADAPS	Assistant Director Army Postal Service
ADS	Advanced Dressing Station
AIF/CSC	Australian Imperial Forces/Combined Selection Centre
ATS	Auxiliary Territorial Services
BAPO	British Army Post Office
BFPO	British Forces Posted Overseas
BM/BEM	British Movements/British Escort Movements
BRA	Brigade Royal Artillery
CAAD	Command Anti-Aircraft Defence
CCB	Close Combat Badge
CE	Combat Engineer (Cmd. Southern Area)
CMG	Companion (Knighthood)
CoFEPOW	Children of Far East Prisoners of War
CRA/CRE	Company of Royal Artillery/Royal Engineers
DDOS	Deputy Director of Ordnance Services
DDSS	Deputy Director of Signals Services
DDST	Deputy Director of Supplies and Transport
DPE	Defensive Planning and Execution
DSD	Divisional Supply Depot
DSO	Distinguished Service Order
EFM	Expeditionary Force Message
ENSA	Entertainments National Service Association
ESO	Embarkation Staff Officer
FEPOW	Far East Prisoner of War
FECB	Far East Combined Bureau
FPOD	Field Post Office/Division
FMSVF	Federated Malay States Volunteer Force
FRUEF (Anderson)	Fleet Radio Unit Eastern Fleet (Anderson)

GEC	General Electric Company
GOC	General Officer Commanding
G&W	Garden and Wood areas
HMS/HMT	His Majesty's Ship/His Majesty's Transport
IGD	Imperial Guard Division
IJA	Imperial Japanese Army
INA	Indian National Army
IPS	Indian Postal Service
IWM	Imperial War Museum
LSTM	Liverpool School of Tropical Medicine
MBE	Member of the British Empire
MC	Military Cross
MEF	Middle East Forces
MO	Medical Officer
MV	Motor Vessel
M&V	Meat and Veg.
NAAFI	Navy Army Air Force Institute
NCO	Non-Commissioned Officer
OC	Officer Commanding
OR(s)	Other Rank(s)
RE	Royal Engineers
RAF	Royal Air Force
RACS	Royal Arsenal Co-operative Society
RAMC	Royal Army Medical Corps
RAOC	Royal Army Ordnance Corps
RAPWI	Repatriation of Allied Prisoners of War and Internees
RASC	Royal Army Service Corps
RIASC	Royal India Army Service Corps
RMS	Royal Mail Ship
RSM	Regimental Sergeant Major
RTO	Railway Transfer Officer
SD	Supply Depot
SOP	Senior Officers' Party
USS	United States Ship
VE/VJ	Victory (in) Europe/Victory (over) Japan
WVS	Women's Voluntary Service

Acknowledgements

After extensive research we cast our thoughts to those who have helped along the way to compile the Second World War story of our dad, Stan Moore. Sincere thanks go to the Anckorn Family, where Fergus – their flamboyant patriarch with his continued zest for magic and storytelling – became our inspiration, and latterly his niece, author Valerie Gordon Anckorn. Our father died in 2001 and Fergus became our go-to PoW. Of course, posthumous thanks go to Dad for writing his little faded diary, and to Mum for keeping this and the box of mementoes safe. An indebtedness goes to many authors (some listed in the bibliography) who dared to write and reveal the conflicts and conditions in the Far East, as early as 1960, under censor. Without them, piecing together our knowledge of the theatres of war in South Asia and the Far East would have been difficult.

Gratitude and thanks to those credited in the end notes, which extends to the staff at the National Archives at Kew, volunteers at CoFEPOW: Keith Andrews, David Brede, and Alan and Chris Wills who work tirelessly to ensure the longevity of the PoW exhibit at the National Memorial Arboretum. To the many members of West Sussex CoFEPOW, including Anne Humphreys, the Spreadburys, and especially Carol Boxell, whose father was FEPOW, RA Gunner George Staples (HAA), who gave Jill an incredible tome – *The Far East Theatre 1941–1946* – which became her bible for learning and absorbing the intricacies of that time.

Thanks to our editors at Pen & Sword and to Simon Burgess for providing the IJA Admonition and High Command capitulation documents. And to Geoffrey 'Jeff' Hoare for his splendid 1945 ceremonial photos of the Padang in Singapore at the official Japanese surrender. To descendants Sally and Tony McQuaid, Judith Quick, Angie Taylor, and the Southwater History group – Patsy Laker and Paula Lucerne, niece of John Rookwood a victim of the march from Sandakan, Borneo. Through these collective groups, often emotional father, uncle, or grandfather tales have been eulogised with compassion and commemorated at social or memorial gatherings.

Heartfelt thanks go to all our family members and friends, but essentially to Andy, Chris and Amber (Jill) and Allan, Harry, Jonathan and Becky (Jan) who have given support in various ways.

> Father made our history. He fought for what he thought would somehow set us free.
>
> Authors, Jill Robertson and Jan Slimming

End Notes

Introduction

1. 'Changi' is the native word for the Balanocarpus tree, some of the tallest trees that used to grow in Singapore. The Story of Changi | COFEPOW

Chapter 2

1. *Railway of Hell*, Reginald Burton.
2. *Railway of Hell*, Reginald Burton.
3. Liverpool Docks and Western Approaches. See Appendix.

Chapter 3 Leaving: Convoys

1. www.britain-at-war.org.uk/ww2/alberts_war/html/winston_s_specials.htm. Includes Halifax and crossing the line ceremonies. In an unprecedented move, the British troops were witnessing the result of Winston Churchill's urgent 'Most Secret' message to Roosevelt asking for US Navy ships to escort their convoy. The 18th Division were reinforcements destined for the Middle East.
2. USS *Wakefield* www.britain-at-war.org.uk/ww2/albertswar/html/winstons. specials.htm. Naval-history.net xAH-WS convoys04-194 1B.
3. Cockney: a slang term for Londoners 'born within the sound of Bow Bells', St Mary-le-Bow Church, City of London.
4. Wolf Packs of German U-boat submarines, hunted and attacked Allied supply convoys in the Atlantic. German Naval Commander Karl Dönitz, gave orders to eliminate Allied shipping by instructing U-boats to track and attack, often after sundown. He wanted to starve Britain into submission. Packs of sometimes ten U-boats, would find the slow-moving convoys, but with Allied destroyer escorts there was often a deadly battle. In the occupation of France, German U-boat stations were constructed at Lorient to launch submarines in the Bay of Biscay. Germany's navy thought it was infallible, but their encrypted Morse code radio messages were intercepted and read by Allied intelligence where, in submarine tracking rooms, U-boat locations were plotted. The intelligence derived provided deciding factors for battle, and Allied convoys were saved when re-routed. The

Battle of the Atlantic was one of the longest battles of the war, but the revelation that Bletchley Park codebreakers intercepted and read most enemy messages did not emerge until the mid-1970s.

5. USS *Ranger* (CV4) in December 1941, was returning to Norfolk from ocean patrol in Port of Spain, Trinidad and Tobago, when the Japanese attacked Pearl Harbor. www.en.wikipedia.org/wiki/USS_Ranger_(CV-4)

6. USS *Vincennes* (CA-44) left the east coast late in November with Convoy WS-12, American transports carrying British troops. USN – US Navy Naval History Center.

7. Quincy sailed with TF 16 for Iceland on neutrality duty which included a patrol in the Denmark Straits from 21–24 September. She returned to Newfoundland with a convoy on 31 October. *Quincy* then proceeded to Cape Town, South Africa, via Trinidad, where she met another convoy which she escorted back to Trinidad on 29 December 1941.

8. Their journey had five different legs. 1) Halifax to Trinidad. 2) From the Caribbean involving zigzagging (doglegging) to places such as Dragon's Mouth and Serpent's Mouth Straits between Trinidad and Venezuela to Montevideo for refuelling. 3) Montevideo to Cape Town. Doglegging on this route entailed several equator crossings and traditional 'crossing-the-line' ceremonies took place, like a rag-week ritual. If you were new at sea and fell into the group of the uninitiated, you were a 'Pollywog'. Pollywogs were caught and forced into some unsavoury action to become a 'Shellback'. The names are believed to date back 500 years. If you had been grabbed and de-bunked it only happened to you once on that vessel. Shellbacks passed on the custom to new sailors. Those who had passed over the equator many times, became 'Golden' Shellbacks. Other ceremonies in non-wartime waters would be wilder affairs including drink. Since the US Navy ships were dry, this was not the case. Ref. source: wamtnhunter.

Chapter 4 Cape Town

1. Delmonico's was a popular bar/restaurant and music venue 1930–1960. Originally opposite the Alhambra theatre, in Riebeek Street, the establishment later moved to the Seamen's Institute in Lower Burg Street, Cape Town.

2. HMS *Prince of Wales* and HMS *Repulse* took part in sinking the *Bismarck*, North Atlantic, May 1941.

3. Pearl Harbor: The New Evidence, Channel 4.com/programmes/Secret History. Based on Andrew Summers and Robbyn Swan's '*A Matter of Honour*'. Japan knew the US Navy was the only battle-force that could hinder their plans to conquer the Far East, its trade and its people. Their strategic presence across the Pacific was crucial for them to succeed.

4. The HMS *Dorsetshire* (*'the Dorset'*), a heavy cruiser, 633ft long with three chimney stacks, was built in 1930 at Portsmouth Dockyard – part of the Royal Navy County Class. She was 'war-equipped' and involved in sinking the Bismarck. After *the Dorset* left the convoy, six escorts remained including HMS *Exeter*, famous for serving at the 1939 Battle of the River Plate against the German battleship Admiral *Graf Spee*. On 5 April 1942, *The Dorset* and *Cornwall* were sunk in battle with the Japanese Navy in the Indian Ocean, 500 miles from Sri Lanka (Ceylon). 424 officers and crew were lost. en.wikipedia.org/wiki/Indian_Ocean_raid, www.bbc.co.uk/history/ww2peopleswar/stories/60/a3808460.shtml, CoFEPOW/Wikipedia www.dorsetshire.pwp.blueyonder.co.uk/

5. A gift from the British government (and Winston Churchill).

6. Under British orders at 0700hrs, the two ships urgently ran at 20 knots towards Bombay arriving at 1600hrs.

7. *Sisters in Arms* by Nicola Tyrer. As part of the tyrannical control prisoners endured over four years under the IJA, survivors incarcerated at North Point were restricted in their letters to conceal Japanese atrocities. But one nurse, Kathleen Thomson kept addresses of next of kin of all those she nursed and wrote to their relatives after the war. She achieved this by writing on a thin piece of paper hidden in a talcum powder tin. From her selfless endeavours many Britons were able to discover the fate of their loved ones.

Chapter 5 Ahmednagar, India

1. *McQuaid*.

2. E W Backhouse. en.wikipedia.org/wiki/Edward_Backhouse_(British_Army_officer).

3. *McQuaid*.

4. The cart or 'jinker' is pulled by a team of bullocks attached to a yoke by a special chain, or rope, for one or two animals. The driver and other passengers sit at the front of the cart, while the load is placed at the back. Traditionally, their cargo was agrarian goods or lumber. *Wikipedia – Bullock Cart*.

5. Khandan: a Noor Jehan musical. *Encyclopaedia of Indian Cinema*, New Revised Edition 1999. *Wikipedia*.

6. Museum exhibit, IWM Manchester, Horner's account re leaving Ahmednagar. *McQuaid*.

7. Conversation with F. Anckorn (*Westpoint*). It is uncertain whether Captain Horner also knew of this during the loading confusion of the USS *Wakefield* and *Westpoint*.

8. The salary Stan received was now US$2.00 per week, except for SA40 Rand, while in Cape Town. *S. A. W. Moore Army Paybook*.

Chapter 6 Somewhere Beyond the Indian Ocean

1. BM11 Convoy and cargo of USS *West Point* and USS *Wakefield* and escorts. The *West Point* carried approx. two-thirds of the troops from India. In all she carried approx. 5,272 men. The convoy was escorted by the light cruiser HMS *Caledon* and later the HMS *Glasgow*. The escort swelled to three cruisers and four destroyers as they approached Java. *CoFEPOW.*

2. Escort ship HMS *Hampshire*, does not appear to be in the convoy as noted in R. M. Horner's *Singapore Diary,* McQuaid. Other source: www.convoyweb.co.uk.

3. *Abide with Me.* A communal comforting traditional hymn; usually sung in times of suffering written by Henry Lyte.

4. In a sister convoy BM12 the *Felix Roussel* primarily carried stores and supplies. Soldier Bill Anderson, of 9th and 11th Northumberland Fusiliers, part of the 55th Infantry Brigade was on board. He recalled: '... a day out of Singapore we were caught in what are called The Roads (The Straits). The Japanese spotted us that day. Some planes came over and our Colonel, a First World War man, said they'll be back the next day and sure enough they were, and we were bombed. The ship behind us, the *Empress of Asia*, was sunk. We received casualties aboard – twenty were killed. We eventually got into Singapore in the second convoy formation.' *CoFEPOW.*

5. *CoFEPOW* – Ships and Chat.

6. Derbysulzers.com/felixships.

7. IWM Manchester, Horner's account. Leaving Ahmednagar. *McQuaid.*

The 17 Day Battle

1. www.roll-of-honour.com/regiments and www.wartimememoriesproject.com/ww2/allied/rasc.php#sthash.KVE6pKCX.dpuf

Chapter 7 Keppel Harbour

1. IWM Manchester. Extracts, McQuaid.

2. Thompson, Peter, *The Battle for Singapore: the true story of Britain's greatest military disaster.* Portrait Books 2005.

3. After a failed people's revolution in 1912, Siam promoted the idea of a Thai Nation. In 1932, at the time of the Great Depression, a bloodless revolution took place when military and civilian officials overthrew the monarchy. The forced transition of power granted the Siamese people their first constitution, ending centuries of absolute monarchy rule. In 1940 during European conflict, anti-Chinese and anti-French policies, the name of the country changed by decree from Siam to Thailand. Japan invaded Thailand 8 December 1941, and the Thai government joined them in a military alliance. They also declared war on America and Britain

though this was not recognised by most Allied powers. www.historytoday.com/archive/siam-becomes-thailand.

4. www.cofepow.org.uk.

5. RMS *Empress of Asia*. www.cofepow.org.uk/armed-forces-stories-list/ss-empress-of-asia. Captain A.B. Smith. On board the Empress of Asia were the Royal Northumberland Fusiliers and other regiments. Equipment from the West Point for the Royal Artillery was included in its cargo.

6. Middle-class families employed three or more staff from the local Singaporean community. Most were trustworthy. However, there was a habit of moving valuable items – say a jewelled cigarette box – towards the door. If an employer didn't notice it had been moved, it was considered the owner didn't care for the item, and eventually it would vanish. If the employee was challenged, they would appreciate its absence had been noticed and would ensure it was returned to its rightful place. An amah is a nursery maid/housekeeper.

7. *The Battle of Pearl Harbor and the Fall of Singapore*. Extract from Cromwell Productions' video of 'Changi Battlefield' S4/E4. Frame: 1:13.445 to 1:13:53, believed to be S.A.W. Moore.

8. McQuaid.

9. Television documentary, Series 4/Episode 4 Battlefield: *The Battle for Pearl Harbor and the Fall of Singapore*.

10. Farndale. Brewster Buffalo Planes and zero materiel. American fighter Brewster Buffaloes were monoplanes used by Royal Air forces in Australia, Britain and New Zealand early in the Second World War. Designed and built by the American Brewster Aeronautical Corporation, they were also used by the US Navy. At the time, compared to lighter-weight enemy planes, they were considered overweight, often unstable and largely obsolete.

11. Ernest Warwick interview and *Tony Lucas RA Gunner Audio BBC R4. The Reunion – Far Eastern Prisoners of War*.

12. Two Audio extracts from Australian film footage: *Singapore 1942: Empire*.

13. Atcherley, p.34.

Chapter 8 Move of Many

1. Teck Hock was a small rustic kampong (Chinese settlement) in north-east Singapore, off Tampines Road. www.singapurastories.com/2015/02/singapura-stories-seminar-four-the-stories-behind-two-unique-kampungs-at-lorong-muallap-and-lorong-teck-hock and en.wikipedia.org/wiki/Defu_Industrial_Park.

2. British troops urgently requisitioned private civilian houses of wealthy businessmen, particularly in the Newton Circus area. These were used for protection and military headquarters for the different units.

3. Farndale, p.54. The surprise night-time invasion between Tanjong Buloh and Tanjong Murai. *Singapore 1942*, Australian Screen.

4. Dalforce (Singapore overseas Chinese anti-Japanese volunteer army), a forces/guerilla unit of the British Straits settlement that recruited ethnic Chinese Singaporeans. It was created 25 December 1941, by Lieutenant Colonel John D. Dalley of the Federated Malaya States Police Force, with 4,000 volunteers, 1,250 armed. The unit was active until heavy defeat on 13 February 1942 (Black Friday). It was part of the Australian 22nd and the 1st Malaya Infantry brigades. Their HQ was at Kim Yam Road. Dalley's Desperados. Ref: Wikipedia Singapore 1942, Australian Screen.

5. *General Wavell Last Order; Letter to General Percival; Admonition.* Ref: CoFEPOW member Simon Burgess and his great-grandfather Captain R. G. Read. Permission kindly granted to the author by Simon Burgess, July 2018. Multiple references – Wavell/Sea Wall fall.

6. Ibid.

7. Ibid.

8. www.cofepow.org.uk/armed-forces-stories-list/singapore-at-war and Wikipedia, Sir Shenton Whitelegge Thomas, the last Governor of the Straits Settlements.

9. www.2db.com/person_bio.php?person_id=113.General Wavell ABDACOM (American British Dutch Australian Command – permission to surrender).

10. Atcherley – Escaping officers.

11. Admonition. Courtesy Simon Burgess.

12. Inaugurated 1939, the Cathay Building, at eleven storeys, was the tallest structure in Singapore. Headquarters to BMBC (British Malaya Broadcasting Corporation), including a cinema and residential properties. The elevated position gave the building prominence and was commissioned for British Army use in January 1942. En.wikipedia.org/wiki/Cathay_Building.

13. Horner's views. McQuaid.

14. Burton.

15. Ibid.

16. Handwritten letter from Yamashita to Lieutenant General Percival. Permission kindly granted to the author by Simon Burgess, July 2018 regarding his great-grandfather Captain R. G. Read.

Chapter 9 Capitulation

1. War of the Roses. Troops training c.1941. Burton.

2. Permission kindly granted to the author by Simon Burgess, July 2018, regarding his great-grandfather Captain R. G. Read.

3. The Japanese Emperor immediately declared Singapore to be the same time zone as Japan, an hour and a half ahead. Reference *Singapore Diary* p.10.

4. Local guides and discussion with personnel at Alexandra Hospital 2015 and The Reunion – Far East PoWs, Captain Parkinson loss. BBC/Sue MacGregor www. bbc.co.uk/sounds/play/b05rl3j8

5. Fort Canning was the RASC Garrison Adjutant's office, overlooking the city of Singapore. It was HQ of general staff and Royal Corps of Signals. It was the first mansion of Sir Stamford Raffles, with tunnels and underground bunkers.

6. Historians say Singapore was not a fortress as northern defences were incomplete. Plans to make the Far Eastern Island the centre of British Imperial defence began in the 1920s, but the British government could not afford to complete the fortification due to debilitating debts from the First World War. Surprisingly, this was only brought to the attention of Churchill a few weeks before Singapore fell. Meanwhile, Malaya and Singapore were considered peaceful and non-hostile. RAF aircraft engineers were detailed to service Hurricanes that would come to protect the island, but none came. They had only 3' artillery guns from the First World War, mounted on undercarriages with wheels. The Reunion – Far East PoWs. BBC/Sue MacGregor www.bbc.co.uk/sounds/play/b05rl3j8.

7. Brooke-Popham fought hard for the resources he considered vital for the area, but priority went instead to the Middle East. Military and government politics were exacerbated by personality rifts with the Secretary of State for War, Alfred Duff Cooper Viscount of Norwich, who had developed a keen dislike for Brooke-Popham. Crippling command spats lead to denials on political grounds – Siam was a neutral country at the time – until it was too late. (Prabook.com)

8. Brooke-Popham Ref: S4/E4 Battle of Pearl Harbor and The Fall of Singapore. en.wikipedia.org/wiki/Robert_Brooke-Popham and en.wikipedia.org/wiki/American-British-Dutch-Australian Command.

9. Churchill's shocking command was to practically sacrifice a million army personnel and civilians. He said explicitly to fight to the last man – meaning any civilian as well as any soldier. Electric Pictures, Australian Screen. Audio Extract from film footage Singapore 1942, End of Empire, Electric Pictures and Screen Australia.

10. en.wikipedia.org/wiki/The_Fullerton_Hotel_Singapore

11. Events leading to the capitulation and its aftermath; extracts from TV's Battlefield series and other film footage reveal Japan's warfare strategy. TV Battlefield series *'The Battle of Pearl Harbor and the Fall of Singapore,'* series 4/Episode 4, expands the enemy warfare strategy that regular British troops and officers would not have known.

12. Sir Shenton Whitelegge Thomas, the last Governor of the Straits Settlements, serving from 1934 to 1942. Felton.

13. In November 1941, the aircraft carrier HMS *Indomitable* set out on her maiden voyage to the West Indies. But she ran aground on a coral reef near Jamaica, which

ultimately caused a fatal delay for the Singapore battle fleet. It was planned for her to join the naval convoy in Singapore as part of a deterrent force against the Japanese – *Force Orange* – but after the delay she went to Ceylon instead. Not until later was she able to reach Sumatra to provide air protection in battle. en.wikipedia.org/wiki/HMS_Indomitable (92).

14. Felton p.33; Wikipedia.org/wiki/malayan campaign. See Appendix.
15. Wikipedia and Peter Thompson: *The Battle for Singapore: The True Story of the Greatest Catastrophe of World War II*. Portrait Books 2005.
16. Fyans p.90 and 91, *The Second World War*, Winston Churchill, Penguin 1985.
17. Bill Anderson, CoFEPOW website.

Chapter 10 Beginning PoW Life

1. Dannert wire, around the perimeter of several barracks, was installed over a large area of the eastern tip of Singapore.
2. Urquhart, p.96. Sook Ching Massacre.
3. Maggots helped eat away infection and stopped the spread of gangrene where there was no antiseptic. However, infected wounds, scratches and sores, often deep and suppurating, attracted flies and their eggs turned into maggots. If not controlled, the infection could penetrate down to the bone. Video sources: Dan Snow: *Moving Half the Mountain – Building the Death Railway, Timeline Series;* Jack Chalker: *Surviving Hell/Stories from the Fall of Singapore.*
4. Major General Merton Beckwith-Smith, DSO, MC, General Officer Commander-in-Chief.18th Division 53rd, 54th and 55th Infantry Brigades.82nd Anti-Tank Reg. less guns, 85th Anti-Tank Reg., 6th HAA Reg. and 35th LAA Reg. Farndale.
5. Brigadier Eric Whitlock Goodman, DSO, M.C. Royal Artillery was born in 1893 at 'Cottesbrooke', Mostyn Road, Merton, Surrey, son of Charles John Goodman, partner in Scholefield, Goodman & Sons (*Buerk's Peerage*). Educated at Wellington College and Royal Military, Woolwich, he served in France in 1915 with 21st Heavy Battery and was mentioned in dispatches 30 November 1915. He was adjutant, 9th Brigade RGA, commanded 119th Heavy Battery RGA at the end of Jan 1918. Served in Iraq 1919–20. He married Norah Dorothy Stackpoole. They had one son, John Whitlock Goodman, also a major general in the Royal Artillery and Army Air Corps. After commanding in the 5th Bombay Mountain Battery, R.A., Waziristan in 1936–37 with DSO and mentioned in dispatches, Goodman senior, commanded 21st Mountain Regiment 1939–40. In 1941, he commanded C.R.A. 9th Indian Division, Malay, and B.R.A. Malaya command 1941–42. www.britain-at-war.org.uk/WW2/Brigadier_EW_Goodman.
6. Table of British and Commonwealth General Officers, extract. Appendix, p.186. Felton.

7. At 0930hrs, General Percival held a conference at Fort Canning with his senior commanders. He proposed two options: either launch an immediate counterattack to regain the reservoirs and the military food depots in the Bukit Timah region, or surrender. After heated argument and recrimination, all present agreed that a counterattack was not possible. Percival opted for surrender. Post-war analyses show, however, that had Percival opted for a counterattack, it might have been successful. The Japanese had reached their last supplies and their artillery had only a few hours of ammunition left. Ref: Peter Thompson, *The Battle for Singapore: The True Story of the Greatest Catastrophe of World War II.* Portrait Books 2005.

8. D. A. G. Brigadier Thomas Kennedy Newbigging held the flags of surrender with Japanese speaker Cyril Wild, who was later known as the tall man who never slept.

9. Multiple published extracts re Fall of Singapore: A deputation was selected to go to Japanese headquarters, consisting of a senior staff officer, the colonial secretary and an interpreter. They set off in a motorcade bearing a Union Jack and the white flag of truce towards the enemy lines to discuss a cessation of hostilities. They returned with orders that Percival should proceed with staff officers to the Ford Motor Factory, where Yamashita laid down the terms of surrender. Percival formally surrendered shortly after 1715hrs.

Chapter 11 Prisoners on the Padang

1. Ernest Warwick Interviews, Private Soldier, 4th Battalion Suffolk Regiment. *Tamajao p.241: A PoW Camp on the River Kwai.*

2. Ibid. The tortured prisoner was Ernest Warwick.

3. Between Havelock Road and the Singapore River, a bottling plant, known as Frazer and Neave's, originally occupied the site. The PoW contingent was eventually sent to Taiwan to work in a copper mine and some were shipped to Japan early in 1945. The group managed to achieve 85 per cent survival – www.cofepow.org.uk/royalengineers.

4. Early working party figures show 5,812 moved to Pasir Panjang, leaving 45,562 in Singapore, Felton, p.104.

5. Officers intervened in civilian torture treatment, Atcherley.

6. 'Nippongo', Burton, p.40.

7. *McQuaid*, p.16–17.

8. Excerpt, Gillies, p.109 and Wikipedia February 2019: At the Japanese occupation Singapore was renamed Syonan-to/Shonan-to, meaning 'Light of the South Island', and included as part of the Greater East Asia Co-Prosperity Sphere.

9. *Shonan Shimbun Times*, Burton.

Chapter 12 Six Months in – a New Order

1. Lycopene is a nutrient that protects against UV rays, cancer and heart disease and contains 40 per cent of the daily Vitamin C recommendation. When cooked, lycopene is released for consumers to absorb antioxidants. Wikipedia.
2. In the British Raj, tiffin was the English/Indian name for customary afternoon tea, later supplanted by Indian practice of having a light meal. The word derived from colloquial English, or slang, 'tiffing', to take a small drink. By 1867, in northern British India, tiffin meant lunch to most Anglo-Indians, but not necessarily a light meal. In southern India, tiffin can also mean breakfast.
3. *Kongsi* means a group or clan among prisoners/men who look out for each other. This proved useful later.
4. The Red Cross is a long-standing neutral voluntary aid society, with roots in Switzerland going back to 1870. In previous wars, captives received necessary supplies and corresponded with family and friends through the service organised by the governments and in this case the British Red Cross.
5. Felton, p96, p100–101.
6. Excerpt, Gillies, p.119.
7. Felton, p.105.

Chapter 13 Divided Working Parties

1. Felton p.85–8
2. Vichy France. Wikipedia and www.cofepow.org.uk/armed-forces-stories-list/events-in-french-indochina.
3. Hell Ships, Kandler p 43–5, 4 April 1942. A regiment of 1,000 men under Commander Hugonin, detailed to work on docks in Saigon. They never returned to Singapore.
4. Quote, Edward (Ted) Brede, LAC, RAF 100 Squadron. 'The Health Farm at Habu,' CoFEPOW Website.
5. Extracts, Burton.
6. Ibid.

Chapter 14 Weather, Ailments, Officers Leave and Religion

1. Climate: www.worldweatheronline.com
2. Trench foot, also known as Immersion Foot, arises by standing in water too long, too often. The ball of the foot becomes sodden, the skin cracks and fills with mud and dirt. Bruising and painful sores develop. If untreated and unprotected, long-term damage and gangrene can occur. *From the Prisoner List.* Reuben Kandler's trench foot experience.

3. References to ailments and medical treatments from multiple sources: Gilles, McQuaid, Felton and Fyans.
4. Officers account: www.britain–at–war.org.uk/ww2/ Brigadier E.W. Goodman, *Tanjong Maru*, Felton p.121.
5. After the war, the church was dismantled and shipped to Australia in 1947, where it lay untouched until 1987. It was incomplete, but with donated money, materials, roof tiles and timber posts, the building was reconstructed and now stands in the grounds of the Royal Military College, Duntroon, Canberra. It was officially opened as a National Memorial in August 1998. A replica of the cross was built at Changi Gaol, outside the prison walls. For many years, visitors found solace in this small place of worship. In 2001, this was moved to the newly built Changi Museum.
6. The handcrafted Lychgate skilfully built by 18th Division Royal Engineers, was dismantled after the Second World War and eventually sent to Bassingbourn, England. It was re-sited to the National Memorial Arboretum, Alrewas, Staffordshire, UK at the FEPOW Grove.

Chapter 15 The Selarang Incident

1. Gilles, p.167.
2. Recreated letter from Colonel E. W. B. Holmes and Colonel Harris was retained by Captain Horner:
3. See Special Order Nos. 2 and 3. S.A.W. Moore personal archive.

Chapter 16 Normality? Concert Parties Recommence

1. Former Cambridge School of Arts student, Sapper R. Searle, No. 2072249, 287 Field Company, RE, left the UK on Convoy William Sail WS12X, part of the Winston Churchill Special, which formed the USA protected Convoy HS-124. *Ref: To the Kwai – and Back War Drawings 1939–1945 by R. Searle.*
2. Aldershot ovens consist of an improvised arched brick and metal covering, often constructed daily.

Chapter 18 Only the Lonely

1. After the initial imprisonment of Hess in 1941, he was put on trial through the War Crimes Commission, found guilty and subsequently imprisoned for life. He died in Spandau Prison, August 1987, aged 92.
2. www.nps.gov/articles/liberty-ships-and-victory-ships-america-s-lifeline-in-war-teaching-with-historic-places.htm

3. *King Rat*, James Clavell. Clavell was born in Sydney, Australia 1921 and educated in Portsmouth, United Kingdom. He enlisted in the Royal Artillery in the 35th LAA Regiment on his eighteenth birthday in 1939. He was captured in Java then held in Changi Gaol. His story was made into a film in 1965. Many FEPOWs would read this book, including Stan.

4. *Ah*: a song adapted for prisoners of war, original sung by comedian Leonard Henry 1929, British Pathé Production.

5. Merton Beckwith-Smith died of dysentery, 11 November 1942 at Karenko Camp, Formosa (Taiwan): Nominal Roll WO361/237 TNA, UK.

6. *I'm A Little Prairie Flower*, The Two Leslies. 1935. (Leslie Sarony and Leslie Holmes) recorded in 1936; Elsie Carlisle with Jack Harris & His Orchestra V. 1937.

7. drive.google.com/file/d/0BwYC2zir-F9ValprcWVrdUNudGc/view. Thai and Burma Railway parties sent to work up-country. The contingent L–X consisted of 8,450 from Changi, with 1,260 classed as Great World Singapore, accompanied by thirteen lieutenant colonels.

8. Self-made cigarettes 'roll ups', made from tobacco and pages from a Bible.

Chapter 19 The Tree Felling and Railway Sojourn

1. BBC – *Building the Burma Railway; Moving a Mountain*. The bridge was a large-span timber construction with Songkurai camp central to the 16km of track. The Japanese were determined to complete this in five months. Songkurai Camp No.2 was situated on Salween Khwae a short distance along the river, depicted by David Lean's *Bridge over the River Kwai* film, 1957.

2. The 3rd prime minister of Thailand Luang Phibunsongkhram, supported fascism and nationalism. In 1939, he changed the country's name from Siam to Thailand. Anti-Axis powers refused to recognise the new name after Phibunsongkhram signed a military alliance with Japan and declared war on the United States and the United Kingdom. When Japan was losing, Thai diplomats secured peace treaties with the Allies while maintaining cordial relations with Japan. In 1948, the Siamese constituent assembly voted to officially change the name of the country to Thailand, with western support. The proposal was accepted on 11 May 1949. Thailand simply means land of the Thai People.

3. Description from Philip Toosey, Fyans.

4. Working Party F Force, Burton, p.74. Forces War Records website.

Chapter 20 Communication

1. 18th Division postal unit: Corporals: Purfitt, Cutler, Gillies, Hall and Tanswell; Lance Corporals: Blunden, Bugler and Rogers. Sappers: Carding, Chambers,

Coles, Cox, Dodd, Gerrard, High, Hill, Joslin, Logan, Parriman, Potter, Prescott, Randall and Smith.

2. All 18th Division postal unit RE were interned. The OC expressed appreciation for their work and recognised their fine spirit and morale under extreme battle conditions. After capitulation, daily records were kept, providing a vital source of information. They were permitted to organise mail services within Changi goal and railway camps in Thailand, for which OC Captain W.A. Border RE was later awarded an MBE. National Archive Kew, WO172/11401, released 1972.

3. 'Captives' Mail Lost' August 1943 – a BOAC flying boat was lost off the coast of Eire, carrying mail from Far East troops, the date of the aircraft's demise was 28 July 1943. The Postmaster General announced 30,000 letters and postcards were affected with only 2,570 salvaged. Newspaper cutting: Daisy Lawrence Archive.

4. Captors burnt letters as punishment. www.CoFEPOW.org.uk

5. *Daily Express*, Vivien Batchelor, 17 August 1943. Newspaper cutting: Daisy Lawrence Archive.

6. www.cofepow.org.uk/hell-ships-casualties/hell-ships-casualties

7. Frenchman Emile Lienard, who risked his life many times, was awarded the King's Medal for Courage in the Cause of Freedom by George VI, Kandler.

8. Telegram. Daisy Lawrence Archive.

Chapter 21 Summer 1943 – Stan's Humiliation

1. *The Prisoner List* – Japanese humiliation p.57

2. BBC 2014, *Building the Burma Death Railway – Moving Half a Mountain*. Interviews with engineers from Japanese Railway Regiment.

3. Gilles, re: John Clemetson's Changi rubber factory.

4. www.iwm.org.uk/collections/item/object/80012489 P. Neild, IWM Audio

5. McQuaid.

6. Burton.

7. BBC: *Building the Burma Death Railway*; *Moving Half a Mountain* (Moylan). After the war, Japanese engineers admitted no guidelines on how to treat prisoners were given. The order was simply 'to make use of them'. They could let as many prisoners as there were railway sleepers die. BBC Radio 4. *The Reunion*, April 2015. Far East Prisoners of War Interviews – Sue McGregor.

8. Colonel Dunlop and Captain Markowitz. *The War Diaries of Weary Dunlop*.

9. Songkurai escapees. www.britain-at-war.org.uk/ww2/Death_Railway/html/songkurai.htm. McQuaid. Horner refers to Captain Jack N. Feathers* Army No. 138995, who lived at 791 Thornton Heath Rd, Croydon, Surrey, close to Stan. He died as part of F Force attempting to escape.

Chapter 22 Autumn 1943 and the Year Ahead

1. H Force, under British Lieutenant. Colonel. H. R. Humphries and Australian Lieutenant Colonel. Oakes was a party of 3,270 that left Singapore 5–17 May 1943. It consisted of approximately 1,141 British, 670 Australian, 588 Dutch and 26 Americans. Malay volunteers and Indians made up another 845. Ultimately there were 885 deaths (27.1 per cent). www.changipowart.com. They left in six train loads, 'and for this purpose were split into parties of 600 (H1, H2, etc.). The RAF party was to constitute part of the first trainload, H1, under the command of Major G. F. Gaskell, RA.' (Recorded by Pilot Officer R. T. Bainbridge, ref: Clare Stanton – daughter).
2. Konkuita is 258km from where the rails start at Non Pladuk, food was in short supply.
3. After the Allied Invasion of Sicily, King Victor Emmanuel III declared the Sovereign States of Italy should surrender to the Allies and support the United Kingdom. The Italian submarine *Comandante Cappellini*, a Marcello Class craft built for the Italian Royal Navy in 1939, was in Keppel Harbour, 10 September 1943, but before it could slip away, the Japanese boarded the vessel and took the crew prisoner, at Sabang, Singapore. She was commission by Germany into the Kriegsmarine as UIT-24, foreign U-boat, assigned to 12th U-boat Flotilla, with a mixed German and Italian crew. She stayed in the Pacific and was seized by the USA at the surrender. After the war she was scuttled at Kobe in 1946. www.military-history.fandom.com
4. Sime Road better conditions. Burton, p.144.
5. Blackwater fever is a complication of malaria which can lead to death, in which red blood cells burst in the bloodstream (haemolysis) releasing haemoglobin directly into blood vessels and urine leading to kidney failure, or in severe cases cerebral malaria which affects the central nervous system.
6. Pellagra is characterised by the 'four Ds' – dermatitis, diarrhoea, dementia and death. The condition, a form of leprosy, was first recorded in Spain in the 1700s. Pellagra had Italian roots, meaning 'Holly Skin' – sour or rough skin, caused through a diet lacking in niacin, a third B complex vitamin designated as 'Vitamin B_3'. Niacin is important for every cell in the body and is part of the biochemical machinery which channels energy when sugar and fat is burned. That energy powers all cell work, from muscle contraction to nerve function to simple everyday maintenance of cell integrity. It is easy, therefore, to understand how deficiency in this vital molecule can produce total body disease.
7. 18th Division Provost Death figures. Fyans.

Chapter 23 State of Affairs

1. Far East Prisoners of War Hansard, Secretary of State for Foreign Affairs, Anthony Eden's, House of Commons Speech. HC Deb 28 January 1944 vol 396 cc1029-35.

2. A letter written to Pat by her mother in July 1944, indicated a postcard from Stan had been received. It was taken to his mother, Emma Moore, by Pat's young nephew and nieces. The letter was rediscovered many decades later and returned to the authors by Pat's niece, Patricia Franklin.

3. In line with wartime secrecy, the methods some people may have used to find more information could have been via intelligence sources. Pat was officially employed as a Foreign Office clerical assistant at Bletchley Park, which now reveals she was a Decoder. She would have had access to some intelligence operations, but whether she used this resource to find Stan is unproven.

Chapter 24 Word on the Wire

1. Kandler
2. Kandler
3. Atcherley, p.225.
4. RASC Broadcast Records, Hastings, Sussex, UK – 8 Feb. 1945. *Codebreaker Girls: A Secret Life at Bletchley Park,* Jan Slimming; Daisy Lawrence archives.
5. Red Cross supplies for prisoners were kept for years at St Andrew's Mission School by the Japanese. The elegant structure was built in 1875 at Fort Canning. With two storeys and rows of tall, arched windows, the rectangular building was the size of two football pitches. Before the war, it was St John's Ambulance HQ and later became a British Council building. During the 1960s, it was the National Library. Unfortunately, the site was razed to the ground, but a section of the perimeter white pillars and white-painted iron railings are still visible. *(Storyboard, Fort Canning Hill. Oct. 2014.)*
6. Major Hans MJ Jensen P/58737, RIASC, ADT Malaya Comm. of Wallasey, Cheshire.
7. Sime Road Camp, *NLB Singapore Infopedia*, Faizah Binte Zakaria (multiple references). Girls' and boys' secret exams, *Straits Times*, 18 December 1945 p.3 *Newspaper SG*. Sime Road Tapestry, IWM, Kennington. See Appendix.

Chapter 26 Freedom

1. Arsenic powder, ref: www.atsdr.cdc.gov.
2. Now they were receiving better rations than the Japanese distributed earlier – rightly theirs all along. Supplies were constantly hoarded and held up but now they were being released. Other supplies were also reported to be arriving from neutral South Africa, and the UK via the Red Cross and Switzerland.
3. Chinese water torture is where water is slowly dripped on to a person's forehead, which allegedly makes restrained victims insane. This form of torture was first described by Hippolytus de Marsilis in Italy in the fifteenth or sixteenth century.

4. The Royal Rescript is a legal speech at the surrender of war. Emperor Hirohito was forced to concede after threats of a third atomic bomb over Tokyo. His rescript was urged by his closest legal advisers. Hirohito had never spoken in public before until the recording of 14–15 August 1945. www.theatlantic.com/international/archive/2015/08/emperor-hirohito-surrender-japan-hiroshima/400328/

5. Count Terauchi Hisaichi, multiple references inc. *The Far East Theatre 1941-46*, Gen. Sir Martin Farndale, KCB.

6. The Far East Combined Bureau (FECB) escaped Hong Kong then Singapore and relocated partially to Australia (Melbourne) and Colombo, Ceylon (now Sri Lanka), alongside Signals Intelligence FRUEF – HMS Anderson (Fleet Radio Unit Eastern Fleet – Anderson). This unit also moved when attacked, and from April 1942 to August 1943 was based in Mombasa, Kenya, before returning to Colombo. Allied receipt of Far East Intelligence was always delayed, unlike in Europe, due to limited methods of communication over a vast area. Refs: *Japanese Codes*, Sue Jarvis, Bletchley Park Trust, p.25; GCHQ and TNA/HW4; Government Code and Cypher School: FECB, Signals Intelligence Centre in the Far East (HMS Anderson): Records | The National Archives; www.discovery.nationalarchives.gov.uk/details/r/C9283.

Chapter 27 Waiting to Leave

1. HMS *Sussex'* brass band: *Sussex by the Sea*, William Ward-Higgs, South Bersted, Sussex 1907. www.sussexhistory.co.uk/sussex-by-the-sea-lyrics.html.

2. Artefacts held by the navy at Gosport since 1945. Artefacts held by the navy at Gosport since 1945.

3. HMS *Sussex* entered Singapore Harbour flying the Flag of Rear Admiral Cedric Holland. General Seishirō Itagaki, commander of the garrison at Singapore, boarded and signed the formal surrender of the army, completing 'Operation Tiderace', the Allied plan to recapture Singapore.

4. en.wikipedia.org/wiki/Louis_Mountbatten_1st_Earl_Mountbatten_of_Burma#Second_World_War. The final act of unconditional surrender to Lord Louis Mountbatten, and author JR's interview with Jeff Hoare, September 2018.

5. On the boat from Singapore to Liverpool, Going Home. (HMT *Sobieski*), 28 September 1945, Malacca Straits Imperial War Museums (iwm.org.uk)

6. www.history.com/topics/world-war-ii/douglas-macarthur

7. www.britain-at-war.org.uk/WW2/Signalman_Waders_Diary/html/body_my_journey_home.htm. The SS *Orbita* was a Harland & Wolf 18,000-ton navigation steamer, the last ship to carry troops home from Rangoon, 11 October 1945.

Chapter 28 Homeward Bound

1. General William Joseph Slim, 1st Viscount Slim, KG, GCB, GCMG, GCVO, GBE, DSO, MC KStJ. V KCB. Multiple references including *The Far East Theatre*, Gen. Sir Martin Farndale, KCB.
2. Battles March–July 1944. Multiple references including National Archives WO172 Regimental War Diaries, British Allied Land Forces and South East Asia Second World War.
3. General Douglas MacArthur, www.history.com/topics/world-war-ii/douglas-macarthur.
4. Veteran interview Bletchley Park 2018.
5. Guard Your Tongue notice, issued to all. See Aftermath.

Epilogue

1. Memories of Fergus Anckorn – A Most Remarkable Man by Valerie Anckorn, and *Surviving by Magic*, Monty Parkin. Anckorn.val.anckorn@btinternet.com.

Authors' Notes

1. Java Club administer compensation for remaining survivors and affected spouses. See: www.thejavafepowclub42.org; Far East Prisoners of War Hansard 24 November 2000 – the API www.api.parliament.uk › written-answers › nov › far-e...; Far East Prisoners of War Hansard 30 October 2000 – the API www.api.parliament.uk › commons › oct › far-east-pri....; https://hansard.parliament.uk
2. FEPOWs have donated their bodies to LSTM for medical research. The LSTM team wishes to hear from other British services people who treated/nursed ex-PoWs. Meg Parkes and Geoff Gill *Captive Memories* www.captivememories.org.uk/links-news/media-interviews
3. Atomic Bombs Apology; President Barack Obama Speech 27 May 2016.

Index